FOR TROUBLED BLACK GIRLS, WHO SOMETIMES CRY

RODNEY THOMPSON

FOR TROUBLED BLACK GIRLS, WHO SOMETIMES CRY

ARPress
ILLUMINATING IDEAS.
EMPOWERING VOICES

ARPress
45 Dan Road Suite 5
Canton MA 02021

Hotline: 1(888) 821-0229
Fax: 1(508) 545-7580

Ordering Information:
Quantity sales. Special discounts are available on quantity purchases by corporations, associations, and others. For details, contact the publisher at the address above.

Printed in the United States of America.

ISBN-13:   Softcover   979-8-89356-422-8
           eBook   979-8-89356-421-1

Library of Congress Control Number: 2024904559

Table of Contents

Rodney Thompson

Trouble Black Girls

If you look really close,
you'll see through their disguise.
They are troubled black girls,
who some times cry.
They know too much sadness,
and that's a scandal and a shame.
'Cause a troubled black girl,
got too many to blame.

But she can't blame her man,
even if he won't be a father to his child.
And she can't blame her son,
even as the streets make him wild.
She can't blame hope,
her faith an agonizing pursuit.
When you're a troubled black girl,
you're not sure what you should do.

If you look really close,
you'll notice alienation in her eyes.
Affection always within sight,
true love and unsustained prize.
Timid is the troubled black girl,
she knows not how to be bold.
Her guide is a tormented heart,
which leads a distressed soul.

But she can't blame her man,
'cause he's been oppressed.
And she can't blame her boy,
ain't he s'pose to cause stress.
Can't blame her prayers,
her spirituality is gone too.
When you're a troubled black girl,
you just don't know what to do.

When you're a troubled black girl, you simply exist.
A while back you stopped living.
'Cause when you've gave everything you've got to give,
the only thing that's left is misgivings.
So you stare into a hole, that once held your soul,
you research tirelessly for a clue.
You are a troubled black girl, and in this world,
You just don't know what to do.

Too Much

If I had to do it all over again, would I have chosen this path? Everybody has a journey they must travel. To put it plain and simple, mine has been a difficult road. Twenty plus years to reach this destination and the only statement I can definitely make is this. Too many parts of this trip I would have preferred not to have taken. I tell myself over and over, what if I had done things differently? What if I'd learned from all the mistakes I'd made? What if, what if, and what if, a question I'll always ask and an answer I already know.

Why does it always have to be this way? Why do the men I love not love me back? Why is it the more I love them, the more certain they are to leave me? Love should be a lot of things but it shouldn't be this damn hard! I will love them regardless of their faults. I will love them in spite of their flaws. I love with all my soul, and what good does it do? I can truthfully say, that my entire life, the people I love always leave me.

My latest is Jamie, fine, fine ass Jamie. When everybody else was against us, I gave you my all.

Whenever you needed me, I did everything I could to meet those needs. It is so sad and ironic, now when I need you most, and you obviously need me just as much, it's impossible for us to be together. The cold reality is that our love was not strong enough to overcome all of the obstacles in our way. I don't know how things got to be like this. All I know is that it hurts like hell. And I'm tired of hurting

My name is Maya, Maya Baxter. Even though I'm only twenty-six years old, I have already shed enough tears to fill Lake Hartwell. Twenty-six years old, dark andif you were to believe all of the men I've dated, at least in the beginning, as sweet as Hershey's finest chocolate. My face is alright, but what turns every straight man's head, and maybe a few of the gay ones, is a body that looks like it was made to be loved hard and often. That's inspite of all my troubles. That's also despite having a baby when I was only seventeen years old.

1

My son's name is Antonio. We call him Ant for short. He is the absolute, most precious child on the face of this earth. When I lay down with those men, I didn't realize that he'd be the only good thing that lasted more than a few minutes, I'd ever get from any of them. One thing that I'm absolutely certain. I'd trade in all of those bad times for my little Ant.

His daddy is named Anthony Madison, but everybody calls him Tony, smooth, slick Tony. He's from just up the road in Greenville. that's the big city in these parts. Tony showed what type of man he was when he found out about me being pregnant. At first he'd began to ease away from me. As time passed, he quit coming around all together. Later on I heard he had three or four bastard children roaming around the Western part of the state. I guess I wasn't the only one to fall for smooth, slick Tony. Now he's back and forth between the county work farm for not paying child support, or some other petty jail time. But that's not what makes me despise him. The thing I hate most about Tony is the way he treats Ant. He can always find time for any whore in a tight skirt, but never any time for this most precious child. His very own most precious child.

Ant's the type of child who just makes you want to smile whenever you see him. It doesn't matter what screwed up things are going on in my life, my baby can make life seem slightly tolerable. No doubt in my mind, he is the best thing that ever happened to me. It's really amazing how he can pick up on how I'm doing. He knows when Mama is a little down. Whenever I am, there he is to give me the biggest hug. Or at least he used to be there to give me that hug.

He started the third grade this year. Since I quit in the 11th grade. I want to make sure he gets a quality education. He is supposed to be starting the fourth, but I let his teacher talk me into holding him back the year before last. I was having problems with another boyfriend and it affected Ant. I realize that it hasn't been easy on him. I promise myself that I'm going to make things better for him. It's just so very hard raising a child without a daddy. My ultimate goal is to give him a decent family life. I want him to have it better than my baby sister Tanesha and I had coming up.

I suppose if you were to ask a psychiatrist, he might say the reason I put up with so much from men is because of my daddy, or the lack of one. We never really know our daddy. He took off for good when I was about six years old. Even before he left, he didn't really do anything for us. I don't have any memories of daddy taking us to the park, or to the County Fair, or nothing like that. If it weren't so pitiful it would be sad. The best memory I got of my daddy is one day he wasn't there anymore. I looked up and he was gone, and he hasn't been back since.

Growing up it was Mama, Maya and Tanesha.Folks who knew her from way back way, except for the drinking say Ilook and act just like Mama, I reckon some of that is true. I got this picture of her when she was about my age, and I sure look like her. As far as acting like her, we definitely had in common of being a magnet for problems.

Lord knows Mama had her problems. She took it really hard when daddy finally left us. I don't know why? All they ever did was fight. He'd always accuse her of running around on him, then he'd jump on her and beat the living days lights out of her, I supposed that's when the drinking started. To deal with those beatings, Mama found a way to cope. Anyway that sounds about as good as anything else I could make up. With Mama, you always needed to make up things. This would help you understand. This would help you to cope.

You would have thought with him gone, she might have slowed down on the liquor. But it was the exact opposite. After he left, she started drinking even more. After he left that's when all those men, those sorry ass men started to come around. The absolute worse part of growing up was Mama's men folk. Even now it's hard for me to think about them without wanting to hurt their ass.

Well Mama died three and a half years ago. It was in the fall of eighty-five. When she died, nobody even knew how to get in touch with daddy. The last we'd heard was that he lived in Detroit some place. To this day, I'm not even sure if he knows Mama's dead. Not sure if he gives a damn.

The doctors said she died from something called pancreatitis and cirrhosis of the liver. I'm not exactly sure what those things are all I know is the liquor killed her that and all those men. Before she died, Mama was pretty messed up. That stuff turned her eyes as yellow as government cheese, and swelled her belly up like she was ten months pregnant.

3

I never told anyone, don't need anybody thinking I'm crazy, but sometimes when I'm thinking about all kinds of things, I talk to her. I guess if the truth be known, mostly I listen to her. I listen to the never-ending criticism. Even from the grave, she calls out to me. Even from the grave I can't manage to please her. That shouldn't surprise me, all my life, I couldn't please her. But still I continue to try.

At her funeral I remember standing there as they lowered her into the ground. All I could think about was the money Tanesha and I had to scrape together to buy a decent burial dress. It's not the fondest memory I have of the funeral but it's the one I recall most often. It seemed like such a damned waste, both my Mama and that dress being put to rest way too soon. And it was such a pretty dress.

The funeral was pretty pathetic. We ended up getting the cheapest casket Miss Robinson had. If you looked really close, you would have swore the thing was made out of a corrugated cardboard box. You would have thought, out of all the men Mama went with, somebody would have offered a little help. None of them son of bitches coughed up so much as a single red cent. So Tanesha and I did the best we could. What else can you do, except the best you can? So we buried Mama, No big send off, we just got her into the ground.

I felt guilty because I couldn't cry. Tanesha didn't shed a tear, but it was different for her, she seemed relieved. I really wanted to cry. I truly did. The tears are like a dam breaking if any piece of a man decides to leaves me. But when it came time to say goodbye to my own flesh and blood, the tears refused to flow. Here I stood, looking down at Mama, in that big cardboard box, with the belly about to come out of that dress, not one tear could I shed. You could have put a sliced onion underneath both eyes and I still wouldn't have been able to force a single tear.

I know folks were talking. In a town as small as Tylerville, South Carolina, people's main form of entertainment is talking about somebody else. Gossiping is right above football in terms of favorite activities. So when Mama was buried in the Tylerville Memorial Rest Grounds, the conversation surely focus on that fact. Although the name sounds quite peaceful and respectful, the truth is it's a place where they buried Black folks who are bums, addicts and basic low lives. So, it wasn't long after Mama was put to rest, that the gossip came alive

I've got to admit that the talking bothered me for a long, long, time Tanesha told me to tell them "all to go to hell" Tanesha is always telling someone to go to hell. Depending on how you look at it, she's either real strong or real weak.

What can I say about Tanesha. She is my baby sister. Even though she is a year and a half younger than me, she has always been the one who kind of takes care of me. She is my protector. My baby sister don't take nobody's trash. She can out curse any sailor and would fight the whole world for me or Ant. Bless her heart, I don't know what in the world I would do without her.

The only negative thing I can say about my sister is that she expects me to be like her. Sometimes I wish I could, but I'm just not that type. One of the words I use to describe her is tough. No one would ever describe me as being tough. I am a lot of things, but tough isn't one of them.

She's always getting on me about the men in my life. She's the type person, who would do without rather than put up with a man's foolishness. She doesn't even need a man to love her. I do. I don't know why I can't pick a good man. Lord knows I've had enough practice with the bad ones. If I'd learned from my mistakes. I would certainly be a love genius. But apparently bad romance knowledge doesn't increase the love IQ.

One of her pet saying is that I'm "a sucker for anything with a dick." She let's me know all too often that I fall in love too easily. I just know that everybody needs somebody, and one day I'm going to find the right somebody for me. I tell her nobody's perfect and that you have to put up with a few faults in a man. Her response was that I "put up with the San Andreas" whatever that is.

It's easy for her to believe that. She is so pretty. She's got this pretty light tan colored skin, with long dark curly hair, and the softest light brown eyes. When we were little, folks around here spread a rumor she was a white man's baby, and that was the reason my daddy finally left my Mama. Blacks folks, at least in these parts, have a double standard. If you're real light skinned, then they all figure that you think you are better than them. How they know what anybody thinks is beyond me. With Tanesha being closer to white than anybody else on this side of the track, then naturally she has had to deal with that self-hatred mentality all her life. Personally, I don't care about any of that mess. She's my sister and I love her

The problem is I love Jamie too. I now know it was asking too much, but if I only she could have gotten along with Jamie. She didn't have to love him, but if she could have just tolerated him. Jamie is my latest great romance. Or maybe would be more accurate to say, he is my last. It's still very difficult for me to accept that it's over. It's difficult to think of him in the past tense. I keep thinking and hoping that there could be some way that we could go back and make things rights. But after what just happened, I don't really know if that is possible. If we can't, then you might as well say the last two years of my life have been shot to hell. All that time wasted.

It seems funny to say this but I'll always be somewhat thankful and regretful for the Tylerville Textile Mill. In between the yarn, the spools, and the machinery is where I was able to find a bit of joy. The ironic part of this is it's also where the road to agony began. That old mill means a lot to the entire western part of this county. If you don't work in the mill, then you are supported indirectly by the mill. That's just the way life is in these parts.

I'd been working at the mill for five years when Jamie moved here. That was in the early Spring of 1992. At that time he was the talk of the town. There was all kinds of gossip floating around about why he'd moved here. I mean who in the hell wants to move to Tylerville, It's only got about three thousand people, two thirdswhite and totally segregated. Old folks tell that when the courts ordered the schools to integrate in the 70's, every white person in town, with money, took there kids out and enrolled them in the private school. Twenty years later the town and the schools or just as segregated as 40 years ago. Time just forgot about Tylerville.

Anyways some folks thought he had to be running from something. Southerners tend to be funny that way. They always think the worse about a stranger. We don't trust nothing or nobody who we don't know their entire life history. Since early on Jamie wasn't saying a whole lot about why he moved here, people thought the worse.

My man Jamie is at least six feet two and built like one of them Greek statues. He's got this olive tanned complexion with this perfect short, curly, dark brown-blonde hair. It's cut real short almost in a bowl cut like some of them young boys wear these days. He's also got this strong jaw, with hazel brown eyes, and full sexy lips not like most white people. It still makes me wet in the right spot just to think about my baby.

For me Maya Baxter, dark as a star-less night sky, to be hooked up with a white boy in Tylerville in this date and time, well it either took a whole lot of courage or a lot of stupidity. The looks and some name-calling were major problems when we first went public. But Jamie didn't seem to mind, after all I got the worst of it. There were several names for me. First of all there was bitch, or a cracker-loving bitch, or on bad days a coal faced, black ass cracker loving bitch.

You don't live on Flint Hill, if you're a sister and screw the slave master. If you are a brother, it's alright for you to get you some white stuff, but don't let them find out a sister is giving it away to a white boy.

Anyway. I put up with it all, I put up with all of the gossip, all of the stares. Put downs and even a threat or two. I put up with it all, because I believed in the power of love. I loved him so much that no matter what we had to deal with, I was willing to do it. The funny part about all of this is that it ultimately wasn't race that lead to our breaking up. It was about something all to common on Flint Hill.

When he moved in with me a little more than a year ago, there were times when I was in Heaven. This was the happiest time in all my life. I had my doubts, but I was willing to live with those doubts What I couldn't deal with where the things I didn't know about. I didn't know about the dark side of this white boy. I didn't know about his demons.

Early on he showered me with love, and tenderness, and gifts. There were flowers, and candy and that bracelet. When my birthday came around, he gave me the most beautiful bracelet. No man had ever given me anything quite that lovely and expensive before. To me that bracelet symbolized how much I meant to him. At least I thought it did.

But just like every relationship I'd ever had, somewhere down the road things begin to change. Near the end, our relationship became more and more like a seesaw. One week we were up, the next week we were down. Seems like every month we'd have some type of big blow up. I would try as hard as I possibly could, but at times there just was no pleasing him. Especially when he was dealing with those demons.

The last month before I ended up in this place, things had gotten as low as they'd ever been. The seesaw wasn't coming back up. The ride was coming to an end, and what an end.

So I simply blamed myself and took on all the responsibility. Somebody must be responsible for a world that has simply fallen apart. Somebody has to be responsible for love gone bad. This is where my journey has taken me. All because I love too much.

HOPE

It's something about Spring that causes hope to bloom. Every year I still get that feeling in spite of Winter being finally gone, those beautiful Pansies will stay through June. Of course every year they are long gone before May's first sunrise. But that doesn't keep me from trying. That doesn't keep me from hoping. Spring is a lot like love, at least like my love life. Each new man brings me a little bit of Spring. If you ever seen a girl who loves too much, well she searching for a bit of Spring. The only thing worse than searching for that feeling, is to give up on Spring ever coming again.

I get finished loading the washers with my clothes. This is the Peach Tree Street laundromat. I push a button and immediately the machine starts twisting and twirling. I sat down in a yellow, plastic, rock hard chair. The hateful redneck, peckerwood owner won't put any decent chairs in here, on account of who has to use the place.

Here I sit with my best friend Caressa. We've been tight for years now. She didn't really have anything to wash, since her Mama is watching her kids she just come on down with me. I reckon she needed a break.

Caressa is totally wild and doesn't have a bit of sense. Everybody knows about her and her reputation. It's the type of reputation no lady really wants but Caressa earned it. Although she's concerned about what people think of her, she already knows that her name can't get any worse. She and I have always needed and supported each other.

She is as sweet a person as ya'll ever know. She puts on this tough front but actually is very vulnerable. In that way she is a lot like my sister. Actually, she is the only person I ever met who can talk more trash than my sister. I mean it, you get her going and she'll shut Tanesha up. Secretly that's always been one of the things I liked best about her.

She also happens to be the biggest whore in town. She has screwed everybody and his brother and his going around for the second time.

9

She got me beat by a long shot. She'd probably screw a snake if its head would stay stiff long enough and it would promise to love her forever. But her search for love has caused her plenty of heartache and pain. One time they had to call her into the county health department on a count of her having chlamydia and the clap. She was virtually a one woman epidemic.

As long as I've known her, she has never had any confidence in herself. When she was in high school she was in love with this guy name T- Dog. He was the star of the boy's basketball team. He set it up where half of the boy's basketball team pulled a train on her. Ever since then she was known as the town's whore, and she has done everything in her power to live up to that title. She was always the one person, no matter how bad I'd feel, that I knew felt worse about herself than I did.

Sitting across from us are two trailer trash white women. One of them is a stocky, double chimed soul dipping cracker named Bertha. I know her from the mill. I think to myself, why do people name their children Bertha? Every Bertha I've ever known has looked just like a sow. Maybe it's the name that causes them to get fat.

The second one I don't know, and don't want to know. She's a friend of that heifer and that's all I need to know. She's a skinny, mushed face bitch. Got a face that looks like she been hit with a two by four edgewise. You could call her ugly but then ugly would have to sue you for libel.

When we came in they had all five of the washers tied up. I had to wait for at least an half-hour. The last thing in the world I want to do is spend the afternoon washing clothes and looking at these two faces.

Whites and blacks, as a rule, in Tylerville don't get along very well. It's not so much that we don't get along, as we just don't associate. It's always been that way, and I guess nobody's in a hurry to change things. What's that old saying. down South you can get big, just don't get too close. If it wasn't for work, school, and stuff like that, I wouldn't fool with none of them, and you can sure as hell bet they wouldn't be knocking down any doors to mingle with us.

I light up a cigarette and slowly inhale. There is a temporary pause in Caressa's and my conversation. We are ease dropping a little bit on ugly and uglier's conversation. I do stuff like that when I'm with Caressa. We got to do something to past the time. We soon find ourselves pretty bored with their conversation. Who in the hell cares what kind of okra and string beans they going to set out this year? I rise up, and walk over to the door. I fake a smile at them as I walk past. That's the way things are done around here, don't know why we smile at one another. It's something we just do.

As I stand there looking out, my mind returns to my current sorry ass life. I just broke up with my last boyfriend. This was about two months ago. The pitiful bastard left me for my own cousin. Around here that type of thing amounts to a pretty fair conversation piece. Even though he wasn't any good, he was my man. The last few weeks, without a man, life done been really hard.

I walk back in as the skinny cracker unloads one of the dryers. She looks up at me and quickly puts the clothes in a basket without even folding them. I don't know why, other than to make small talk, I observe.

"Well it want belong now."

She fakes a smile. I notice some stained nubby teeth

"Child I hope so. I got a thousand things I need to be doing."

"You and me both."

"If Bud would put more machines in here then nobody would have to wait."

"Well my washer is finished. I guess I'll just load up the dryer now."

"Bout time gal. I ready to get outta this bitch."

I proceed to walk over and load the dryer. This causes me to have to move closer to those Southern Belles. As soon as I finish. I turn and walk back to the luxury of my plastic chair, relieved to escape the vicinity of those two. By now Caressa has nodded off. The girl can fall asleep anywhere. She's sitting there head nodding with her mouth open and a little bit of slobber escaping from the corner. I decide there must be something more pleasant to look at than these three.

As I reach for a magazine that has to be two years old, the door squeaks open. I look up in time to see by far the best looking man in the city, hell in the whole doggone county. I think to myself I wouldn't mind getting a little bit of that. As a matter of fact, I wish I were those blue jeans he has on. If them pants knew the words they'd be singing praise be to the Lord.

I had seen him around the mill the past two or three weeks. You can't miss him as fine as he is. Besides that he don't look like any of the folks from around here. He stands out like a marigold in a weed pitch.

I look up and then away as he nears me. I feel kind of shy. I done been with more men than I want to remember, but still feel afraid of them. I still don't trust them.

He slings an old green duffle bag full of clothes down on a table. He flashes the most gorgeous crooked smile and speaks.

"Ladies how y'all doing today?"

I assume he's talking to the two white women, especially since Caressa is sawing wood, so I don't say anything. Bertha and old mush face are both about to drool over themselves, answer in a made up syrupy voice that stills crackles from their redneck background. You can take the redneck out of the country, but you can't take country out of the redneck.

"We doing just fine."

"We sure are. And how 'bout yourself"

"I'm just fine ma'm." He then announces, apparently talking to me."

"Look like your friend having a rough day, and how you making it Maya"

Hearing this I just about fall out of my chair. How in the world does he know my name? I look up into those sexy hazel brown eyes and at a smile that's so sinful they'll make your panties just fall off. I stutter nervously.

"HHHow you know my name?"

He slides down beside me and whispers, so as not to wake Caressa, in a voice that will make your heart skip a beat.

"I got special powers. If ya'll give me your phone number, I'll tell you 'bout them later on."

I think to myself, Damn! I've never been hit on by a fine white man, anyway not one that looks this good. I'm not sure what to say.

For some reason I look up at the two women across the Laundromat. I wonder what can they be thinking? I mean they had to hear him come on to me, otherwise they wouldn't be looking like they had just seen General Sherman with a torch in his hand.

"Well pretty lady are you gonna give me that number or am I gonnahave to use them special powers again?"

"I can't give you my phone number."

"Well why not?"

"I don't know nothing 'bout you".

He rises up from his chair and playfully sticks out his hand for me to shake.

"Hello, Maya Baxter, my name is James Edward Cook. My friends all call me Jamie."

The sounds or just the realization that there was a good looking man around must've awaken Caressa. She stretches like a two hundred plus pound cat, rubs the spit from her faces, struggles to open her eyes, then looks with her head crooked at Jamie.

I smile uneasily, not really sure what to do. He continues talking as I reach out and shake his hand.

"And I sure hope that one day ya'll be one of my very best friends."

Caressa never one to act shy jumps right in the conversation. If a good looking man even looks in her direction she gets a case of the hots.

"Well you sure didn't shake my hand. What's up with that?" Jamie just smiles and extends his hand to Caressa.

"How you doing ma'm. I didn't catch you the first time 'cause it looked like you was sleeping."

"I wasn't sleeping. I was just resting a bit. Now who might you be with your fine self?"

"You can call me James."

"And you can call me Caressa."

"How's it going Caressa?"

"Sitting in here looking at you it's going damned good. Matter of fact if it get to going any better I wouldn't know what to do with myself."

Caressa's smiles like a hungry fox in the hen house with the farmer gone to town.

I can't do nothing but smile myself, as he sits back down next to me. He is smooth white boy. He has got player written all over that handsome tanned face.

"Now that we been formally introduced, what do you say?"

I pretend I don't know what he's talking about. "What do I say 'bout what?"

"What do you say 'bout that phone number, and while we talking 'bout that, we may as well set up the time I can pick you up tonight?"

Before he can finish I cut him off. He may be fine, but he doesn't know the deal.

"Whoa, whoa, whoa, hold up. You're not picking me up, as I ain't going out with you, Uh-uh no way." Caressa jumps dead in on that.

"Sweet thing if she ain't available tonight you can pick me up at six, or Seven, or eight or whatever damn time you can get there."

I look at Caressa with my best shut the hell up expression. She gets the point.

"You know what I'm gonna go outside and smoke me a cigarette. That way y'all can handle y'all's business."

She slowly eases her big wide ass up from the now happy chair. She can't help but look back as she exists. If she were cat then she'd be dead as hell. I now focus totally on Jamie.

He looks at me puzzled like. Then in a voice like a small curious child, he asks.

"Is it cause of the color of my skin, I mean if it's cause of my skin color then you know that's not right." I lie.

"No it ain't cause you're white."

In a surprised voice and a shocked expression.

"White! Who says I'm white?" I laugh.

"I say you white, and that ain't got nothing to do with why I won't go out with you."

"Whew I'm sure glad to hear that. If it was 'cause of that then I'd have a real problem. I'm not really sure if I could do anything to change that."

I shake my head in disbelief as he continues to smile. This boy doesn't have the sense he was born with.

"The reason I'm not going out with you, is 'cause it's like I done already said, I don' know nothing 'bout you. I mean you can't just walk up in here and expect me to just go out with you. That ain't how it goes."

As Jamie and I continue talking, for a short time we must've forgotten about the other two people in the room. But Old Mush Face decides she'd heard enough. She jumps in to add her unwanted, unsolicited two cents worth.

"I'm not trying to be nosy or nothing, but I couldn't help but hear what you two were talking 'bout Lemme just say this. I personally don't have nothing against nobody, white nor colored. As far as I'm concerned a person can go out with whoever they want. But it only seems right, at least for as long as I been alive, that people feel more comfortable sticking with their own kind." Jamie counters

"Ma'm what kind am I s'pose to stick too?"

"What Gertie was saying" suggests Bertha, "Is that in Tylerville folks have always stuck to their own race. You know whites marry whites, and colored they marry colored. This mixing up the races just ain't done 'round here. A lot of folk just want except it, they see it as down right scandalous."

I look at Jamie not knowing what to say or what to do. I'm from this town, born and raised here. I know a lot of what fat ass and snuff mouth are saying is true. In Tylerville you don't cross the race line. It's simply not done.

"Ma'm what's so wrong 'bout a man like me and a woman like her getting together for a lil' fun. Hell we ain't even held hands and you two got us married off."

"Son you're not from around here. It's like Gertie says people don't go for that sort of thing. It ain't nothing against either one of you two.

It's the way things have always been done, and you can't force them to change the way they feel 'bout that type of going ons."

"Miss you here to tell me that it's wrong for God's people to care 'bout one 'nother?"

Bertha continues on what now is becoming a bit of a tirade. By now her eyes are bulging and veins are stretching out in her neck. She looks like she's about to have a stroke.

"Son you hear me and hear me good. You don't know nothing 'bout the way things are in this here town. You come in here talking 'bout what's right for God's people. Well lemme tell you one thing, you want find no better people than right here in Tylerville, South Carolina! These are fine folk, God fearing. Christian folk."

"That's right young man. You listen to what Bertha saying. People in this town believe in the Bible, I personally read mine almost every single day. And I can promise you this one thing, that nowhere in that Bible do I see where one kind of people s pose to mix with another kind of people. In fact, it is the exact opposite. That kind of thinking is only gonna cause problems."

"Well ladies, I really do appreciate that fine Bible school lesson, And I really glad to know that ya'll don't have nothing against all of God's people trying to get long. You know if we only could get the rest of these good folks to believe like ya'll. It's not often you see people so concerned "bout someone else's well being. But ladies and I say this with the utmost respect and I do hope ya'll take it that way, it's like this...I don't given fat babies ass 'bout what you and the rest of these fine folk think. As a matter of fact, all you good Christian folk can go dig a hole straight to hell. Then I want every last one of ya'll good folk to go and jump in that hole. And if y'all will do that, I most certainly will take the time to cover y'all red necked ass up."

The looks so their faces say it all. In Tylerville you can count on the Tyerville mill producing fabric. The Confederate flag waving on the Fourth of July. And the Son's of the Confederacy reenacting the Civil War. But until now I'd never counted on a white boy going against his own and taking up for a black girl.

No, no, no, no, and no once again. It takes them a minute or so to get over there initial shock. As soon as that happens the queen and princess of the trailer park hurriedly gather up their still damp clothes from the dryers and haul ass out of the Laundromat. Before they leave they manage to give both of us a look that would not be fitting for good Christian folk. Hell it wouldn't even be fitting for the worst sinner.

Jamie turns to me, shrugs his shoulders and smiles this perfect, did I say something wrong smile. I laugh out loud and shake my head. I think to myself this is one crazy ass white boy. I also think this boy can be trouble. But even though he could be trouble, I can't help but feel special. Hell I've never had anyone I could depend on but my sister for as long as I could remember. If he'd stand up to these crackers, maybe he's okay. And I sure haven't had anybody who was all right in a long, long time.

"Boy you know them two gonna trash your name in this town. What you just did is gonna be all over that mill by Monday evening."

"I don't care. Somebody needs to stand up to people like that."

"What you mean, you don't care? You had better care. This is Tylerville."

"I mean I don't care. Who are they to say who I can, and can't be with? Who are they to sit back and judge people? To say this one is better than that one. I don't buy it. As far as I'm concerned you are one of the prettiest women I've ever seen." I blush.

"I mean it Maya. When I first saw you at work last week, it was like nothing or nobody else was even there. Girl you are fine!"

"Boy you need to quit your lying."

"Lying? Maya lemme tell you this and I swear to goodness it's true. You are one beautiful chocolate lady. I mean it. You just don't know how pretty you are. And I'm here to tell you that I'm just the man to let you know."

I look adoringly into those gorgeous eyes. I think damn this boy is fine, even if he is white. But there is no way I'm messing with a white boy. Everybody I know, especially my sister, would have a duck dying fit. Besides that, he's too smooth with those lines he shooting at me. I done been down that road way too many times. Just because he's not a brother, deep down, he's still a man. In my book that makes him a dog. A different shade of the same breed, and sooner or later a dog is going to show itself.

"With that gorgeous chocolate skin, and them big ol' pretty eyes. And don't think I'm trying to get too-fresh. Believe me I ain't trying to be fast. But girl you got a body that's made to be adored. I'm talking 'bout from your head down to your toes. Girl you are so beautiful that I've been dreamin' 'bout you since the first time I saw you at work. I don't know what it'll take for you to give me a chance to know you better, but whatever it is, I'm more than willing to do it. Hell any man who wouldn't appreciate you, well something's bad wrong with him."

I hope God may kill me! This boy has got my head going. I'm glad we're not anywhere private. Otherwise, I'd have to give this boy a big hug, and believe me if he were to even touch me, heaven forbid if he was to kiss me. I don't know if there has ever been a case of panties evaporating, but if this boy was to kiss me, well these panties might just turn into vapor. I have to tell myself to slow down. How many men done shot me some line to get some ass, then they end up dogging me. I remind myself that he's just another dog spouting the same old bow-wow.

"Jamie what you saying sounds good and all that, but the truth is I'm not all that sure 'bout going out with you."

"Now Maya you told me it didn't matter 'bout my skin color.

Besides that's all it is, color."

"Well I lied. I just can't see it happening. Not in Tylerville."

"So because I'm a different shade than you are, you gonna let them rednecks, who don't give a damn 'bout you decide who you can be friends with."

"It ain't just them. I live down on Flint Hill."

"So."

"The West Side of town."

"So

"The Black Side of town."

"So."

"Is your answer to everything So? Do you know how much hell I'd catch from being with a white boy and living on Flint Hill? Half the people on Flint Hill blame the white man for all of his problems.

The other half only blame most of their problems on ya'll. I got to live there, and here you are thinking I'm gonna just go out with you."

"You know what?"

"No I don't and I'm not sure if I want to know."

"Well I'm gonna tell you anyway. You worry too much 'bout what other folk think. Them people can't live your life. You end up going to your grave, miserable as hell worryin' 'bout what them people thinking. You need to worry 'bout Maya and what makes her happy."

"And that's exactly who I'm worried 'bout. I can't change the way things are done 'round here. This is Tylerville. In this town, whites don't go out with blacks. As much as I'd like to get to know you, them two old ladies were right. That type of thing just ain't done."

He, kind of slick like, smiles that damn crooked smile. If it is possible, I hate it and love it at the same time.

"And what you find so amusing?"

"Nothing much."

"Then why you smiling like the cat that ate the canary?"

"Well, in between all that talk 'bout Westside and Flint Hill, I heard you say as clear as day, that you'd like to get to know me better."

"No I didn't."

"Yeah you did."

"No I didn't."

"I heard you girl. You can't take it back now."

"Well even if I said it, it don't mean nothing. I'm still not going out with you. So you might as well wipe that jack o lantern grin off your face."

The smile disappears from his face.

"Aw c'mon Maya. Just give me your phone number. I want even come over. We'll just talk for a while 'til you can make up your mind."

"My mind is already made up."

"I reckon I'm gonna have to work on changing that mind of yours."

"You can work as hard as you wanna. I won't change my mind. So you might as well learn how to take no for an answer."

"If I didn't have this feeling that you were so special, I'd walk on outta here and leave you alone. But I won't do that. I mean it Maya, if I have to I'll beg. If I have to I'll get down on my knees and beg like a dog."

As he says these words he literally get down on his knees. I look at him and then back up. Looking through the window, observing it all, is nosy ass Caressa. She smiles at me and I wave her away, Jamie turns and smiles at her as she nimbly like a 200 plus pound cat jumps back out of sight.

"Girl I don't care who don't like me, as long as I can be with people as sweet and gorgeous as you. When I look at you, I know you're the right one for me."

"Fool you don't know nothing 'bout me, and get your ass off that dirty floor before you really do turn black." He laughs.

"This floor could stand a good scrubbin." We both laugh as the buzzer on the dryer sounds.

"See there, you already having a good time with me. I'm telling you Maya, it can be like this all the time. One thing 'bout me is this, I don't make promises I can't keep. I'll spend my days and nights trying to make you happy, and that's a promise."

This is too much for me. I rise up and walk over to the dryer. As I unload my clothes, I try to take in what's going on. A white boy, a white boy, that's all I can think about. If he were black, I wouldn't hesitate to go out with him. If he were black, I'd have already given him the digits. If he were black I'd already be planning on what I was going to wear, Without looking at him I respond.

"Jamie I done already told you no. I don't know what else to say." I continue loading the clothes into my basket.

"Do this for me Maya, promise me that ya'll at least think about what I'm saying."

"I done already thought about it Jamie."

"Just say you'll think about it some more. Will you do that for me?"

As I finish unloading the clothes, I pick up the basket and start toward the door.

"If I say I'll think it over, will you leave me alone?"

"Yes ma'm, I promise."

"And do you promise that you'll respect my decision?"

"Absolutely."

He grabs his duffle bag and walks with me to my car. Caressa notices us leaving and she walks over toward us. As we reach the car, he opens the door for me and then for Caressa. She eases into the passenger seat and pretends like she's looking the other way. I know her nosy tail well enough to know that she's got those ears wide open, I load the clothes in, and walk around and get into the car.

"Well, Jamie it's been an interesting conversation, but it's time I get on back home."

"Yeah Maya don't believe I've had this much fun since I hit town. You take care of yourself and think about what I said. Caressa you take care of yourself too."

"I will baby, and you think 'bout my offer. If Miss Maya want do right, you can call me anytime." She grins and he smiles.

"Think about it Maya."

"Oh I imagine I won't be thinking about nothing else. Well we gotta get on home now."

"You already said that."

"I kinda feel like I'm leaving you. Why don't you go on back in and wash them clothes?" As soon as I say this, up pops that old sinful smile.

"Well if the truth be known, I didn't really come here to wash no clothes."

"Huh?"

"It's like this. You see that boarding house 'cross the street. Well it just so happens I was looking out the window, when who should walk to the door but the girl I been dreaming 'bout for the past week. So I threw a bunch of stuff in this bag and flew over here as quick as I could"

I shake my head in disbelief.

"You are one strange white boy."

"Strange and nearly crippled too. I just about broke my neck getting over here before you left."

I smile, turn the keys in the ignition switch, it refuses to crank. I turn the switch a second time, a third time and finally the car cranks up. I shift into drive and the car cases away. He runs behind me a few steps and shouts.

"Bye bye beautiful. And don't forget to think about me." Caressa is the one to answer his request.

"Think about you, hell I'm gonna be dreaming about you baby. And it's gonna be one damn hot, wet dream." I laugh at her horniness.

I proceed to drive Caressa home. I am really glad to get rid of her. All she wants to talk about is whether I'm going to give the white boy some pussy. When I say I don't know she says I got to be out of my head. Hell, she would've given it to him right there on the dryer.

I head on out to my sisters house and pick up my son Ant. He of course is playing basketball in the park and doesn't want to come in. I finally get him inside and gather up his belongings.

Tanesha wants us to stay awhile longer, she always wants us to stay awhile longer, but by now I'm dog tired. Ant and I load up and head on for home. Just as soon as I get him down for his nap, and everything put away, I hear a knock on my door. I think now who in the world can this be. The last thing I want is somebody dropping in on me.

I walk to the window and peek out. I think this must be amistake. Outside is a white boy, probably nineteen or twenty years old. My first thought is he must be lost. In his hand he's holding a bouquet of flowers. I can't recall a lost white boy with flowers in this neighborhood. I think these can't be for me. I haven't had a steady man in over a month, and on top of that, I have never had a man send me flowers before. I curiously open the door.

"Yes ma'm, I'm looking for Miss Maya Baxter."

"That's me."

"Miss Baxter, I'm from the Tylerville Florist and I have a delivery for you. Would you please sign this delivery form?"

"Sign? Sign for what? I ain't ordered no flowers."

"No ma'm. Somebody else ordered them for you."

"For me?"

"Yes ma'm. If you're Maya Baxter of 313 Orr Drive."

"Yeah that's me."

"Then these are for you."

"And I don't have to pay for 'em?"

"No mam."

I sign the pad. He hands over to me the most perfect, the most beautiful, the most gorgeous flowers I've ever seen. They're a dozen long stemmed burgundy colored roses. I rip open the card attached to the flowers. Inside is a note. I read it out loud.

Just so you wouldn't forget about me. I sent this little reminder. Here's to wishes and dreams that somehow come true. Stay beautiful.

Love Jamie

I immediately start grinning like a preacher with a full collection plate. I don't know what I was feeling before, but right now. I want to dance. For the longest time, all I can do is to stare at those flowers and bust out smiling.

I think maybe Jamie's right. Maybe I do worry too much about what other people think. After all look at where it's gotten me. Maybe I need to look out for myself. If I want to get me a little white stuff on the down low, it's nobody's damn business. I can just keep it a secret and see how things go.

I look at the flowers and again I smile. This is the first time in a long time that I had anything to smile about, regarding a man. I think to myself, girl you can get this white boy. You put this chocolate loving on him and he'll never go back. Who knows this might just work out? It might be a reason to hope.

CROSSING OVER

Here I am rushing, rushing all around this house. As the saying goes, tonight's the night. I feel like everything has to be perfect. Jamie is coming over for the first time. This means no more sneaking around. For over a month that's all we've been doing. No more secrets, no more lies. Tonight, just like this damned Carolina Summer, it's going to get real hot. Tonight, we're going to cross the line.

Before, when we went out, Tanesha would have to look after Ant. Right of the bat she was questioning me about who I was going out with? And why the big secret?

The fact is I didn't want to tell her about Jamie. Tanesha, as light skinned as she is, has heard the rumors all her life. Rumors about, "why is it that Maya and your Mama so dark and you being so light?" Rumors about her daddy not being a black man. This is the kind of nonsense she'd heard all of her life. I had kind of figured she go off when she heard about Jamie, and boy did I figure right. I can still hear her screaming "You doing what? Are you outta your god damn mind!"

That was about the nicest thing she had to say.

Tonight all of the hiding would be over. Jamie was going to catch a taxi over, and we'd all meet for supper. The mere thought of Jamie, Ant, and myself sitting in the same room had me as nervous as I could ever remember. My sister had damned near said I was crazy. I don't know what I'd do if Ant doesn't like Jamie. Quite frankly, I'm not sure how he is going to respond.

The truth of the matter is I don't want to lose this white boy. It's a damned shame, but nobody else has ever treated me so nice. It's not just the flowers or the cards he gives me, it's much more than that. The first time he stood up when I walked up to the table, I asked him "Were he was going?"

He always tells me how beautiful I am, and how lucky he is to be with me. I think I'm falling in love, as a matter of fact I know I am.

I have had plenty of experience related to love, most of it bad. But I do know about falling in love, and this time it's with a brown-blond haired, soft hazel-eyed white boy. Hell if he wasn't white, I'd been done gave him some pussy. Well tonight white or no white, he's going to get him some of this loving.

But still, there is the problem of his being white. I just can't feel really comfortable with him in public, I keep wondering what other folks are thinking? I pray that won't matter quite as much if Ant likes him. If Ant likes him, maybe this thing can work.

As I set the plates for the table, I anxiously look up at the clock. Jamie is supposed to be here in fifteen minutes. I double check everything in my head.

The house is clean, spotless. I got a box of lubricated rubbers in the bedroom, banana flavored. I smile at the thought of using them all. Ant is, where is Ant? My thoughts again return to Ant. If I can only get my baby on my side. I've got to get him liking Jamie. I call out to him.

"Ant, you ready yet?"

"No ma'm."

"And why ain't you ready?"

"Cause I don't want to wear these punk clothes."

"Boy don't you start with me tonight. Get yourself out here and lemme look at you."

Out of his room he meanders. He's moving about as fast as molasses on a cold day running uphill. He's decked out in the cutest navy blue shorts and a pink Polo shirt. He looks absolutely gorgeous.

"I look like a punk."

"You don't look like no punk, and I better not hear you saying that again."

"But Mama, I don't like these clothes."

"Well you gonna wear them, whether you like 'em or not."

"Why I gotta wear 'em?"

"Cause I say so."

"Why you say so?"

"Ant, you gonna wear those clothes and that's that. Besides I think you look real cute, and stop tugging on that collar."

"It itches Mama."

"Well leave it alone and it'll stop itching."

"No it want."

I walk over to him and button his shirt.

"Aw Mama, Ain't nobody button the top button."

"I do."

"I don't know why we getting all dressed up for anyway."

"I told you earlier today, we're expecting company tonight."

"Another boyfriend?"

"Now why you asking that?"

"Cause I know you ain't dressed like that for no lady."

"Well if you must know smarty, it is a man friend." A frown crosses his face

"Aw Mama, why you gotta get another boyfriend? Can't it be just you and me and Auntie?"

Although it shouldn't have, his response surprises me. I sometimes forget that these people come not just in and out of my life, but in and out of his life as well.

"I didn't say he was a boyfriend."

"But he's gonna be."

"He might, and he might not."

"I hope he ain't."

"Ant, why you saying that? You don't even know Jamie."

"Well I hope he ain't like the rest of 'em."

I smile, and think to myself, well be sure doesn't look like anybody I've ever dated before. I wonder if this is the right time to tell him about Jamie. Is it the time to tell him that Jamie is white? I decide to wait for a better time. I'm not sure when that will be, but I'll wait just the same"

"He's really a very nice man, who Mama is gettin' to know. So you be real good you hear."

"Yes ma'm."

"And mind your manners."

"Yes'm."

"And quit tuggin' on that shirt."

"I can't help it. It itches."

"Go sit on the couch and watch TV 'til our company gets here."

"I wish he'd hurry up. I'm hungry."

"We'll eat when our company gets here and not a minute sooner." He walks over and bounces down on the couch.

"What you cooked Mama?"

"Let's see I got some fried okra, some rice and gravy, fried chicken, and some field peas."

This brings about the expected response from a small child.

"Okra and field peas. Yuck. I don't want no okra and field peas."

"You gonna eat 'em. Ain't nobody got any money to be wastin'"

"That stuff's nasty Mama."

"There's nothing wrong with good food."

"What we got for dessert?"

"You ain't got nothing if you don't clean that plate."

"I know, but what we got anyway."

"For dessert we got a big ol' peach pie. The kind that just melts in your mouth."

"Yeah. Now that's what I call dinner. You know what Mama?"

"What sweetie?"

"I don't think I need to eat too much okra and peas. I might fill up too much and can't eat no pie." I walk over to him and sit down on the couch.

"I don't ever remember a time when you couldn't eat a peach pie."

"I dunno Mama. I'm a lil' boy. It don't take a whole lot to fill me up."

I laugh at this comment. Before I get a chance to respond, the headlights of a car flash through the window. I run over to the window and see the taxi. I run back over to Ant.

"How do I look? How do I look?"

"You look good Mama. Is that him Mama?"

"Yup that's gotta be him."

Ant rises from the couch and walks to the window.

"Good. 'Cause I'm ready to eat."

"Ant you let him in. I'm gonna check and make sure my make up is on right."

I rush into the bathroom and check myself out. I got on this skintight black skirt. It is so tight that if I had a quarter in my pocket you could tell if it was head or tails. It shows enough thigh to get any red-blooded man's attention. A low cut pleated blouse that's down over my shoulder, with a push up bra. I want to show him a little bit of what he's going to be getting tonight. Ant calls "Mama it ain't him."

"It's not."

"No it's some ol' white man and he's coming up on the porch."

I walk out of the bathroom. I feel a bit unsure and slightly embarrassed. I guess this is the proper time to tell him about Jamie.

"That's probably him. Our dinner guest is white."

"Huh?"

He rolls his eyes as he stands there in disbelief. His look says "I know she didn't say a white man was eating dinner with us."

"What for Mama?"

I don't know how to answer that question. How can I answer his question when I'm asking myself the same thing? What for Maya? I look away from him and proceed to open the door. As I pull it open Jamie, smiling that naughty smile, steps into my home and into my life. In each arm he holds a package.

Before now it had been just Jamie and me sneaking around. Before tonight it didn't matter as much. We could call it off at any time and nobody would ever know. Tonight meant the sneaking was over. The two most important people in my life now know about him.

He kisses me lightly on the lips and hands me a box containing a fifth of Seagrams V-O. I take the box and look at Ant to gauge his response. Those two big eyes say it all.

On my baby's face is a look that clearly says, what the hell is going on! He looks at me in total disbelief. There is something to be said about the instinct of a child. He then looks down at the floor. Children are normally so trusting and optimistic. I do not see those qualities on my son's face. What I do see is an array of things, but not one of them is trust, or optimism. He, for whatever reason. does not look straight ahead. There is no comfort in his eyes. He doesn't look skyward for hope. There is something about the instinct of a child, My child looks down at the floor.

"Hey there partner. You must beAnt." "Maya's little Ant"

In a whisper of a voice, while never taking his eyes from his shoes, he responds.

"Yes sir, I'm Ant."

"Ant this is Jamie. The person I was telling you 'bout." Or should have told you about.

"Hey there."

"He's a friend of mine and I just wanted you to meet him."

He rolls those saucer sizes eyes up without saying anything. A few seconds drag and drag some more until what seems like a minute has past. It's real clear. Ant would rather have a pork chop tied around his neck, in a pen with hungry pit bulls, than to be here. To make matters worse, right now, I'm not sure if I wouldn't prefer to be right beside him.

"Hey partner, I bet you can't guess what I got for you?"

"Jamie you didn't have to bother with no presents."

"It no bother. I been dying to meet this fella for over a month now. Feel like I already know him. So I thought I'd get things off on the right foot."

He extends his hand out, and reaches the package toward Ant. Ant is unsure of what to do. On the one hand he's curious about it and very much wants the gift. On the other hand, he's never had a white man give him anything except a hard time. He looks at me and then at the package. He takes a second look at me. I anxiously nod for him to take it. I don't want to hurt Jamie's feelings.

He shyly moves forward and accepts the package, all the while keeping his eyes fixed on me.

"Now what do you say to Mr. Jamie?" In a voice that sounds more like it's coming from a mouse. "Thank you Mr. Jamie."

"Well you're welcome, and you can just call me Jamie."

I nervously smile as Ant takes the package back to the couch. I lie.

"That seemed to go alright. I just believe once he gets to know you, y'all gonna get along just fine."

"No question 'bout it Maya. One thing 'bout me, kids they love me to death."

Ant getting over his initial suspicion tears into the packet. He pulls out a large green basketball jersey. On it are the words BIRD and CELTICS. There is also the number 33. He innocently asks.

"Who's Bird?"

Jamie responds in disbelief.

"Who's Bird! Ant, I thought you knew your hoops? I want you to know that you're holding the jersey of the great Larry Bird. He and Michael Jordan are the greatest basketball players of all time."

Now that was going to just about do it. If there was one thing even I was certain of, there was only one basketball player ever mentioned on Flint Hill.

This was a Michael Jordan house. There was only one greatest and he sure wasn't named Larry or Bird.

"I know Michael Jordan is but ain't nothing special 'bout Bird."

"Man Larry Bird in his prime was the best basketball player on the face of the earth."

"That Birdman ain't the best basketball player in the world. There ain't but one best and that's Jordan."

"You're a lil' bit young son and probably don't remember how good Larry Bird was, but I'm tellin' you that Bird was just as good as Jordan"

"Everybody knows Michael Jordan's the best basketball player."

"Now Ant, son I'll give you a lil' credit. Jordan is good, real good, but take it from me. Bird is a better shooter, a better passer and a better rebounder than Jordan. Bird did it all, and he's got three championship rings."

"Jordan's got one and he's gonna win another one real soon." A noticeable pause.

"Well Bird's got 3 MVP awards."

"Michael's already got 2 and a Olympic gold medal, and he always leads the league in scoring."

"Well Bird played for the Celtics. The greatest team of all time.

Nobody even the Bulls got more titles than the Celtics."

"Nobody 'round her cheers for the Celtics. Nobody wears no Celtic stuff."

By now I'm certain this conversation is going nowhere. There is no way Jamie nor anybody else is going to convince Ant that Jordan isn't perfect. I decide I need to step in before things head further in the wrong direction.

"Now Ant that's enough. I want you to thank Jamie for the gift."

"Why I gotta thank him for something I ain't gonna never wear?"

"You are gonna wear it." In a hushed tone.

"No I ain't."

"What you say?"

He sticks out his lips, rolls his eyes and gives his standard reply when he knows to say otherwise means a butt whipping.

"Nothing."

"Now you thank Jamie for that present."

"That's okay Maya, if he don't like it I can get him another one. Besides! got it on sale for half price."

"No it's not okay. He's gonna take this jersey and be glad he's got it. Now Ant what do you have to say to Jamie!" A pause. "Well Ant I'm waiting." The pause continues as Jamie stands idly by, not knowing what to say

"Antonio, do I have to get a belt out?" This announcement brings about the desired words.

"Thank you."

"Thank you who?"

"Thank you Mr. Jamie."

"Thank you Mr. Jamie for what?"

"Thank you Mr. Jamie for this jersey."

I sigh heavily. This is certainly not the way I'd hoped things would start out.

"I'm sorry Jamie, I don't know what gets into this child."

"Ain't no problem Maya. Once he gets to know me a lil' better, we'll get along just fine. How 'bout we sit down to a nice supper and forget the whole thing."

"That sounds like a good idea. Y'all have a seat at the table and I'll fix the plates."

"You need any help?"

"No I'm just fine."

I hope I'll be able to say those words an hour from now. We all proceed to sit down to what has got to be the longest dinner in the history of mankind. If time had went any slower, it would have had to go backwards. The few times Ant picks his head up from staring at the design on his plate, it was to ask if he could be excused. He didn't even want to stay around for dessert. When Jamie and I tried to involve him in the strained conversation, he would only move the food around his plate and politely say, "yes'm and no sir."

Ant is a child who usually will not go to bed unless he's kicking and screaming. Tonight when I asked him to get ready for bed, he was like a prisoner who'd been pardoned by the governor. I bet he was thinking "Free at last, free at last, thank God almighty I am free at last.

In a way this was a moment I both dreaded and longed for. We'd staggered through the evening for the opportunity to be together. Now that we've reached the destination, I again question myself. Would the journey be worth it? I anxiously walk over to the C.D player. I don't even know what music to put on. I decide on some Anita Baker. While I do this, Jamie rises from the couch to fix himself a second drink.

"From begin to end, three hundred and sixty-five days in the year, I want the same old loving."

You can't go wrong with Anita. I walk over to the couch, next to it is a lamp. I look at Jamie, he looks at me, do I want this light off or on? I turn the light off. I sit next to him on the couch. It takes a minute or so for my eyes to adjust to the darkness. Before I can say or do anything, he leans over and kisses me softly on the cheek. It's a wonderful feeling, except for the slight smell of alcohol on his breath. He proceeds to kiss my neck so, so gently all the while he's caressing my shoulders and back in small circles.

He continues to lovingly massage that area of my back, moving back and forth not missing a spot. This goes on for several magnificent minutes. A slight moan escapes my lips, he kisses away the moan and soon it becomes a soft wail. I call out his name. He answers by leaning back on the couch and pulling me down on top of him. I now can feel my skirt rise up over my thighs. His hand slides down my back, over my hips and between my now parted legs. He kisses me with more passion and desire. I can feel the hardness of his erection rubbing against my legs. He seemingly has more than two hands and they all know what to do. One is stroking my lower back in a manner that is as gentle as the wind on a warm Spring night. It makes all of my senses come alive. The other hand is massaging my inner thighs so teasingly that my panties are getting moist with jealousy, And Lord knows what he's doing with that tongue of his. It seems to be tracing a delicious path up and down my neck that's leading to the bedroom. This goes on for minute after joyous minute. I feel my breathing coming in rapid breaths. It has to do this simply to keep up with my pulse.

All the while, Anita extends herself reaching one of those notes that very few humans have the capability of reaching "I love you just because, just becaaaaaauuuuuse I do..." as she hits her climax I join her with mine. I gasp, at the same time I grind my pelvis into his, thrusting hoping to have him penetrate me through clothes and all. I want him inside, all the way inside. But he has other ideas.

He slides, slithers, or somehow maneuvers himself from underneath me. His hands are beneath my skirt firmly tugging at my underwear. They come off with no resistance. He proceeds to kiss me on my knees. I can honestly say, I've never been kissed on my knees before. However, he doesn't remain there very long. That tongue of his is slowly gliding up my thigh. Each movement sends a tingling sensation throughout the lower half of my body. I didn't realize a tongue could produce electricity. At this moment it could light up every house in this country ass town. As he moves higher and higher, he pushes my legs and thighs back a little farther. Soon my legs are moving in opposite directions, and open invitation for further discovery.

My breath is coming in rapid burst. I am no longer able to speak. That is an understatement, the only sounds heard are from pure animal passion. They are simply grunts and groans. This delightful instrument overloads several of my senses. As he penetrates me with that extraordinary tongue, I am no longer able to control my own body. I am his. I do not belong to myself. At this moment I'm his possession. He probes and nibbles, licks and kisses. An then there is simply an explosion. With legs gyrating and pelvis pulsating I almost slide off the couch. He stops for a moment.

"Are you alright Maya?" I smile and weakly respond. Barely audible I announce.

"I am better than alright."

Through the dim light I sense that old crooked smile. I thank goodness as he resumes, right there on the living room floor. Right now I'm thankful for two things. One is that he found his way back to the same spot and two that there is shag carpet on the floor.

He eases my skirt off, while not lifting his head from what is now my favorite spot for more than a second. Soon after the skirt comes off he slides his now naked body on top of mine. How he got naked that quick I don't know? I'm just thankful he didn't take time away from what he's doing. I feel the warmth of his thighs, the strength of his hands. He opens my blouse and explores my breast. They heave and respond immediately to his touch. Involuntarily my thighs open farther to allow him total access.

My mouth opens and he kisses me. As he does, I can feel him seeking entry. I reach out and rub his erectness. I smile to myself, I guess all the stories aren't true. I guide him inside of me and we merge into each other. He begins to thrust and I notice our joint moaning. We have truly joined. While not jumping the broom, I have certainly stepped over to the other side, and for the time being, it sure feels good.

Faces

Rrrr bang, rrrr bang, rrrr bang, rrrr bang, as that noise repeats a seemingly endless pattern, the only other sound to be heard is whizzz clank, whzzz clank. whzzz clank, whizzz clank. This is the sound of weaving and doffing machines as they produce the incessant clatter of the Tylerville Textile Mill. It goes on 24 hours a day, seven days a week, fifty-one weeks a year. There has been talk lately about the old mill shutting down. The owner and the bosses talking about something called NAFTA being signed earlier this year. It suppose to cause jobs to be shipped out to Mexico for slave wages.

I don't know about any of that. As long as I can remember this mill has been churning out the cloth for towels, sheets, pillowcases and what not. As long as I can remember there has been the Tylerville Textile Mill. I don't guess that'll be changing. If this mill ever did shut down, I reckon the town would be right behind it.

The break whistle is about to sound. Besides a half-hour for lunch we get two fifteen minute staggered breaks. The bosses good about giving us our breaks. They aren't good about giving raises, or promotions for Blacks but they will give us a fifteen-minute break. I look up at the clock, through a dull haze. The cotton dust makes it look like it is late evening inside here. This is in spite of the high-powered lighting system. I also look up for Jamie. This is his last week on first shift.

There is a flashing of lights as the break whistle sounds. Immediately everybody heads for the canteen area. I hesitate as I wait on my man. The canteen area consists of two Coke machines, and some other vending machines. There are about twenty long rectangle tables for the workers to sit. Everybody walks past me at the entrance. I give a friendly smile to the ones I know and greet them. Most speak but some choose not to. The big news on Flint

Hill is not about the upcoming holidays, but Maya Baxter had a white man move in with her and her son.

I look up for Jamie, he works in the spinning section, and it takes him a bit longer to get over here. Finally I see that crooked smile. I think, my goodness he's fine. He strides on over to me holds the door and we walk inside. We take off our goggles and pull out the earplugs. We look around for a place to sit. All around us are coworkers black and white. They are mostly segregated by choice. We decided that since we'd made the commitment to live together we might as well get our relationship totally in the open. Besides after this weekend it wasn't like it was that much of a secret.

He spots a table where there are a few chairs together. He leads me to the table. To the surprise of all the onlookers he pulls out the chair for me. I blush slightly and sit down. This is certainly going to be the longest break of my life.

"You think they know??"

"I don't care."

"I know you don't care Jamie, but I do."

"Why?"

"Why! 'Cause this ain't Atlanta, Greenville, or even Spartanburg. This is Tylerville, South Carolina in the year 1992 and in this town I can never remember when a white and black couple lived together on Flint Hill. I mean never."

"Well in Tylerville people live together and that's all we are two people who love each other. So don't even think of me as being white. And as far as these good folks, they need to get ready for some changin' times."

"I wish it was that simple."

"It is that simple and if other folk don't see it that way the hell with 'em. I'll be damned if these rednecks gonna tell me who I can and cannot fall in love with."

That's Jamie. The more I'm with him, the more I realize he's not an easy man to be persuaded. To compare him to a jackass does the jackass a disservice. He is very, very stubborn. However I don't share his confidence and strong will. What I do share is a love that is very special.

At the table to my right I see big fat ass Bertha and her Confederate crew. I can only imagine what they are saying. Whatever it is, I'm sure the word black bitch is included. To my left is what looks like a localbranch of the Klan. These guys all could be called Bubba, and Bo and whatever other name cousins who marry call their children.

The Black tables aren't much better. The only real difference is I know those characters. It is because I know them that I know what they are saying. I know what they are saying because if it were not me with the white boy, I'd be sitting with them and saying some of the same things. Hate doesn't restrict itself to one color in this neck of the woods. It is not reserved for only one table.

Through the door walks my friend Janetta. I've known her for at least ten years. She stops at the soda machine and appears to be looking around for somewhere to sit. I wave at her. She apparently doesn't see me. I stand and wave a second time. She still doesn't see me.

"Who you waving at?"

"My girl friend." I call out to her.

"Netta, over here."

She acknowledges my existence. She waves back and gestures that she'll be silting at another table. She walks over to one of the Black only island and squeezes in between Marguerite and this other girl Shelia.

Marguerite is a good friend of my sister. Actually, she and Tanesha have been best friends since high school. She and I kind of tolerate each other for Tanesha's sake. I've always felt that she looks down on me, that somehow or another she seems to think that she's better than I am. I suppose this new situation won't change things very much.

I sit back down. I realize it's already happening. I'm being looked down on.

"Don't be lookin' all sad now. If they really your friends, they gonna stand behind you on any decision you make. Am I right?"

"I guess."

"You know I'm right baby. They'll come 'round, just you wait and see."

As he continues talking, I look up and glance at the variety of faces studying us. I try to do this discretely. I don't want to look directly at some of the expressions. Who wants to peer into the soul of hatred? For some strange reason I feel guilty, as if I'm the one who's done something wrong. I remind myself that the only thing I'm doing is being with the person, with whom I've fallen in love.

Some of the faces are easy to read, too easy. I've seen that look before. It says Nigger! Some of the faces are more difficult to read. They look on for the sake of curiosity. It's as if they're asking themselves what in the hell do you do with this thing? It is so foreign to them that it is a bit unreal. It's like going to the circus for the first time. You know tigers and zebras and all those animals exist, but the first time you actually see one it's a bit of a spectacle.

"What's going on Home girl?"

My thoughts are interrupted by my friend Caressa. She's still my oldest and probably my dearest friend, and the person I've told the most about Jamie. I don't associate with her too much because Jamie doesn't really care for any of my friends. He says he doesn't like "the way Caressa carries herself." At times I feel like he's trying to control me.

He doesn't even like for me to talk with her on the telephone. He doesn't know her very well but for some reason he chooses to dislike her. I find myself easing away from my best friend as my love for Jamie grows. The sad part is she so desperately wants to be accepted by anyone especially by anyone close to me.

"I said what's going on?"

She sits down at the table before either myself or Jamie can invite her and opens up a pork chop sandwich, a bag of potato chips, and a diet soda. She's always got a diet soda. Even though she weighs over two hundred pounds she keeps that diet Coke. I would guess that it isn't working.

She, as is her style, jumps dead into our conversation. It doesn't matter that she knows nothing about the conversation.

"It is hot'n a hell in here! Damn it's January, they ought to put a air conditioner in this bitch."

I look to Jamie and he to me. By reading the expression on his face I can tell he doesn't particularly care for Caressa's presence. Even though she's the only person who'll sit with me. I hope that he'll see this. Out of an entire mill, she's the only person who will dare support me. She is the only person without coercion or force who voluntarily sits at this table. That has to be worth something. I think, if he'll only take the time to gets to know her. If he does he might at least accept her. I don't need to be laying off any friends at this point in time.

"Jamie ain't you gonna say hello to Caressa."

Caressa cuts me off before I can finish talking to Jamie. She also manages to put her foot in her mouth. I didn't want her to let him know how much she and I had been talking.

"Child you don't have to be telling Jamie to say hi. As much as you been givin' me the 411 on him. It seems like I done known him for the longest. Heyyy Jamie how you doing."

"I'm just fine Claresha."

"It's Caressa, and if I was doing any better I wouldn't know what to do with myself."

She continues talking without slowing down one bit except to occasionally take a bite of her sandwich.

"Girlfriend I guess y'all know, you and Jamie are the talk of this mill. Hell y'all the talk of the whole damn town." Jamie looks at me as if to say what the hell is this person on.

"I don't know what the white folk talking 'bout, excuse me Jamie, but all anybody from up on the Hill can talk 'bout is Maya and her white boy. Excuse me Jamie. I mean it. They want to be all up in y'alls business. Like they ain't got nothing else to worry 'bout. I mean it. The way I see it a person can be with whoever they choose to be with. Ain't that right Jamie?"

"Yeah you right 'bout that."

"I know I am."

She takes a bite from her sandwich and a big gulp from her soda, while continuing to talk.

"It ought not make a bit of difference if you white and she black. It ought not make a bit of difference to no body if you was purple and she was polka dotted. If you wanna be with her and she wanna be with you then that's that. Ain't that right Jamie?"

"Yeah you right again." She continues.

"Me and Maya done been friends for as long as I can remember and she'll be the first one to tell you that I've always stuck by her and I always will. I don't care who she goes with. As long as you make her happy then I'm down for y'all and the hell with all these other sorry son of bitches."

"Caressa we don't have to be talking 'bout what these people feel. We ain't hurtin' nobody."

"Who you tellin sister girl. If I was y'all I'd tell all of 'em to kiss my fat, black ass, and I mean it too. Excuse me Jamie for saying that."

He smiles and kind of shakes his head. I don't think he has ever met anyone quite like my girl Caressa.

"And another thing 'bout them bastards up on the hill they just mad 'cause a white boy gonna be gettin' a sisters stuff. And they know if he get it good enough, they sorry ass ain't gonna be smellin' no more of Maya's ass."

I stop her.

"Caressa, Jamie don't wanna hear all that."

"It's the truth! And you know the truth will set you free. Hell all this time they could've been doing right by you and what they do, try to be slick, Thinking they some kinda players. Well they done played slam out. I mean it too. Jamie if you got any nice white boy friends who wanna jump the fence you just lemme know. Hell I might just try me somebody outside of Flint Hill."

He again laughs. But this time he doesn't really appear to be amused.

"Well I don't have a whole lotta friends in town and I might not bemakin' a whole lot, but if I find somebody I'll be sure to let you know." Just as he finishes, the break bell sounds. It's time to return to work.

"Damn is time up already? It sure didn't seem like fifteen minutes."

She inhales the last of her sandwich and chips and gulps down her soda. As she does a loud belch escapes.

"Excuse me. I'm sorry y'all but this rushing to eat a snack just messes with my digestion. I reckon I'm gonna head on back in. Maya I'll call you this evening. Jamie it's been good talking with you."

She gives me a wink and a knowing smile as she prepares to leave.

"The same to you Caressa."

"I guess it's 'bout time to get back inside this hot ass bitch."

She picks up her trash and throws it in a plastic trash can. She moves through the door and back to work, I look at Jamie. He smiles that perfect crooked smile and announces.

"Well beautiful, sweet, lady, I s'pose I'll be seeing you at home this evening. Damn that sounds good to say."

I smile from ear to ear. These words from him mean so much, most importantly I don't have to be lonely. Tonight and I pray for a long time to come, I don't have to be lonely. I don't know what hell I'm going to catch for loving him, but as long as he loves me, I'll put up with it.

The hours at work were as long as the time I had to hold my breathe in the closet when his wife came home early. How could anything move this slowly?

And talk about being cold, ice had nothing on the frigid stares I saw today. I read the looks correctly they either said, "A Cracker loving nigger bitch", that was from the brothers. Or they'd say "A thieving charcoal nigger bitch", that of course was from the white girls. It's kind of funny, but the looks on the sister's faces only appeared to be that of curiosity.

Eventually the day ended and I was able to escape home. Home to the one I find myself falling deeper and deeper in love with.

Tonight, lying in bed in his arm, they could no longer hurt me. In his arms I found my sanctuary. At that time, in that place I felt safe and loved. As he gently massaged my shoulders and back in the smallest roundest circles, I feel alive. I could feel the love pulsating throughout my entire body. There had been a time recently when I wasn't sure if my heart still worked, but now I know. All this old heart needed was someone to beat for. I can feel his touch reaching down into the depths of my soul.

He peels away the nightgown that I'd hoped he'd peel away, all the while pulling me closer to him. I could feel the warmth of his beautiful body. I kissed the contours of what has to me a most perfectly developed chest. As I do so, he ran his tongue down the side of my neck, stopping to nibble on my ear. His hands continue to explore the softness of my upper body, deciding not to miss a single inch. I could sense myself becoming more than warm. The heat rises within my body. I can feel my body longing to become one with his. He gently rolls me over unto my stomach. The caress of his hands changes to a silken tongue. Every nerve in my body responds to this wonderful touch. I don't know if you can go to school to learn how to use a tongue like this, but if you can, my Jamie sure can be the teacher. As it glides down the small of my back, stopping only to kiss the curvature of my longing buttocks. I now experience mounting pleasure as he licks and nibbles my entire upper body. I arch my back to provide him all the access he might need. He slides his hands underneath me as preparation is being made to enter me fully and completely. My body tremors with anticipation. I surrender control to my lover.

Suddenly what sounds like a small whoosh breaks into my consciousness? I have made love hundreds of times before with dozens of men, and never had I ever felt a whooshing sensation. To my dismay Jamie pauses for a second. He raises up from over me, gets out of bed, and walks over toward the window. My eyes follow his torso through the darkness, but outside in the yard there is a small bright light. I think too myself there is no light outside this window.

I now rise from the bed and join Jamie at the window. I look out to see this object burning in our yard. In sharp contrast to the darkness of the night is a blazing T-shaped object. Then it dawns upon me, that's not a T. It's a cross, a burning cross.

I look up at Jamie and he down on me. This time there is no perfect, crooked smile on his face. This time there is no cool disdain for those who would judge. This time there is a look of genuine concern. Welcome to the neighborhood my brother.

Getting' Chilly

Christmas was really special in certain ways, and not so special in others. It was exceptional not because of any gift, but for the first time in many years. I wasn't alone. I'm not talking about being with Ant or Tanesha, or even those pieces of men I'd had in the past. I wasn't alone because of Jamie. He made everything so wonderful, simply by being there with me. Since the mill was shut down for a week, we got to spend a great deal of that time alone, except for Ant. We would make love almost every opportunity we had. We spent the days sneaking some not so short quickies and the nights in heated passion. I can truly say that it was a most wonderful time, except for Jamie occasionally drinking a bit too much. Since it was the holidays I didn't say too much about it. After all we were still together.

Christmas was terrible in that Ant was upset about what he didn't get. Basically all I really could afford was clothes. You would think that with the two of us working, things would be better financially. But that wasn't necessarily the case. Jamie did manage to buy Ant a decent bicycle. This would have been great except Ant refuses to ride the thing, except when Jamie isn't around. I'm pretty sure it pisses Jamie off. I can truthfully say that he has been trying to bond with Ant, and I love him very much for that.

It was also terrible in that Tanesha didn't come over for Christmas dinner. She had promised that she would. We had this big bash all set up and she calls al the last minute and cancels. It wouldn't have been so bad, had she not did the same thing for Thanksgiving. She doesn't like Jamie and it seems the feeling is becoming more and more mutual.

The time after Christmas has always been depressing to me, and this year things are basically the same. All the trees are empty and bare. The nights are really cool and that's not just from the weather. It's late February and the only thing to look forward to is Spring. It's near the end of February and Jamie's still celebrating the Holidays. His drinking to bring in the New Year was just a bit of celebrating. Now it's February, Who in the hell drinks to celebrate President's day?

These days, it seems I've got a lot of time to think. That's because lately I'm spending my time waiting on Jamie. Too much time waiting on him, and not enough with him. Things are getting kind of chilly between us. And that's a shame because I do love him, and I feel pretty certain that he loves me too.

My main activity these days seem to be looking at a damn clock. Imagine how frustrating that can be. Every time it ticks, it just makes me more and more lonely. It reminds me that I'm supposed to be lying down, sleeping in my bed with his arms around me. Well I'm not putting up with it any more. I've seen this picture before. If I don't do something about it, Jamie's will turn out like all the rest of them, totally taking me for granted. We barely been together a good six months and he's putting me through this all because of a damned softball. But tonight it comes to an end. I'm get his ass straighten out. It's best to do it now before it's too late.

With March being just around the corner, in Tylerville it's time for softball. Every year the mill sponsors a softball league. It's one of the most popular social activities in the entire county. Come late March there'll be all kinds of moments throughout the Summer. Folks will come from all over the Upper State to watch and play. The competition is really fierce.

If it's one thing in this town that will temporarily overcome racism and prejudice, its sports. In the Fall it's high school football. In the Spring it's softball. When it Comes down to sports, it doesn't matter if you're Black, White, Red or in between, if you can hit that damned ball over 300 feet then everybody will love you. It turns out that Jamie is pretty good.

When he first mentioned joining one of the teams at work, I really thought it was a good idea. After all it would help him get in with both the white boys and the brothers. When they saw how good he could go to the hole and get the deep grounder, they temporarily forgot that he was going to my hole. The team he hooked up with was mixed, talk about ironic. They decided his living with me wasn't a big deal. If he wanted a little dance on the dark side, who were they to stand in the way. For the time being, he could keep stroking me as long as he kept stroking that ball. So even though things were getting better for him at work, for me there wasn't as great a change. More than anything, I was being tolerated.

Back at home, things however were getting worse. It seems like every time they had a practice, it meant male bonding. Testosterone being what it is, that would mean the guys had to stop at Red's Grill, shoot some nine ball and have a few beers. I'm finding out more and more that Jamie has a problem with stopping at a few beers. The few beers lead to a couple of shots, which lead to him coming home late at night, with his pockets empty. It also seems he can't start drinking without playing those poker machines, the South Carolina version of Las Vegas. As good as Jamie is at making love, and playing softball, the opposite is true about his gambling.

As soon as he comes in I'll let him know how I feel. If we are going to have any kind of future, it's best to let him know I'm not putting up with this stuff. I've learned my lesson a dozen times over. I'm through letting men run over me because I might like their ass. And he better have some money.

As I look up, I see a single headlight shine through the window. I been asking him to fix that light for the past week and he hasn't fixed it yet. If it were his car, he'd have fixed it by now. And I bet he has driven all the gas out too. He acts like the damn thing runs on air.

I get up, anxious like, and go to look out the window. Jamie gets out, slams the door and walks slowly up the gravel driveway. I think hopefully, at least he isn't staggering. Maybe he's not drunk this time. Maybe he didn't drank too much tonight. Maybe he's even got some money to pay on all these bills. Maybe he want be too hard to get along with tonight. He reaches the top step stumbles and almost falls. I frown, so much for his not being drunk.

He fumbles with the door a few seconds then manages to open it.

He walks up to me.

"Hey baby, sorry I'm late." He slobbers all over my mouth. I can taste that nasty ass liquor.

"I was just hanging out with some of the fellas from work. We stopped off after practice down at The Grill and shot a lil' Nineball." It's clear by his voice that he's had more than one too many.

"I thought Red's closes at midnight, what y'all been doing for the last two hours?"

He sits down at the kitchen table, and slides the keys to my car across the table and on to the floor. I pick them up.

"You know, we, we hung around outside dranking a few beers."

"All this time?" He smiles.

"Yeah, all this time. What else you think I'd be doing?"

"I dunno, you been spending so much time out dranking and playing them poker machines the last few weekends, I don't know what you doing half the time."

"Well I ain't been doing nothing, so let's just let that go. I didn't come here to be questioned like I'm no five-year-old child. Besides I'm hungry. How 'bout fixing me a sandwich or something?"

I sit down across from him. It sounds stupid but even drunk I can't help but appreciate how damn good looking he is. But I don't want to get distracted.

"I'm not your maid. Come in here at all times of the night talking 'bout fixing you a sandwich. Fix your own damn sandwich."

"Ah c'mon now. I said I was sorry 'bout being late. I'll make it up to you tomorrow. We'll go out to dinner somewhere. Maybe go over to the fish camp and have some of that peppered catfish you like so much."

"You think anytime you say you're sorry that's it? All you gotta do is smile at me and just say, I'm sorry, and that makes everything perfect. Well Jamie! been hearing that too much lately. I'm sorry don't mean nothing when you don't make no effort to change what you're sorry 'bout."

He frowns and fires back. For the first time you can notice his voice began to rise.

"What you want me to do Maya? Huh! You want me to sit around here on my day off looking at the damn walls! Looking at the stove, the 'frigerator. Hell, I went out to have a little fun. Now you tell me what's wrong with that? I got a life besides working and coming home."

"I know you got a life Jamie, but I'm s'pose to be a part of your life too. What do you want me to do when you go out and stay all night long?"

"You can do whatever you wanna do. Didn't nobody say you need to sit 'round this house waiting on me."

"That's just fine. Two weeks ago you had a fit when I went to Greenville with my sister and her girlfriend. Now you sit here talking 'bout it's okay for me to go out." He lies.

"That was different. You out there with your sister. She ain't got no man waiting on her at home. She out there looking for somebody."

"Tanesha ain't out looking for no man."

"Oh, so what she too good for a man?"

"Hell no! She ain't like that. She just not the type to be running around after no man. She got more pride than that."

"Well I still don't like you going out with her. Let her come over here if she wants to see you. Hell we invited her for both Thanksgiving and Christmas and the only reason she didn't come is 'cause she thinks she's too damn good for me."

I can't believe this stupid drunken bastard sits here criticizing my baby sister. Realizing you can't argue with no liquored up logic, I do my best to remain calm.

"That's my sister Jamie. My only sister. If I can't socialize with her, who can I hang with?"

I can sense now that he's about to lose it. I have seen that temper flare up a few times the past month or so.

"Did I say you can't socialize with her? I said I don't like you going out with her. She can come over here anytime. I don't like y'all hanging out at clubs and places like that. You know what kinda men out there."

"I'm not looking for no man Jamie. Lord knows the one I got is handful enough."

I immediately regret those words. As quick as quick can be, the look on his face turns nasty and hateful.

"And what that s'pose to mean?"

"It don't mean nothing."

"The hell you say. You talk like I'm not good enuff for you. I was good enuff for you when I had your legs jacked up in the air and you head banging up against that headboard the other day." I frown at this comment.

"It ain't all 'bout sex Jamie. It's about you letting me be part of your life. It's about us respecting one another's feelings. It's about you caring enough to spend some time with me, like it was when you was first trying to get up with me. Can't you see that?"

"I can't see a damn thing, but I sure as hell can hear that big ass mouth of yours. I tell you the truth, if I live forever I'll never understand women. Can bitch 'bout me spending time with you, and as soon as I hit the door, you trying to run me off with that mouth. I want you to do one thing for me, get off my ass!"

"Jamie all I'm asking is for you to take me out every once in a while. We used to sneak off to Greenville and go to the movies and out to dinner, all I want is to do those things every now and again."

"Okay, okay, I promise next weekend me and you are gonna spend so much time together that you gonna get sick of me. Are you happy now?"

"I'll be happy if you don't forget. You know how you forget things when you been drinking a lot." He's immediately annoyed by this comment.

"And who says I been drinking a lot? Did I say how much I had to drink? Well did I?"

"No."

"Damn woman lives with you awhile and she thinks she knows everything. The fact is I had a few beers and the three of us split a pint. So I'm no ways near being drunk."

I accept this obvious lie. I can feel his anger rising to a fever. I know what'll happen if I keep on disagreeing with him about his drinking. That's how I got my face slapped the last time we got into it.

"I didn't mean to say you was drunk."

"Well that's sure the way I heard it. A woman who don't even drank but once every blue moon, gonna tell me 'bout my dranking."

"I wasn't telling you 'bout your dranking. All I was saying is sometimes when you been dranking, you just don't remember everything."

"So what you saying Maya? You saying you can tell what I'll remember next week? Hell baby I didn't know you could see in the future? Can you tell me what lottery ticket to buy? How 'bout telling me who's gonna win the World Series this year? What about you and me going to Atlantic City. Yeah we can go to Atlantic City and make a killing. Then I want even have to worry 'bout all the money I lost tonight on that damn pool table."

This immediately catches my attention. Jamie had sworn to me that he'd quit gambling.

"I know you didn't go out and blow money gambling after what happened last week! What we gonna do 'bout all these bills thats due? I don't even have money for the light bill."

"I don't know what you gonna do? Them bastards gonna have to wait if they want some money from me."

"You promised me no more gambling."

He laughs at me as if this whole thing is somehow one big joke.

"I promised you no more gambling on the poker machine. I didn't say nothing 'bout shooting pool."

"It's the same thing! Gambling is gambling."

"It ain't the same thing!"

"Then you tell me how it's s'pose to be different then. You just tell me what the big difference is?"

"It's different 'cause I didn't break my word to you. I have never broke my word to you. I kept my word just like I promised!"

He laughs again. Only now it's real cynical and mean spirited. "It's not funny Jamie. 'Specially since you blew your whole pay check last week."

"To hell with last week. I do what I damn well please with my money."

"And what am I s'pose to do? I been paying the rent, the car payment, the.." Before I finish he angrily cuts me off.

"You s'pose to pay those bills. The lease is in your name. The car is in your name. You gotta feed your child. So why should I be kicking in all my cash to make your ends meet?"

"Jamie you know when you moved in we agreed to split all the bills."

"Well that was then. Lately I done reevaluated things."

"Reevaluated? Reevaluated what? You hardly gave me a penny in the last month and a half. Not since Christmas."

Instantly, you can sense that the rage has spilled over the top. His fury can no longer be contained in this vessel.

"Is that what it's all about? Huh bitch? Is it all about how much money 1 bring here? Is that what it's about?"

"You don't have to be calling me no bitch."

He explodes up, knocking over the chair and hitting his leg on the table. I've not seen this picture before, not at this level. It scares the hell out of me. I also rise up from the table, but I instinctively move back a step.

"Answer my damn question Maya. Is that all I mean to you, how much money I can pay on some bills."

"No Jamie, how can you say something like that? You know what we been going through. You know how much I love you. You know its 'bout more than that."

"Not from what I've been hearing lately. The only thing that comes outta your mouth is money, money, money. Not 'bout how much I mean to you, nothing but how much you got for this or that. You love my damn money so much, you go on and take my last."

He proceeds to reach into his pocket. He pulls out what appears to be about three dollars and some change. He then holds out the money for me to take. Call it instinct, but I understand all to well, that if I reach out for this money, money is not what I'll be getting.

"There! That what you want? Huh? You asked for it. Is this what you wanted?" He steps toward me. I continue to retreat.

"I don't want the money Jamie. I just want you to do what's right."

"That's what I'm doing. I'm doing what's right. I'm giving you every single penny I have. Now you take it!"

"I don't want it Jamie." He takes another step towards me. I realize I have nowhere to go.

"You take it right now, or I'm gonna kick your ass all over this house."

I look into those once beautiful eyes and all I now see is rage. I don't know this man. This man who has me in fear for my very own safety. I'm terrified. I want to back up another step, trying somehow to escape before he decides to strike, predator against prey. But before I can move far enough away, he draws back and flings the money at me. I try to move, but a piece of change catches me right on the forehead. An ache shoots through my temple. I think to myself, I didn't realize a quarter could hurt so doggone much. I scream out in pain, I kneel down to the floor. I can feel the tears flowing. They are partly from the physical but mostly from the emotion ache. I scream at him loud enough to wake every soldier in the Confederate cemetery.

"Jamie! Why you doing this to me?" He stalks over to within a few feet of me.

"Shut up! I mean it. You shut up right now."

I try to stifle the sobbing and moaning, but I can't. "Bitch! I told you to shut up."

But I can't. It has now come to a head. He draws back an open hand. I'm grateful for that. I raise my arms to block the blows that I now know are coming. But before he can hit me, standing in the doorway in Flintstone pajamas, Ant calls out in my defense.

"Why you hitting on my Mama?"

Both of us look over to Ant. He's obviously been awakened by our fighting.

"Boy you get your behind back to bed before I put my foot up your narrow ass."

"I ain't going nowhere 'til you leave my Mama alone."

I plead to him. Ordinarily, I wouldn't be as concerned, but tonight Jamie has totally lost it.

"Ant, Mama's alright. You just go on back to bed."

"He better take his nappy ass head somewhere."

While Jamie is sidetracked, I half crawl and half scamper over to my baby I'm trying to reassure him as well as protect him. I hug my child in a embrace, trying somehow to cover him up. I become a human shield. Jamie momentarily forgets about his planned attack on me. He seems to be unnerved by Ant's presence. While he tries to make up his mind, I look back at Ant. He's at Jamie, the looks in his eyes is that of pure loathing. One so young shouldn't know such evil feelings.

"Boy if you know what's good for you, ya'll quit looking over this way, and get back to bed."

"Leave him alone Jamie. He's only a boy."

"I don't give a good got damn what he is. He ain't gonna be looking at me that way. And it's 'bout time he learned to do what I tell him to do anyway."

"I ain't got to do nothing you say. Your white ass ain't my daddy!"

In life we make all kind of decisions, good and bad. I can truthfully say, that as soon as those words leave Ant's lips, this was not a good choice. As soon as these words touch the heated air, I know any hope for peace tonight has now been lost. Things instantly have gone from bad to worse. Jamie goes ballistic. He stomps over, knocking over a chair, and grabs Ant by the arm. I'm totally panic struck. I don't know what to do.

"Lemme go. Lemme go." I plead. "Jamie please leave him alone."

He continues as if I had said nothing, too consumed by his present state of mind.

"I'm gonna leave 'em alone alright".

Before Jamie can utter another word, Ant takes matters into his own little hands. With a loud grunt, demonstrating all the strength he has, he kicks Jamie squarely on the knee. Jamie stunned by the impact staggers, stumbles, and falls. He bellows in agony.

"Son of a bitch! Son of a bitch!"

Ant, realizing the magnitude of his action is suddenly engulfed with fear. We are terrorized at what is being played out before us. Jamie gets up on one knee. The look on his face goes beyond suffering and anger. He whips the belt from his pants in one swift motion. He stands as best he's capable, considering the combination of alcohol and the kick to his knee. Ant looks to me first, and then he looks to run. Before he can make his escape, Jamie lashes in on him with the belt. Ant cries out in agony. This is a most painful night, of a most painful existence.

"Owww! Mama, Mama."

Jamie slings him against the wall to keep him from running away. He continues to swing with all of this strength. The force of the belt striking flesh brings forth continuous pained screaming from Ant. I can't stand it for another second. I run over and grab onto Jamie, holding him as best I can. As I do this, Ant slides down to the floor.

"You bastard, leave 'em alone! What's wrong with you?"

We wrestle for a second. Then he takes the back of his hand and smacks me right in the jaw. It is as if somebody has cut the legs right out from under me. I collapse to the floor, clutching my face.

"Bitch! Don't you know better'n to grab me like that? I want have it Maya."

"What's wrong with you Jamie? Why you doing this to us?"

"Shaddup! You hear me! Just shaddup!"

"Why you doing this Jamie? Why?"

Before I can say another word, he turns to me with that belt. I try to move away, but before I can move, I feel the sting of the belt on my back.

"Ow, oh Lord, oh Lord help me."

"Didn't I say shaddup? Huh?"

Another swing, and still another, and another. I crawl trying to get away. Except there will be no escape. He follows me. He won't quit. In the midst of all of this, I look up to notice my son cowering against the wall, looking on terrified. What must he be thinking?

Here is his mother getting a whipping, like a damn slave from her white ass master. As the tears pour from my eyes, if the belt wasn't enough, he decides to add a good kick in my side. I feel all the air go from inside of me. Were it not for the sheering pain exploding through my entire body, I'd be worried about not having any breath. I'm now too afraid to move, too hurt to fight. I simply agonize and suffer on a shag carpet that once brought me pleasure with this same man.

"Now the next time I come home through that door, it better not be a damn thing said to me. You got that!"

He looks at me and my child in contempt. Even if I could answer, that look demands that I say nothing. He tosses the belt to the floor, turns off the light and walks back into the bedroom, slamming the door.

For what seems like forever, everything is a blur, I dare not move. I had never realized before, but fear can cause time to become irrelevant. Time is frozen but I do not care. Finally, after catching my breath, I'm able to focus. The only light in the room is coming from the moon. As best I can, I rise up to a sitting position. I locate Ant, huddled against the wall. He's trying to stifle the tears. I want to rush over and comfort him. As I move I began to notice the slight pain in my side. Realizing this, I choose to inch over to him. We hug and comfort each other. I gently caress his face, in a whisper of a voice, so as not to wake up that bastard I ask.

"Are you alright baby?"

He nods his head yes as he sniffs. I rub the welt marks on his arms. This causes me to tear up. I decide in an instance.

"Sweetheart, don't say nothing. Go into your room and get as many clothes as you can tote." He nods.

"Put on some shoes and put that stuff in the car. You put the keys in the switch and leave the door open on my side of the car."

"Mama you ain't gonna go in there are you? Don't go Mama."

"Yeah baby, I got to pick up a few things."

"Mama don't go in there, please Mama please. He's gonna start up with us. I know he will."

"Don't worry precious, nothing's gonna happen to Mama. Now you go head and get your stuff."

I strain to see the pained look on his face. But he does as I asked and quietly walks back into his room. In the dark, I grope for and find the car keys on the floor beside the kitchen table. I crawl across the room and open the door to the bedroom and peer in. As I do so, the door creaks slightly. This causes my heart to pound, my pulse to race, and my palms to sweat. I can make out the image of Jamie lying across the bed, out cold.

Before I tip toe into the room, Ant reappears with an armload of clothes. I hand him the keys and send him to the car. He complies. I pause briefly, reconsidering my decision to go in for clothing. I enter the darkened room and move to the nearest dresser. I inch it open, and pull out some pants. I repeat this process in another drawer, and grab what I hope to be a few blouses.

Just then Jamie rolls over and groans. My heart jumps into my throat. I feel a slight tingling sensation between my legs. I realize I've slightly wet my pants. I, afraid to turn my eyes from Jamie, begin backing out of the room. Just when it looks as if everything is going to go off smoothly, I stumble over one of his shoes. I bang into the door, then regain my balance. A groggy Jamie, snorts, rubs his eyes and looks up. I move a little faster out of the room.

It must've taken him a few seconds to register what was going on. I don't wait around to see. I haul ass to the door, ease it shut and run to the car. Ant has the door open just like I told him. As I throw the clothes in the back seat, I turn the keys in the ignition switch. I look up and see the front door opening.

"Oh shit." I immediately turn the switch. As I do I hear Jamie roar. The engine tries to turn over.

"Maya! Where the hell you think you going?"

He moves out onto the front porch, I turn the key for a second time. The motor spins but refuses to turn over.

"Maya! I said where you going?"

I turn the key again and frantically pat the gas pedal. Still no success.

Getting no response Jamie leaps down off the porch. This turns out to be a mistake for him but a blessing for us. He lands upon a sharp rock and injures his foot. He screams out in pain.

"Damn!" Ant screams to me "Hurry up Mama!" Jamie hops around on one foot. I call to Ant.

"Lock the door Ant, lock the door!"

He complies. I try the ignition a fourth time. It spins, and spins and finally catches. The engine fires up. Jamie limps over to the car and pounds his fist on the hood. I put it in reverse and speed out of the driveway. He tries to follow cursing at the top of his lungs. The car throws gravel and dust high into the air. Once out of the driveway, I put the car in drive and squeal off. I speed past Jamie, who drunk or not knows to get the hell out of the way.

Relieved to have escaped, I allow myself to breathe. I look over at Ant. I know he is absolutely shaken by all of this. He too can now breath. Just then, a red light begins to blink. It's the fuel gauge. The car is on empty.

Tanesha

Knock, knock, knock, and knock. Well this is totally screwed up. Here I am knocking on a door I don't want to be knocking on. Here I am three o'clock in the morning standing at my sister's door. Why? Because I just got my ass whipped and run out of my own house. If you were to come up with reasons to visit your family, this would not be on top of your list.

Knock, knock, knock, knock. Here we are, my child, my baby and myself out in this cold night air. When he ought to be tucked in a warm bed. He's out here because his Mama can't protect him, or doesn't know how to protect him. Through the tears, I look inside the house. All the lights are off. It is dark inside, pitch dark.

I knock on the door again, this time a little harder. Feeling a bit frustrated, a bit desperate, I take my resentment out on the door. Bam, bam, bam! I guess Tanesha's here. I see her car in the parking lot. I hope she's here. I panic at the thought that she might be on a date or something. Maybe she's out and want be back tonight. I have the key that she gave me, but I don't want to use it if she's inside. I ask myself where will I go if she's not here? I guess I'd have to let myself in.

I knock again, this time with even more desperation. I think if I have to beat any harder that I might wake up the whole apartment complex. As I continue beating, I notice from around the corner of her apartment complex two teenagers. There's a park with a basketball goal and swings and stuff in back of her building. The kids all hang out there. I look at the two boys out of the corner of my eyes, not wanting to make any type of direct eye contact. I'm happy when they cross the street and head toward another building.

"Mama is Auntie at home?"

"I dunno sweetheart. I sure hope so."

Just as the last words leave my mouth, a light goes on in the back bedroom. I am torn between relief and dread. My sister, bless her heart, is the sweetest person in the world. She'll do anything for me. Of course she's going to give me a million dollars worth of hell to pay for it.

I know she's going to have a thousand questions about what happened tonight. Then she'll get mad at Jamie. Then she'll get mad at me for being with Jamie, and I just don't feel like hearing it tonight. Unfortunately, it's the price I have to pay for landing on her doorstep.

She approaches the door and pulls back the blinds. Ant sees her face and immediately a smile covers his once sad face. You can feel the love that radiates from him. There is absolutely no doubt about one thing, my boy loves his Auntie.

"There's Auntie Mama. She's at home!"

I hear the lock being unfastened. In a navy blue housecoat, there stands my sister Tanesha in the doorway, one hand on her hip, another on a 38 pistol. She looks at me in disbelief.

"What the hell? Maya?" She looks at Ant.

"What y'all doing out here? Why didn't you call?"

I'm not exactly sure what I should say to her. I feel so embarrassed. That problem is quickly solved. She fires question after question to me, not giving me a chance to say anything.

"Maya? What's going on? And what is that on your face? What's wrong with your face? You been fightin'? Who you been fightin' with? Who's been beatin' on you?"

Before I can say anything, the tears start pouring like a spigot. I blurt out.

"I don't know. I mean it Jamie."

"Don't cry Mama." Tanesha immediately reaches out and embraces both of us.

"It's gonna be alright Maya. Y'all c'mon in here and let's get this child to bed. C'mon now, don't y'all worry 'bout a thing. We're gonna get this mess straightened out. Maya you sit on down on the couch. I'll take care of Ant."

We obediently march into the apartment. Following Tanesha's instructions, I simply flop down on the couch with a fatigued thud.

She looks at me as she moves to her role as protector.

"I'll take care of Ant".

She bends over and stares him directly in the eyes.

"I know you're wore out, I can see it in your eyes. Let's say we get you to bed. It is way too late for you to be up".

He smiles innocently only as a child can. In spite of what he has experienced and witnessed tonight and on previous occasions, he smiles. In spite of everything he knows that he is loved by his auntie and that he is totally safe.

"Auntie is there an extra blanket on my bed? It's cold out there"

"I tell you what, I will get you one and in the morning I am going to get up and make you the best breakfast you have had in a month of Sundays"

She gently takes his hand as they proceed to his room.I slump on the couch listening to them from the back bedroom while also dreading when she finishes with him.

"Auntie can I have some Frosted Flakes"

"Frosted Flakes" boy I'm gonna make you some sausage and eggs with grits and homemade buttered biscuits. Now don't that sound better than some old frosted flakes?"

"Not to me"

She playfully scolds him.

"You just want that mess 'cause its full of sugar. How you gonna grow up to be big and strong by eating cereal?" He giggles and rationalizes.

"I will just have to eat two bowls".

She laughs slightly and calls.

"I bet you would like that. Come 'ere boy and let me give you a big ol' wet kiss."

I guess he complies because I immediately hear the sound of and exaggerated kiss and Ant complaining.

"Ewww, Auntie that was too wet."

"Well if you don't get your pencil thin behind underneath them covers then I am going to give you another one." Another giggle is heard.

"Goodnight sweetheart".

"Love you Auntie"

"I love you more. And no fooling around. I wanna hear some zzzzz's coming from this room in due time".

I look up from my position on the couch and notice the lights go off.

Tanesha comes back into the room bringing that look with her. It's the look I've seen too many times before.I proceed to straighten up the blanket on the couch. It's amazing that to this day I still feel the need to respond to her like I do. I still feel slightly intimidated by my baby sister. Anyway, I know the interrogation is about to begin. She walks back in and sits down at the opposite end of the couch.

I want to tell her I don't want to talk, but she's already decided that we will talk, and I don't have the energy to disagree with her at this moment. So I do what I usually do when we disagree. I hold my tongue. She starts the conversation with a voice that is loving but firm.

"That's a good boy we got there Maya. It'll be a shame if he gotta go through too many more nights like tonight. We can't let 'em go through too many more nights like this."

I nod in agreement. There's nothing else I can do. I know she has already figured out what happened. That probably took all of thirty seconds. After all, she has seen this picture before. The only thing that's different is this time it's a white boy that's whipping my ass.

"You know what we went through as chaps. Ain't no need in putting that boy through no whole lotta of hell."

I look straight ahead for two reasons. First, I feel a need to avoid her eyes. Those eyes know every thing about me, especially the past. I don't like to be reminded of the past. Second, those eyes can consume my hopes like a fire does to kindling.

"Now I want you to give it to me straight, with none of your sugar coating things. You tell me exactly what happened tonight."

I shake my head wearily. My eyes again start to overflow as if the dam had just collapsed. Tanesha automatically moves closer to try and rebuild the structure. This has always been one of the things I love most about her. She might curse and scream and criticize, but eventually she'll reassure and she will never fail to show her love.

"Just take your time Sis. You get some tissue and wipe your face."

"Can't we just talk 'bout this in the morning Tanesha? I'm awfully tired." She refuses to go for any excuse.

"If you're tired I'll fix us some coffee. But I wanna know what happened? I Wanna know what that bastard did to you."

"Me and Jamie had a fight that's all."

"I can see you had a fight. And from that bruise on your face, I believe you got the worst of it. What I wanna know is what were y'all fighting 'bout? What make him think he can beat on you like that?"

"Tanesha I really don't wanna discuss it."

"Discuss my ass! A discussion is talking about some kind of problem. When you get your ass whup like a rented mule, ain't no such things as discuss. It's time for some answers! You come busting up in my place at three o'clock in the morning with a small child and your face swelled up like a damn Halloween pumpkin, and you talking 'bout "you don't wanna discuss it? I don't think so Sister. You sit here talkin 'bout."

In a mocking tone "Me and Jamie had a fight, and I don't wanna discuss it."

"Unh, unh, if that son of a bitch done jumped on you he gonna pay for it. I just wanna know the what fors and the why comes!"

"You know Tanesha it's really none of your business." The look on her face is that of being astounded.

"You right, it ain't my business how your face beat the living hell outta his fist. Don't even go there homegirl! I ain't the one! When you came over my house, whether you wanted to or not you made it my business. And besides that, anything that affects you and that boy is my business. Ain't none of my business. My ass! You put up with that bastard's mess and tell me it's none of my business."

"I didn't mean no harm by it. What I meant was all couples have fights, and it's no big deal."

"No big deal my ass. I done saw what kinda crap you put up with from that poor white cracker. I mean it. I wish the son of a bitch would ever raise his hand to hit on me. Who he think he is? He ain't your Master, he your boyfriend, and a pitiful one at that. That son of a bitch must think you his property! Think he can beat on you like you ain't nothing but his purchased Nigger! Ol' hell no!"

"Damn that! I wanna know what that cracker think Maya? You ain't his to beat on. You don't belong to him."

"No Tanesha, he don't think that."

"That bastard better not. My sister ain't nobody's property. And I tell you this if he put his hand on Ant that's it. I'm gonna go over there right now and blow that crackers brains out. I mean it. His mother fucing mama gonna be wearin a black dress."

I lie to keep her from really going off. As mad as she is right now, and the way she's always felt about white people she's liable to do it.

"No Tanesha, he didn't touch Ant. It was just him and me. Now please sit back down."

"I don't wanna sit back down."

"Please Tanesha." She reluctantly sits back on the couch.

"Okay I'm sitting. Now you tell me why he was beating on you?"

"He didn't really beat on me."

"Then what you call it Maya. What was he doing? Tryin' to put your makeup on? That's it, he was tryin' to put on your makeup when his hand slipped. That's what happened isn't it? You know I can't stand it when you take up for these worthless ass men."

"What?"

"What my ass! Some coward beats the living daylights outta you, and you say he didn't really beat me. Damn!"

I look at the floor and shrug my shoulders.

"When you gonna open your eyes? He done went from shoving you 'round to punching you. You told me two weeks ago, yourself that he ain't paying no bills, he want help with Ant, dranking all the time, and gambling on them poker machines all night. What you need him for? Just tell me that. What you need him for? Then you lie to me and try to protect him."

"Cause if I tell you, you just gonna get mad."

"Mad? Hell I'm already past being mad. Don't tell me 'bout tonight, it don't even matter. Just tell me this, what you need this pitiful bastard for?"

"He's got some good points."

"Yeah like what, a long tongue and a hard dick?"

"You got something to say 'bout every man I ever been with."

"That's cause ain't none of 'em been worth a damn. I mean it. You got to have a magnet for trash. And it wasn't enough with the niggers, now you gotta go and pick out this sorry, worthless cracker. Over 100 hundred million white boys in this country and I be damned if you don't go pick the sorriest one in the whole county, if not the whole doggone state." I simply turn my head.

"You have gotta be the worse in the world at picking out men. Nobody, 'cept maybe Mama had any worse luck. Hell I guess you got it honest. Like Mama like daughter." She stands back up and paces to the back of the couch.

"I don't know. Maybe it's something in the blood. I swear neither one of y'all can pick out a decent piece of a man."

By this time I've had enough. I guess it's a combination of fatigue, anguish and pain, but I have had enough.

"Well I'd rather have a piece of a man, than nothing at all."

This causes her to stop in her thought. It surprises her that I've drawn the line.

"Don't even go there. I know I can get damn near any man in this town if I was to put up with they lying, and screwing 'round. But I'll be damned if I'm gonna settle for a worthless dog just to say I got me a man. I will do without before I put up with what you go through. That thing you got, hell I ain't gonna call him no man. He ain't no real man. A real man wouldn't go 'round beating on his woman. What kinda man would put his woman and her child out on the street? And hell it's your house. It's your damned house! He ain't no man. A real man know how to take care of home. That thing you got is no way near being a real man. Damn piece of poor white trash!"

The entire time Tanesha's talking, I feel myself getting more and more frustrated. She doesn't have the right to talk about Jamie like that. She doesn't know him when he's not drinking. I feel for sure that if he hadn't been out drinking with those so-called friends of his, the ones who used to make those rude remarks at work, then he wouldn't have been so angry. If he'd just quit the drinking and gambling, I really believe things would go back to the way they used to be. I want to say this to Tanesha, but I don't dare do it now. I know my sister too well. Right now it would do no good to speak up for Jamie. When she gets into her no good men mood, the best thing to do is to shut up.

"Do you hear me Maya?"

"Yeah I hear you."

She takes a few steps over so that she's looking down at me. I guess she does this to make sure I'm listening.

"What do you need him for? Just tell me that."

Without thinking I blurt out. "I love him."

A crazed look spreads across her face. It's obvious that she can't believe what I just said. With what happened tonight, I'm having a hard time believing what I just said.

"You love him!...Why?"

"I dunno. Right now I dunno."

She walks away from me. It's as if she can't trust herself to be so close to me. I guess she's afraid of picking up something and knocking the living day lights out of me. She repeats the phrase to make sure she's hearing me right.

"You love him....you love him,...well that's just fine. You love him."

She shakes her head and continues.

"Now lemme see. A year ago you loved School Boy Walker. You let that son of a bitch play you like a guitar. Wasn't he s'pose to be the one. And he left you for your own cousin."

"You know that girl ain't no kin to us."

"That don't matter none. What matters is he wasn't worth a damn."

"Well don't be sayin' she no kin to me"

"Maya that's not the point. The point is before School Boy, there was Robert Lee Mitchell. Now you sho'nuff loved him. Loved him so much he used your car to go to Greenville and ride other whores 'round in. Before him there was Jackie Simpson. Yeah fine as Jackie Simpson. Wasn't he fine? Nigger so fine didn't even lose him to another woman. First it was the pot, then the heroin took 'em. Last I heard, he's either screwin' faggots for twenty cent pieces, or they bangin' him."

"I get your point Tanesha. And as far as I'm concerned that's all in the past."

"No it ain't Sis. You keep thinking things gonna be different with Jamie, but it won't. He ain't nothing but another shade of the same dog. Mama used to think some man was gonna come along and make everything okay. It never happened. You gotta make yourself okay. You can't keep on acting like Mama."

I jump up to defend myself. These words bring back too much pain. I can't be compared to her.

"I'm not like her! You know I'm not."

"It hurts me to say it Maya, but you're acting just like her. You put your hopes on men, and they just break your heart. You keep making the same mistakes over, and over again."

"What you want me to do? You want me to sit at home all alone, night after night? You want me to stay stuck in the house looking at the walls? I can't live like that Tanesha. I can't live like you. I need to be loved."

"Then love yourself first Maya. You don't have to be abused to be loved. You don't have to accept any man."

"I need someone to hold me Sis. I don't know why I need it so much, but I do. I can't take being alone. I can't stand not to have somebody holding me and telling me how beautiful and special I am. I need to be loved." |

"And I'm telling you, you gotta do those things for yourself first."

"I don't know how. I just don't know how"

Tanesha covers her eyes as if to say I give up. She slides next to me, and puts her arm around my shoulders.

"You gotta stop treating yourself like this Sis. You're so much better'n all of this. You're better'n all the Jamie's in the world. But 'til you realize it, nothing gonna change. Nothing gonna be right for you."

She reaches up and, only as a sister can, tenderly caresses my face

"It hurts me to see you like this. All that we've been through together has made me love you more than anything on the face of this earth."

"I know that you love me. I just wish you loved me enough to believe in me. To believe that I can do something right. I know things don't look too good between me and Jamie. but lemme make up my mind on what I need to do."

"I wish I could. It's because I love you and Ant so much that I can't see you keep on like this with Jamie. Tomorrow morning we gonna take care of this mess. I be damned if my sister gonna be beat on and put outta her own house. You work too hard for that lame stuff to happen. We'll get the police to put his ass out."

"Do we have to do it tomorrow?"

"The sooner the better. I don't mean no harm, but I know you and that soft heart of yours. The longer we wait, the easier it'll be for you to take his sorry white ass back. So as soon as I get Ant some Frosted Flakes from the store, you and me gonna take care of some business. Okay?"

I nod my head in agreement. Tonight my head tells me it's the right thing to do. Tomorrow I don't know what my heart will say. Right now it's already speaking to me. If it's possible, I can already feel the loneliness setting in.

"Now I want you to go 'head in there and take my bedroom tonight."

"I don't wanna do that. I can sleep right here on this couch, so as to not put you out."

"You stop that. You ain't a bit mo puttin' me out. Besides you been through enough tonight. I'll just get me a blanket and crash out right here."

"You sure 'bout that?"

"Yeah I'm sure. You go on in there and get some rest. Things gonna look better in the morning."

I obediently head into the bedroom and prepare for bed. As I turn back the covers, I notice Tanesha picking up the phone and beginning to dial it.

I think to myself who in the world can she be calling this late. I immediately think of Jamie and panic. I run to where she's standing.

"Who you calling Tanesha?"

"Don't worry 'bout it, just go on back to bed."

"But who you calling?"

I hear the phone ring and ring and ring. She refuses to respond to a question that I already know the answer too. My heart is pounding as if I just finished running a race. I pray that he doesn't pick up. Once again, prayer not answered.

"Hello."

I think to myself, if that's Jamie in his frame of mind, and Tanesha feeling the way she does, well the fireworks are fixing to fly.

"Well if it ain't that women beating, drunk ass low life son of a bitch, s'pose to be a man."

Damn Sis didn't waste any time. She jumped dead into his stuff. I ease over closer so that I can hear what he's saying. That's really not necessary. He instantly begins to scream so loud that we probably don't even need the phone. I'm sure that half of Flint Hill that he woke, up when he was chasing that car, can now hear his drunken ass screaming.

"I don't have time for your bullshit Tanesha. Just lemme talk to Maya."

"You can speak to her. You just bring your trifling, sorry, pitiful, ass on over here and I'll let you talk to her." I cut in.

"Don't make him madder than he already is."

"I'll make the motherfucker mad alright..."

"Who you calling a mother fucker, you half white stuck up whore."

"I'll be your half-white whore. You bring your sorry, women beating, punk ass on over here! I know how much you like to beat on women, you punk ass bitch. I got another woman for you to beat on. So you come right on over and get some of this half-white ass."

"I done told you Tanesha. I ain't going for your shit. Now you jest put Maya on the phone before I come over there for real and haft to put my foot up your high yellow ass."

"Looka here you sorry, po' white peckerwood, as God is my witness, if you come over and I do mean ever try that shit on me, Miss Maybelle Robinson's Funeral home gonna have some business. I will put so many holes in your pathetic ass that every rat in the upper state gonna think they got them some Swiss cheese. And I promise you that."

"Bitch you ain't promising me nothing."

"I promise you this, if I ever see bruises on my sister face 'cause some low-down dog done jumped on her, you gonna regret the day your peckerwood mammie brought you into this world."

"Bitch! You put Maya on this phone right now, or I'll see your ass at work on Monday and we'll see how much ya'll be talking then."

"You wanna speak to her? Here she is right now."

She slams the receiver down so hard that part of the mouthpiece explodes off toward the couch. Instead of retrieving the phone part, she turns and looks at me with that look I've seen a thousand times before. It's always when she had to take up for me. Always when she had to fight for me a fight that I shouldn't have been involved in. The air between us is too thick with tension to breathe. I don't know what to say.

"Sis, I'm sorry 'bout this thing with Jamie." She rolls her eyes at me and half smiles.

"What you sorry 'bout? Who did you beat up? You ain't done a thing wrong."

"I'm sorry you always gotta be taking up for me. I'm the oldest, seems like it ought to be the other way 'round." She walks over to me and gives me a big, queen-size hug.

"I love you Maya. When you really love somebody, sorry ain't really necessary. Let's go to bed Sis."

Dreamin'

The sound of firecrackers are heard exploding in the distance, on this hot, steamy night. Inside a different type explosion is going on. Mama's got a big tip board party winding down. It's a little past midnight and about seven people, besides Tanesha and myself, are still here. I am 13 years old.

Mama, everybody calls her Lil' Gal is always got something going on at our house. We're known as the party house in town. Just say Lil' Gal's, and everybody knows where you're talking about. In a way we're kind of a Tylerville landmark.

It's past the first of the month and the rent's already two months behind. This wasn't all that unusual. Being a part of the Baxter clan, we learned how to live from crisis to disaster. Mama would have these so called parties to get up money for some emergency. She always seems to pull it off, temporarily keeping everything together.

Mama told us she needed another five hundred dollars. She could always talk old Mr. Peters into letting us stay. I don't know what she would say to him. Old Mr. Peters would come by and he and Mama would go into the back bedroom to discuss the rent. An hour or so later Old Mr. Peters would come out just as friendly as can be. But Old Mr. Peters was getting set to retire. He had turned the business over to his son, and that boy wasn't nearly as friendly. Apparently Mama didn't speak his language. So she needed at least five hundred dollars.

She and Mr. Rob had hoped to do at least fifty books tonight, clearing a few hundred a piece. On top of that she'd hoped to sell about a hundred dollars worth of fishplates and another hundred worth of shots. With what was left of her welfare check, she'd have what she needed and maybe a little more. After all yesterday was payday at the mill.

It was always exciting when Mama had a tip board party. The party would mean all those people would be in the house. In a way it was like a television show or movie. There was always an interesting cast of characters. Everybody laughing and drinking, and eating and having big fun. The only way to describe it was a mixture of smoke, catfish, liquor and adrenaline. You put all that stuff in the air and something has to be going on.

"One thing, one thing" calls out Mr. Rob. He's one of Mama's old boyfriends. Even though they don't go together anymore, they still get together every now and again. I always liked him. He'd buy Tanesha and me stuff. None of Mama's other boyfriends ever did nothing for us. The only bad thing about Mr. Rob was when he and Mama would be drinking; he'd be getting all up in your face with that old smelly liquor breath and scratchy beard, thinking somebody like him that way.

"I got a end" shouts out Cyclops Jessie.

Tonesha and I called him the Cyclops because he didn't have but one eye. He really had two, but one was all gray and cloudy and he couldn't see out of it. We didn't like him because he was fast as hell. He was worse than Mr. Rob was because he was fast all the time. If Mama was out of sight, his hands would get awfully frisky. It's gotten to the point where he'd be trying to sneak a feel on me or Tanesha's butt all the time. It got so bad that he used to try and rub up against me with his thing. I thought to myself, one of these days I'm going to take something and stick him in that other eye.

With him was his girlfriend Peaches. I don't know why they called her that. They should have called her frog, because that's what she looked like. She was big and fat with big pop eyes. Mama would say "Peaches think she something 'cause she got blind ass Jessie. Hell I know I can take him from her anytime I want, but who would want him unless they was as blind as him."

Miss Peaches weighs about three hundred pounds and has these long hairs coming from that big double chin.

"I got a end" hollers out Calvin.

Calvin has got to be the darkest man I have ever seen. He's so black that his shadow is lighter than he is. He's beyond blue black. He seemed like a nice person but he stutters and stank something awful, and he looked like he'd never come face to face with a toothbrush. He got these yellow, cat butter teeth. All twelve of them.

He's got Miss Mattie all up on him over by the couch. I don't think she's his girlfriend. Mama told Ju Ann, that Miss Mattie aint nothing but a five dollar whore. I don't know if she a whore or not, but I know she too old to be wearing that dress she's got on.

I heard Ju Ann tell Mama, "Mat will sleep with a dog if it had ten dollars and hadn't been neutered." I guess Mr. Calvin got at least ten dollars and the necessary parts tonight.

Ju Ann is short for Julia Ann, but don't nobody call her that. She is Mama's best friend. They always hang out together. I like Ju Ann a whole lot. She always talking about how grown up I'm looking and how I'm starting to look just like a woman. Sometimes she'll let me wear some of her makeup. Ju Ann wears make up all the time. She must get out of bed with it on. Tanesha says she looks like a clown, but I don't think so. And she's got the biggest tiddies I've ever seen. She's a real lady.

"I got a end too" Ju Ann announces, as she does a little dance.

Blind Jessie strains to see Ju Ann shake her butt. Peaches just frowns. All the men love it when Ju Ann dances. It causes her tiddies too bounce up and down.

Mama calls out to no one in particular.

"Any of y'all want some mo' of this fish?"

She's slurring her words a good bit because she's had three or four too many. It's okay because nobody else will notice. They are all in about the same condition.

"I said do any of y'all want some mo' fish?"

Peaches responds. "Chile no. I can't eat another bite. I'm 'bout full as a tick."

Tanesha whispers to me.

"She ought to be full. She done ate 'bout five sandwiches."

We giggle. It's pretty hard to imagine Miss Peaches ever being full.

"Alright y'all, ain't but three ends been called out. That means one left on the book. Might be the one. It ain't but seven pulls left on this book, who wants one?"

Pulling tips is kind of like taking a name out of a hat, you only need one number to win. All the slips got numbers on them. If your number matches the one behind the seal on the book, you're the winner. Each slip would cost fifty cents, and there would be a whole bunch of slips to be pulled off. The winner gets four dollars and fifty cents. Mama and Mr. Rob would get four dollars and fifty cents, per book.

Calvin is the first to call for the book. The liquor done made his stuttering worse.

"Ga, ga, give me ta, ta, two mo' pa, pulls." Miss Mattie squeals.

"Calvin ain't you gonna let me pull another one?"

This brings a smile to Calvin's face. Looks like enough butter to bake a cake. He knows he's going to get him some stuff tonight.

"Why sure ba, ba, baby. You go a, ahead and pa, pull one mo'."

They both complete their selection and past the book back to Mr. Rob along with Calvin's money.

"Rob, hand me the damn book 'fore it's picked all over" demands the Cyclops. He's always like that, real nasty to folk.

"Shet your face, you blind eyed fucking bat" shouts Rob, while reaching Jessie the book. He pulls the slips and announces.

"That's one, two pulls. I got two. Here's your dollar."

Peaches clears her throat to get Jessie's attention.

"You gonna let me pull one baby?"

"Hell you can pull as many as you like."

"I mean is you gonna pay for 'em?"

"Hell no! What you mean? Me pay for 'em. What's wrong with yo' damn money?"

"You see how Calvin paid for Mat's, and she ain't even his woman."

"Damn that. I ain't Calvin. Maybe if you promise him some pussy he'll pay for yours too."

Mama looks over at us as she straightens out the Cyclops. She doesn't appreciate his language.

"Jessie you need to watch your mouth while you in here 'round my chaps."

Mat also jumps in to defend herself.

"And for your information, you blind son of a bitch, ain't nobody promised nobody nothing to get them to do nothing for me. And even if I did, it ain't your pussy to be worryin' 'bout." The Cyclops addresses Mama,

"Now Lil' Gal you know for yourself, them chaps ain't got no business in here with these grown folk. I fault you. They ought to have they asses in bed."

"Lemme tell you one damn thing! These my chaps. Don't you be bringing your evil eye ass into my house telling me how to raise my children. Hell everybody in this house knows you ain't took care of none of them lil' dirty bastards of yours."

"You don't know what I did Lil' Gal."

"Wh, wh, why don't we all ja, just forget it and fa, fa, finish the ga, game."

"Shet up Calvin. He don't be talking 'bout I done promised nobody my pussy for no tips."

"Looka here Mat. I wasn't doing nothing but jiving with you. But everybody in this town knows ya'll screw a man out of his paycheck and send him packing home to his woman."

A knowing look appears on everybody's face except Calvin.

"I ain't never screwed your ugly ass outta nothing."

That's 'cause I ain't gonna pay for none."

"If you had a dick you wouldn't have to pay for none. I hear tell your pecker 'bout as useless as that raggedly ass eye of yours."

Tanesha and I just look at each other. There are usually some disagreements when Mama has a tip board party, but this is better than usual. Calvin gently pulls on Mat attempting to calm her down.

"Ba, ba, baby da, don't pay Ja, Jessie no attention. He da, don't know na, nothing 'bout you and ma, mc."

"You damn right he don't know nothing 'bout me. I bet he'll know me if I commence to cuttin' on some ass up in here."

This again causes Mama to jump into the fray, but first she decides that Tanesha and I have heard enough.

"Hold it! Hold it right there Mat. Maya you and Tanesha get y'all asses up and get ready for bed. In here listening to grown folk talk."

We look at her with our best let us stay up for another hour look, but this time it doesn't seem to work.

"Y'all heard me. Get y'all skinny ass behinds in that bedroom and go on to bed."

We drag our feet as we reluctantly leave all the excitement behind. Tanesha tries to crack the door so we can still hear.

"And Tanesha."

"Ma'm."

"If you don't shet that door all the way, I'm gonna come in there and slap your high yellow ass into next week."

We immediately slam the door shut but keep our ears open to listen to what's going on.

"Now Mat you ain't gonna be starting no shit in my house 'boutcutting on no ass." Jessie speaks up.

"Aw hell Lil' Gal you ain't got to worry 'bout that. Mat just talking".

"Talking my sweet ass! You keep on runnin' off at the mouth 'bout something you don't know nothing 'bout. You better watch what you're saying or else we'll see if it's just talk."

"Both of y'all need to watch what y'all saying in my house. Damn niggers can't get together and do nothing without a bunch of cussin' and fightin'."

Mr. Rob steps in, it sounds like he wants to get things back on track.

"Alright, alright, now let's everybody forget 'bout all that nonsense and get back to these tips."

"You, you right Ra, Rob."

"Now who want these last coupla pulls?" No one answers Rob.

"Alright now, y'all mess 'round and leave the winner on here for the house."

Still there is no answer. Jessie is obviously still irritated by the previous conversation, roughly instructs Rob to move on.

"Damn all that Rob. Break them last few tips down and bust open that seal." Mama agrees, hoping for a house win.

"Go ahead and bust it down Rob." Mr. Rob opens the tips and announces.

"Here's that last end. Y'all should have got it."

"Ba, bust it on da, down Rob."

Mr. Rob pops the seal. He then announces and shows the house the winning number.

"It's the eleven. Y'all left it on there. The house wins."

"Damn" cusses the Cyclops. Miss Peaches aggravates the situation.

"I told you to let me get them last pulls. If you hadda listened to me, we woulda had the money."

Mat tries to gig Jessie, but in the process manages to piss off Peaches.

"Maybe if you hadda promised him some pussy he woulda let you pull 'em."

"What you say? No you didn't! I know you didn't go there? Girlfriend, lemme tell you one thing. You done already talked your shit to my man. I know good and damn well you don't wanna start up with me! I know you don't."

Now it's one thing for Miss Mattie to take on the Cyclops, but nobody in that house wants any parts of Miss Peaches.

Besides being the biggest and the ugliest person in the place, and that's saying a lot with the Cyclops and Dairy Teeth in the house, Miss Peaches is known around town for kicking ass, men and women.

"Peaches I wasn't raggin' on you. All I was doing was straightening out your man."

"Well you better direct your talk to him. Don't even put me in none of y'all mess."

"I wasn't puttin' you in nothing."

"It sure sounded that way to me." Jessie jumps in.

"I wish both you arguing ass women jest be quiet. All that stuff is over and done with."

"It ain't over 'cause you say it's over. It ain't over 'til I say it's over. She had no business cracking on me in the first place."

"I didn't say nothing to nobody 'til Jessie's skinny ass started up on me. All I was doing was gettin' back at him. He didn't have no business bringin' me into nobody's mess."

"Ba, ba, baby why don't you ja, jest say you sa, sorry to Peaches and we can jest move on."

"And why don't your no talking, charcoal ass, jest ma, ma, mind your own damn business."

Mr. Rob suggest, "Why don't everybody tell everybody they sorry, and we can go ahead and run the rest of these books."

"I ain't tellin' nobody a damn thing. All I know is that skinny bitch better not say nothing else 'bout me or my man, 'cause I will turn this place slam out."

"Hold on now Peaches. Damnit! Ain't nobody turning my place out. Now if y'all wanna fight, y'all gonna have to take that mess outside."

Miss Mattie, realizing she wants no part of Miss Peaches continues to speak in an apologetic tone, while I'm sure, secretly making sure her knife is close by.

"Peaches know I didn't mean her no harm. I was talking to Jessie."

"Why don't all y'all drunk ass, simple Negroes shut up, and sit y'all Bama asses back down, so I can run these last few books."

"Damn them books, Rob. Mat done totally pissed me off. If it weren't for a lil' bit it would be hell to pay in here."

It's beginning to sound more and more like Miss Peaches is getting ready to whip some ass. Tanesha and I giggle as we imagine the beating she'll put on Miss Mattie. But that will not happen tonight, Miss Mattie all one hundred pounds of her must've decided it's time to do the safe thing.

"Well Peaches I done already told you I wasn't cracking on you. If you gonna keep on acting like that I'm leaving."

"Your ass better leave. 'Fore they be coming to carry your skinny butt out with a damn sheet over your head."

"C'mon Calvin we getting outta here." Mr. Rob pleads. "Y'all ain't got to leave. Hell, I got twenty mo' books here." Miss Mattie moves toward the door.

"You coming Calvin?" This causes old Cyclops to laugh out loud.

"You better go 'head Calvin. Otherwise you done wasted your money."

Calvin hesitates to think for a second. He then chases behind Miss Mattie.

"Ya, ya, y'all take it easy. Hold up Ma, Mat."

They exit from the house, along with Mama's chances of making the money she needed. The room, just moments ago filled with all kinds of sounds, instantly falls silent. Mr. Rob is the first to speak.

"Well we down to three and the house. Y'all wanna keep going?" Ju Ann swears.

"Hell no. Ain't nobody buying all those tips, to win a few dollars. Especially with the house winning the last book."

" That's right" adds the Cyclops.

"Y'all mess 'round and win too much if we don't buy all the pulls and I'll get to wondering if them books ain't been steamed." Mama still hoping to salvage the night seeks to cut a deal.

"We can raise the size of the pot. We can give the winner six dollars from a full pot. How that sound to y'all?"

"That don't sound worth a damn to me. I think me and my woman gonna hit the road. Don't know if I like these odds. You ready to ride Peaches?"

"Yeah baby, I'm 'bout ready."

"Well how 'bout a drank or a sandwich? Anybody wanna drank? It's plenty of liquor left."

"Nah Lil' Gal. I think I'm gonna just head on out to the club for a while. You wanna hang with me?"

"Maybe later Ju Ann. I guest me and Rob gotta get this money divided up first."

"Jessie how 'bout you and Peaches dropping me off at the club?"

"I'll drop you off, but it's gonna cost you five dollars."

"Five dollars! You going right by the place."

"I don't care. Damned if I'm gonna be runnin' my gas out for nothing."

The threesome gather's up their possessions and moves toward and out the door. From the porch you can hear Miss Peaches seeking to help out Ju Ann.

"Jessie it ain't gonna kill you to give her no ride."

"Yeah and it ain't gonna kill her to give me five dollars. Hell a taxi would cost at least that much."

As they leave you can hear Miss Peaches voice.

"I tell you what, c'mon Ju Ann. I'm gonna drive. Jessie's already half blind and now he's half drunk on top of that. Any fool can see those two don't go together. So Jessie you jest hand me them keys."

"I ain't giving you my keys."

"Fool you better hand me them keys, I ain't got time to be fooling with your drunk, blind ass. Can't half see even when you sober."

As their voices fade into the night, Mama and Mr. Rob begin tallying up tonight's profit. While they're doing this, a minor disagreement starts over how the money will be split up.

"Damnit Lil' Gal, I can't do it. I can't just up and give up no hundred and fifty dollars."

"I ain't asking you to give me nothing Rob. Just lend me the money for a coupla weeks. Hell you still will be 'head over two hundred."

"And ya'll be close to five hundred."

"I'm gonna give you the money back. I wouldn't even ask for it if'n it wasn't for the rent. You know I can't get put outdoors with those two little girls."

"Nah Lil' Gal, I ain't gonna do it. If you need some mo' money, we need to run the rest of these books tomorrow."

"You know we done had damn near half the folks in this sorry ass town through here the last day or so, and I ain't even got four hundred dollars. These people ain't got no mo' money. You know for yourself this is one of the best take we done ever had, over seven hundred dollars between us. These people done spent everything they gonna spend. In the morning they gonna be heading for church. After Rev. Dubois get through beggin', money is gonna be scarcer than hen's teeth."

"It's some mo' out there. You just got to try harder."

I can't be runnin' tips and sellin' liquor on a Sunday. Them damn police would be all up on my ass. I wouldn't be asking you Rob if'n I wasn't desperate. I gotta have that money by first thing Monday morning or else me and my chaps gonna be in the streets. How that gonna make you feel?

"I'll feel almost as bad as if I gave away all my money to you. I can't help you Li'l Gal. You might as well stop asking me. Now pour me another drank of that Bumpty."

She hands him the bottle and he pours himself a drink.

"Why don't you ask Ju Ann for the money? She might have it."

"Ju Ann barely got a pot to piss in, and you know it."

"Maybe Peter's will take that three hundred and sixty you got and let you give 'em the rest next week. 'Specially if you give 'em a lil' something to tide him over."

"If it was the old man that might work, but his son don't seem to like no black stuff. He done already told me, Five hundred or nothing."

"Why he being so hard?"

"I dunno Rob. Could be he can rent it out for a few more pennies. Some white folk act that way. Hand me that bottle back." He does so.

"Rob if there was any other way."

"Lil' Gal, you talking 'bout a hundred and fifty dollars. Hell I wouldn't give my mama a hundred and fifty dollars if she was gonna be put out doors. That's just too much damn money. Anyways I'm tired of talking 'bout money. Let's me and you go on back in the bedroom and have some fun. We can talk 'bout that money in the morning."

"Oh no! You think you gonna screw me in my house, in my bed, but want help me from gettin' put out. Nigger you gotta be out of your mind."

"I said we'd talk things over in the morning."

"Talk my ass. You can give me a hundred and fifty dollars tonight or you ain't seeing no parts of this sweet black stuff."

"Bitch you the one who crazy. You'd have to give me some cock every day from now 'til Christmas 'fore I gave you all that money. A hundred and fifty dollars for some cock I done had fifty times."

"Well I just hope that pecker of yours don't get hard tonight, 'cause if it do, you gonna be in a world of hurt."

"That's a helluva lot better'n my billfold hurtin'."

"I told you I'm gonna give your damn money back!"

"I tell you what, and this is my last offer. Let's go on back in the bedroom and I'll give you fifty dollars right now. We can talk 'bout the rest of it tomorrow. Now how that sound to you?"

"That sound like a horny bastard who think I'm going for that in the morning mess."

"Well that's the best I can do. Besides it ain't like I ain't had none of yours before. I guess I might as well head on up outta here. I'm gonna need to find me somebody who ready to do something. Somebody who'll do something for a helluva less than a hundred and fifty."

He gets up from the chair and prepares to leave. That's pretty much all I can be definite about. As I stifle a yawn, I find myself drifting off to sleep right there at the door. The rest is kind of a sleepy blur where I have to fill in some of the blanks.

"C'mon Rob. You know how much I need the money. I ain't got no other way. You my only hope please don't make me beg."

"I'm sorry Lil' Gal. I ain't uppin' all that money. Fifty dollars is better'n nothing, no tellin' what might happen tomorrow. You might just be able to hustle up on the other hundred. So you better go head and take that fifty dollars, why Ol' Junior here is ready for some hot action."

As he makes the last statement I can imagine him reaching down to grab his penis through his pants. When he and Mama was going to get together, sometimes he'd talk like that.

"Well tell Ol' Junior to give up at least a hundred and he can ride Miss Kitty all night long. And I'll give you fifty back no later than the first of next month."

Mr. Rob rubs his scruffy old chin as the bartering continues. Finally, he comes forth with another suggestion. A new proposition.

"I tell you what Lil' Gal, I'll give you a hundred dollars. But there ain't but one way."

"I need a hundred and fifty."

"Just a second ago you would've taken a hundred."

"I would've taken a hundred but I need a hundred and fifty."

"I tell you what. I'll give you the whole hundred and fifty" he hesitates for the slightest moment, but it ain't you I want this time."

"What you mean it ain't me you want this time? Ain't nobody else here?

"Well there is somebody else."

A pause ensues. It must've taken a few seconds for whatever Mr. Rob was talking about to register with Mama. For the next minute I was awaken by some serious cursing and screaming. With Mama's screaming loud enough to awaken the dead, I can't really make out but a few bits of what Mr. Rob was trying to say in his defense. Since I'm unable to make out the conversation, I drift back off to sleep.

"Son of a bitch! I know you ain't talkin 'bout one of my chaps? I know good and got damn well you ain't talkin 'bout screwin' one of my girls."

"Now here me out Lil' Gal."

"T'll hear you out alright. I'll blow your damned brains out!"

"It was just a idea Lil' Gal. You ain't got to do it. I just figgered you wanted the money."

"I do want the money, but what make you think I'm low enough to let you screw one of my babies? What kinda mama you think I am?"

"Lil' Gal them gals of yours ain't nowhere near being no babies. I bet you was near they size when you done it the first time? If it's they first time?"

"You damn right it'll be the first time if I was to go for it, which I ain't."

"Well I understand that. I just figgered somebody got to get it the first time, and you know 'round here it won't be too much longer. Them young boys already eying that high butt on that oldest one, and the boys already flocking like flies 'round that pretty high yellow one."

A long and heavy pause hangs over the room before Mr. Rob continues.

"The way I see it, it'll kinda be like helping out the family. It ain't gonna do nobody no good for y'all to be sitting outdoors."

She speaks this time in a noticeably calmer voice. This time the cursing and screaming and threatening are absent.

"Rob you'd better just hush your mouth."

"All I know is some pimply face snotty nose boy gonna end up gettin' it and that ain't gonna do nobody no good. Hell one of them might end up puttin' a baby in them girls. You know I ain't got no mo' babies in me."

"I don't think so Rob."

"Lil' Gal it ain't like they ain't got to learn. And I'll be real slow and easy like so as not to hurt 'em."

"I dunno Rob."

"I tell you what Lil' Gal, I'll make it two hundred dollars. You need a hundred and fifty dollars. I'll give you two hundred for that pretty lil' yellow one. Just think two hundred dollars for a few minutes."

"This ain't right Rob. Why don't you just take me? I'll do anything you want me to, and I'll pay you the money back."

"We done covered this before. You can take it or leave it. You go in there and get the dark one outta there, and just give me thirty minutes. And to show you I ain't putting you on, I'll give you the money right now."

He reaches into his pocket and pulls out a wad of money. He begins to count.

"That's twenty, forty, sixty, eighty, one hundred, one hundred and twenty, one hundred and thirty."

As he counts Mama's eyes must've been fixed on the money. Mama always had this thing about money. It talked to her. I'm sure once the money came out of his pocket; the decision got to be a whole lot easier.

"One hundred and forty, one hundred and fifty, one hundred and sixty."

As the count nears its conclusion, it becomes harder and harder for her to say no. I know I was near sleep, and maybe through the years I just wrote what happened in my mind, but I can't remember her saying no. Even though I was lying there next to the door, I can't remember hearing the word no. Even in my imagination there was Mama, once the money came out of his pocket, the words coming from her mouth did not include no.

"One hundred and seventy, one hundred and eighty, one hundred and ninety, one hundred and ninety-five, two hundred dollars."

He reaches out the money to her. I'm sure she thought about protesting, maybe she did protest just a little bit more. At least I hope she protested.

"This ain't right Rob. It just ain't right."

"I promise to you Lil' Gal, I promise on my mama's grave, I ain't gonna do nothing to hurt that child. You know my dick ain't even that big."

Somewhere in the next few minutes, he reaches the money to her. His arm is extended out toward her. In it he holds what she needs most. The money starts talking to her. She probably pauses for a moment to finalize her decision. She rationalizes, just this one time, and finally decides to accept the money.

"Okay, I'll do it this one time, but if you ever mention this to anybody, I'll call the police on you and say I didn't have nothing to do with it."

"Oh I want tell a soul, you can count on that."

"And it's gonna have to be Maya, Tanesha still a bit too young."

"Now Lil' Gal I told you I wanted the yellow one."

"Well you ain't gettin her. Now you can take Maya or not."

He pauses to think and decides to accept the offer.

"Okay, I'll take the black one but you gotta pay me back fifty"

"Twenty-five"

"Okay twenty"

She must've nodded her lead in agreement.

"Anyway I reckon she'll do."

I didn't hear Mama when she led Tanesha out of the room. The only thing I remember was being lifted onto the bed. Then I feel these rough hands rubbing between my legs and over my bottom. I smell this terrible liquor odor. As 1 become mindful of what's occurring, there is this wet slobbering breath trying to kiss on me. I try to scream, I try to fight, but nobody came to help me.

"Mama, mama!"

"Don't worry child I ain't gonna hurt you. I put some spit on it so it'll go in easy."

"Mama, Mama! Somebody help me. No, no don't do that, please, stop it. Stop it. Mama! Please stop."

I awake in my sister's bed with tears flowing down my face and Tanesha holding me.

"Don't worry Maya, don't worry." "Tanesha it's so terrible. It's so terrible."

"I know sweetheart, I know. All them times they hurt us is over with. He ain't gonna hurt you again. I won't let nobody hurt you again, it's just a bad dream. It's just dreamin'.

After Dreamin'

After reliving that old familiar nightmare, this day starts as another dreaded occurrence. It begins with me waking up in a strange bed. To arise in an unfamiliar surrounding makes you a bit confused. I look all around the room and gather my bearings. I see the sunshine through the side window, and immediately realize where I am. I don't like it. All too often in my life I've felt this way. What a terrible feeling, to not want to get out of bed. What an awful feeling it is, to not want to face the day. If I could, I'd just lie hear with the covers over my head and cease to exist.

I rise up, too fast, from the bed. A painful jolt, from slightly bruised ribs, reminds me of last night's encounter. I feel about my face and realize that most of the swelling has gone down, and there is but a slight pain in that area. Far worse than any pain, is the anxiety of today. Tanesha was easy on me last night. I know that is subject to change.

When you are alone, you put up with stuff. I don't have nobody else, at least nobody who I can go to for anything. Since I started living with Jamie only a few people will even talk with me. It hurts so badly, and not from the beating. I've given up so much for that bastard. I've given up myself. At least that part of me that I know about. I've never been exactly certain of the whole person.

Despite the pain, I manage to rise up and move toward the living room, hoping and not hoping to find my sister. As I past through the living room, I hear her humming some song behind the swinging kitchen doors. I call out to her without entering the kitchen.

"I'm glad somebody's feeling good this morning."

She calls out to me from behind the doors. I can't see her face, but I know that she has that look on her face. The one that says when are you going to learn.

"You say something Sis."

"I said I'm glad somebody's feeling okay."

"Huh"

"I'll wait for you to come out from the kitchen, and then I'll tell you what I said"

"I'll be right out."

I sit down at the dining room table and begin wondering. What is she going to say? What am I going to say to her? What am I going to do about Jamie? What about Ant? For me to have just gotten out of the bed, I suddenly feel very, very tired.

I rub my eyes to see if that will help. It doesn't. Things are just as confusing. It is so frustrating to never know which way to turn, or who to turn to.

I look up as I hear the kitchen door open and close. It has an annoying squeak. In walks Tanesha, already dressed and looking quite pleasant. As a matter of fact she looks a little too pleasant. It's not like her to be almost glowing. She's just too sensible and cautious to be bubbly. In her hands are two cups of coffee, I assume one is for each of us. She reaches a cup out to me.

"Here you are Sis, something to get the morning started." I gladly accept the coffee and begin to sip on it.

"Thanks, I need something to help me get going."

"Well you know I'm here to help. I don't want you feeling all sad and pitiful. Things got a way of working themselves out. Ya'll see."

I think to myself, here comes the lecture. I figure I might as well get it over with. I merely nod, so that things can start working themselves out.

"Now I'm gonna run out to the store before Ant wakes up. Every time he comes over he's gotta have those Frosted Flakes. But just as soon as I get back, we gonna make some calls to see what can be done 'bout that boyfriend of yours." I sigh and complain.

"Do we have to do that today? I don't feel like being bothered with no police or nothing today."

"Whether you feel like it or not, we gonna get it taken care of today. I know you girl. If we don't jump right on this thing, ya'll be back with that low down dog in a week's time."

"You don't know that."

"Yes I do. I hate to say it but, I done seen it too many time with you and your So-called men. You probably already got in your head that you're gonna take his ass back."

"That don't have a thing to do with it. I just don't want to do it today."

She raises from her seat mildly frustrated, but unwilling to change.

"Now Maya you know how much I love you, but I'm not gonna let you change your mind 'bout this lowlife cracker. You didn't have to open that door last night and see your face, swollen and scared to death. You didn't see Ant's face. How in the hell do you think it makes me feel?"

I look into her eyes and I see the hurt. She tries to stop them, but in the corner of her eyes the tears begin to leak out. As soon as she starts, my tears have to join in with her. All of my life it has been difficult for me to see anybody cry. Pretty soon both of us are standing and hugging each other. She actually squeezes so hard that it slightly hurts my bruised ribs.

"Ouch."

"You okay?" I lie.

"I'm fine."

"I'm sorry Maya but we gotta do this before that white son of bitch hurts you real bad. Now we gonna get this taken care of today. I'll be back in 'bout an hour or so. If Ant wakes up don't feed him nothing, 'cause I'm gonna get my baby his cereal. If Marguerite calls while I'm gone, you tell her she don't have to come over early to help me get ready."

"Get ready for what?"

"Don't you remember, it's our spades day. Marguerite, Janetta, and Caressa are coming over to play cards today. Marguerite was gonna come over to help me get ready."

"Since when you been playing cards with Caressa?"

"Since my sister dropped outta the group, Caressa has sit in with us a buncha of times. So if you don't mind, just pass that message on to Marguerite."

"What was that message again?"

"Tell her she doesn't need to come over early to help me set up."

"What kinda help you need to get ready for a spades game?" She hesitates briefly as she thinks about it.

"Well we lay out chips and stuff like that. Why do you ask?"

"No real reason."

"It's just Marguerite's nature to be helpful. She is the type of person who don't mind coming over a bit early and helping out."

"Okay I'll be sure to tell her."

Tanesha continues toward the door. She opens it. Before leaving she turns back to me and speaks.

"And Maya."

"Yes Mama."

"Don't be smart. You don't need to be talking with him while I'm gone. If he calls you hang that phone right up." I pause and say nothing.

"You hear me?"

"I hear you. I'm not deaf."

"I know you're not deaf. I'll be back in a lil' bit."

She walks on out the door. I sit in total quiet for what seems like hours, but is only minutes. Time can be many things when you are troubled, but all it seems to be to me is a personal tormentor. I nervously tap on the table. I know what she's saying is right, but I love him. To me it is that simple. When you love someone you do not give up on him without first giving your all. I'm not sure if I've reached that point yet. That fact and the fear of loneliness make me consider all possibilities.

For as long as I can remember, I've dreaded being alone. Already, less than a day away from him, I feel the loneliness creeping in. All my life I've been abandoned. My daddy abandoned me. My Mama abandoned me, and every man I've been with left me. You would think I'd be used to loneliness, but isolation is something someone like me can never get used to.

Now I find those feeling are made worse because Tanesha will be having friends over. I don't want anybody to know. I can either stay in a room, hiding like I did something wrong. Or I can come out for all to see, and become an ongoing gossip piece.

I used to have friends in this town. Before Jamie, I'd be included in the spade games. Before Jamie, I'd hang out with Janetta and Caressa. I was never really that close to Marguerite, even with her being Tanesha's best friend for years. She always seemed kind of resentful of me, looking down on me.

One time I think she believed I wanted her hound face husband, Isaac. The boy is so homely, he looks like he'd been beaten with an ugly stick. I don't know why Marguerite would think I want his ass.

I used to have friends before Jamie. Most people would still talk to you and all that. But it was different. You soon realized that they were treating you very different. Too much unseen pressure, but you sure as hell felt it. People acting all funny about it. On my side of town, I wait and wait for my people to accept the fact that I'm living with a white boy. They don't so much accept it as simply tolerate the strangeness of it.

Even the one's who still would fool with me, Jamie doesn't like them. It has gotten to the point that he doesn't even want me leaving the house except to go to work. So more and more I drift away from my old friends. In a way it was just like when we were kids, the only person I truly could count on was Tanesha.

I have even back slid from going to church. It wasn't like I was a Holy Roller or nothing, but the longer I was with Jamie the more I drifted away. I wasn't going to be looked at and talked about. It didn't bother Jamie that I quit. He never went to church anyway. It just became too much of a problem.

A couple of the boys in his Bible Study group started picking at Ant real bad. Children can be so cruel. You can't really blame them. They get it from their parents. In this town, God's children loves us all, until you cross that color line. Then those good Christian folk tend to pick and choose.

I don't know what to think anymore. If I do break up with Jamie, will any of these men fool with me? I mean really fool with me. I know if their thing gets hard, they want say no to Maya or no other woman. Say what you will about Jamie, in spite of everything I really do believe that he loves me. I don't know if I can go back to being used by a man, and not being loved.

What if I don't break up with Jamie? What will Tanesha say? She sure as hell want like it. And what about Ant? If I don't break up with him what will I tell my son? How can I make things right for Ant? I just don't know what to do.

From my seat at the table, I stare at the phone. I ask myself why hasn't he called? He probably is getting over one heck of a hangover. Will he call? I rise up from my seat and walk over to the phone. I glance down at it. Inside my mind I ask do I really want it to ring? If it doesn't ring, what do I do? Do I call him? If I call him, what do I say? Thank you for beating my ass, and by the way I still love you. I look down at that blessed phone, as if I expect it to tell me what to do. It doesn't, so I speak to it.

"Well aren't you gonna say something? I need some damn help! I need somebody, something to tell me the right thing to do. I need that bastard Jamie to call and say we are going to be all right. I need him to call and say he was wrong and he'll never do it again. I need him to change and become the type of man who is everything I need and everything I want. I need him to say he's sorry and that he still loves me."

Ringgg!

The ringing of the phone startles me. It's as if it was the firing of a gun to start a race. Except the only thing that's racing is my mind. I think it's got to be Jamie. What should I do? Now that he's calling, what will I say to him?

Ringgg!

There it goes a second time. I remember Tanesha's words. Don't talk to him. Don't talk to him. I lift up the phone almost like I'm picking up a dirty diaper. With a slightly loose mouthpiece nudged against my cheek I speak.

"Hello."

Before I can say anything else the subtle, soft voice of a woman surprises me.

"Well hello yourself. Are you ready for me?"

"Huh?"

"I said ..." Then a distinct pause as if there is a realization that something is not what it should be.

"Who is this?"

"This is Maya. Who is this?".

"Oh Maya, I'm sorry. This is Marguerite. I thought you was Tanesha."

"She's gone to the store. I expect her back in 'bout half a hour."

"Oh. I was just playing a lil' joke on your sister, disguising my voice. She had wanted me to help her clean up and set up for the game."

"I know she told me to tell you that you didn't need to come over and help her with that."

"We still gonna play this afternoon, aren't we?"

"Yeah, she still planning on y'all playing." A pause ensues.

"So I'll be sure to tell her you called."

"Thanks. Are you gonna be there when she gets back?"

"Yeah, I might be here for a day or two."

"Oh, Tanesha didn't mention that to me."

"I reckon not."

"Well be sure to tell her I called. And tell her to give me a call".

"I will"

"See you"

Click and then only quiet. As I place the phone back down, from behind me I hear the tiny voice of a child. This is not Ant's usual tone. There is a hint of fear.

All this time I'd been thinking about what should I do. I'd completely forgotten about Ant.

"Mama"

I walk over to him. Just to hug his neck. He looks so innocent and vulnerable, standing there in a cartoon tee shirt. I kneel down and wrap my arms around him. As I do so he tries to squirm away in protests.

92

"No Mama! Don't hug on me."

"But I love you so much. And anyway, what's wrong with a Mama hugging her baby?"

His eyes, as if pulled by a magnet, looks down to his feet. Before he can answer, I feel a slight dampness on my arms. An embarrassed look spreads across his face. He mumbles.

"I think I wet the bed."

"You think."

"Yes'm, I believe I wet the bed."

"Ant! I tell you the truth."

"I'm sorry Mama. I must've had too much to drank."

I'm not totally sure why, but the last few months Ant has started back wetting the bed. About two years before he'd had a problem with the same thing. Out of the blue it has started again.

"Are you mad at me Mama?."

"No sweetheart. Mama's not mad. You go take off those wet clothes and strip Auntie sheets. We gonna have to let that mattress air out. We'll get those clothes washed later on."

"Okay Mama."

A relieved Ant bounces back into the bedroom.

"And you get in that shower and get some clean underwear on."

"Yes M'am."

I walk back over to the couch and sits down next to that taunting phone. It is so absolutely tempting to pick it up and make the call that I'm dreading. All I have to do is dial a few numbers. In just a matter of seconds I could be hearing his voice

"Mama" "What Ant?"

"Where am I s'pose to put these clothes?"

"Put them in the dirty clothes hamper."

"Okay."

I turn back to the phone. If this was a contest of will, I'd be losing. I tell myself to look away, and for a moment I focus on the items in this room. I look over at the fake fireplace with the shovel and iron poker. I examine the pictures on the walls and the carpet on the floor. But this is all to no avail. My thoughts and attention soon return to the here and now. I tell myself that if I called no one would know the difference. I hastily pick up the phone and dial my home. It rings once, then twice, then a third time. It continues over and over until finally someone picks up.

"Mama." I slam the receiver down.

"What Ant?"

"I need a towel."

"Well go look in the linen closet."

"What kind should I get?"

"Whaddyou mean what kind? It don't matter."

He turns and heads to get his towel. As soon as he exits the feeling of loneliness revisits me. The numbing quiet filters down on me. I look longingly at that demon phone. Damn you telephone.

I get up from the couch and walk over to the dining room table. I feel the urge to get away from that taunting phone.

I tap anxiously on that table. I feel like I'm in a prison. I stand up from the table and walk to the door. I look out and then back to the phone.

I ask myself even if I do call what am I going to say? How can you treat me so special one day, then whenever you take a notion, knocks the daylights out of me? I don't understand.

What can I say? Jamie I love you so much, so please stop whipping my ass.

"Mama I'm finished."

I look over to see Ant, just as proud of himself as he can be. "Finished? Finished what?"

"I finished taking my shower and putting on my clothes. And I cleaned up after myself."

"Well we'll just see 'bout that."

I walk over to inspect him. I kneel down so I can look at him eye to eye. He stands before me at attention, like a good little soldier.

"I do have to compliment you on one thing."

"What's that Mama?"

"You're the only person I know who can take a shower in thirty seconds."

"That's 'cause I'm little."

"Is that so."

"Yes'm. Ain't that much to get dirty."

"Let's see then. That face looks pretty clean."

He smiles as I place my hands on his shoulders and gently turn him around.

"That neck looks pretty good." He softly giggles.

"So I guess you're pretty clean. But if I remember right, I know a certain lil'boy who forgets to wash his ears."

As soon as the words leave my lips his eyes give him away. He'd better not get in this spade game today. He can't bluff worth two cents.

"Ah man, I forgot to wash my ears."I playfully mock him." Ah man."

Then I lovingly hug him as warmly as any mother is capable of doing. He wiggles mightily. This is to be expected of a small boy who doesn't want to get hugged by his Mama.

"Ah Mama, you don't have to do that."I laugh.

"Oh yes I do. All lit' boys who forget to wash their ears either get a hug or a butt whipping, Now which one you want?"

By now we're both laughing and tussling. I don't realize just how strong this rascal really is. He lets out a playful scream between giggles.

"I don't want neither one."

He tries with all his might to pull away from me. As he does, I lose my balance and we fall to the floor. Ant on top of me.

"Ouch."

I call out in noticeable pain. Ant jumps up clean off of me, like he done touched a hot stove. Them big eyes look fearfully at me.

"What's the matter Mama?"

Ant's landing on my ribs brings back the pain from Jamie's playing football with me. I'd almost forgot how much it had hurt.

"What's wrong Mama?" I lie.

"Mama's alright son. I just landed a bit hard. Gimme a second to catch my breath."

The fear on his face eases a bit. Lord this child has been through enough without him having to worry about hurting me. I sit motionless on the floor without another word passing our lips. Ant scoots over and sits beside me. That same hug he was running from a few seconds ago now is gladly accepted.

We sit quietly for a few seconds as the pain in my side lessens. Just then the key noisily turns in the lock. Ant screams lovingly.

" Auntie."

"Well hey back at you."

Tanesha looks at me in a quizzical manner, as if to say what in the world is she doing down on the floor? She enters with a grocery bag in her arms.

"You won't believe what this one bag of stuff cost."

Before I can answer she pushes the door close and continues. "This one bag cost almost sixteen dollars. Sixteen dollars!

And for what?"

Ant promptly moves over to Tanesha. "Auntie you got me some Frosted Flakes?""Yes I did."

"Thank you Auntie!"

As he hugs her in gratitude, I gingerly rise from the floor, I don't want her to see my discomfort nor remind her of last night's occurrence, and move to the couch.

"Now there is one thing you gotta do to get this cereal."

"What's that Auntie?"

"You gotta take this heavy bag into the kitchen, put everything up, and eat 'til your lil'ol of belly 'bout to bust wide open."

"I can do that."

"And one mo' thing."

"What's that Auntie?"

"A hug ain't good enough for two bowls of Frosted Flakes, No you gotta give Auntie a big, big ol' kiss right on the jaw."

"Shoot, for Frosted Flakes I'd kiss a hungry doberman."

She bends over and they complete the transaction. Ant picks up the bag and takes it through the kitchen door. As he leaves the room he announces.

"It ain't even heavy."

Tanesha smiles and walks over to me. She sits down. Without hesitating, without beating around the bush she asks.

"You ready?" I play dumb. "For what?"

"You know what."

"Can't we just hold off on that for a while?"

"No we can't. Ain't no po' peckerwood son of a bitch gonna be beating on you for nothing. We gonna get his ass outta there 'fore I been done killed him. Or he done killed you."

"That ain't gonna happen."

"How you know?"

"As many times as Jamie done been mad at me, there's no way he's gonna hurt me real bad. I don't even feel no pain from last night."

"Well I guess he hit you in the head, 'cause you ain't makin' a bit of sense. I just wish you'd take the time and listen to yourself".

She reaches over to an end table and picks up a phone book. She scans through the book and locates the number she's searching for. I dread this moment. My heart begins to beat faster. I can feel the pulsing sensation all the way up through my temple. She takes the telephone in her hand and begins dialing. With each number she spins, the pounding in my heart gets more intense. The pressure in my head nears a point of explosion. Then as if those two body parts weren't enough, my stomach decides to join in.

"Hello my name is Tanesha Baxter and I need to talk to somebody 'bout getting somebody evicted from a house." She pauses to listen.

"No it's not my home , it's my sisters place." Another pause.

"Sir you don't understand, it's like this. The man who's staying with her ain't no damn good. He messes his money up on liquor and God knows what else. He won't pay no bills, and lately he's been beating on my sister."

She looks over at me. I glance in another direction. I feel totally useless, totally powerless.

"Yeah it's my sister's place. She rents, but she was living there way before this guy moved in. The lease is in her name and everything." Still another pause.

"I don't understand what you're saying. So you telling me she can't have this no good bastard put out?" A brief pause.

"Why she gotta give him thirty days? It's her place. Well what if he decides to beat the living daylight outta her again in the next month, what y'all gonna do 'bout that?"

A look of disgust appears on her face.

"Well that's a stupid ass law. Okay so what we gotta do now?" She nods her head as she agrees with whatever is being said to her.

"So we need to c'mon down town and sign the eviction papers, and if she chooses she can sign a petition for Domestic Violence. Well I don't know if she wants to do that, but she does want to sign them eviction papers."

She nods her head again.

"Monday morning! Why we gotta wait 'til Monday morning to sign eviction papers? Why can't we do it today?"

The answer must have been no. The look on Tanesha's face said as much.

"I bet if it was the mayor's daughter getting her ass whipped she wouldn't have to wait 'til no Monday morning. And she wouldn't be waiting no thirty days. Well I just guess we'll be seeing y'all on Monday. Is there anybody we need to ask for?"

She pauses to listen.

"So we need to ask for the Magistrate. Anything else? Alright, thank you very much."

She hangs up the phone.

"Yeah thanks for nothing. We got to wait `til Monday morning to even take out papers. Then he gets thirty days to move his belongings from the premises. I swear a woman ain't no better'n a dog in this town."

"Monday ain't that far off Sis."

"It's far off for you. `Cept I'm not about to let you change your mind. Come Monday we gonna get them papers signed. In the meantime I don't want you talking to that sorry boyfriend of yours."

"I'll try to remember that."

"Don't try to, do it. I'll get the police to go over there on Monday to pick up your clothes and stuff."

"Why we gotta do that?"

"Child you gonna need some clothes 'fore thirty days over with." It dawns on me that Tanesha has no plans for me to go back home. At least while Jamie is still there.

"You just plan on living with me for the next month. It'll be a lil' tight here for a while. But we'll make due."

She must have noticed the pitiful look on my face. She tries to reassure me.

"It'll be fun Sis, you and me and Ant. ya'll see everything gonna be just fine."

"I guess."

The sound of something crashing on floor in the kitchen and a worrisome Oh Oh, redirects Tanesha's focus.

"Boy if you break one of my good plates I'm gonna beat your behind. Well I know. I'm gonna go in here and help Ant out 'fore he tears up something. Then I'm gonna get ready for my card game. You oughtta join us, it'll be like ol' times. Besides it can help take your mind off of things."

I think to myself, yeah a card game is just what I need. That ought to fix all my damn problems.

"I might just do that. I'll see how I feel later on."

She reaches over and gently holds my hand. In a soothing voice she announces.

"Trust me on this Maya. You don't have to put up with stuff like this just to say you got a man. Believe me we're doing the right thing."

I weakly smile. Deep inside of me I know she's only looking out for me. But her being right don't hug you on a cold night. Being right don't kiss you all over your body until you tingle inside. Being right don't always feel right.

Suddenly there is a crash coming from behind the kitchen door. A second. "Oh oh."

"Oh oh my ass!"

Tanesha jumps up and races into the kitchen. I'm left all alone with my feelings, mostly depression. I ought to feel comfortable with depression, since we go way back. I can't remember being without it. I also can't remember being this tired and beat for a long time. I feel like I done ran a Marathon. I look at the clock. It's not even 11:00 AM yet. I decide to go back to bed. Maybe when I wake up, I'll feel better. Maybe when I awaken, this thing that I call a life, my life will somehow be straightened out. One thing for certain is it can't be any worse. It couldn't possibly be any worse. That is, unless I dream.

Hanging Out

Hearing the sound of voices and Whitney Houston crooning, "I'm saving all my loving for you". I jump straight up and awaken from a deep sleep. At first, I can't determine who's speaking. As they continue talking, I'm able to distinguish them from their voices. I also realize I have a pounding headache.

"Y'all sorry whores can't do nothing with us today."

Let's see it's Marguerite, Janetta, Caressa and of course Tanesha. But I'm not immediately sure what they're doing.

"And I'll say it again. We kickin' some natural born ass up in here, ain't we partner? Tanesha 'em thought they had us with that pitiful ass Queen."

Janetta replies "Now they sho' did."

Tanesha responds in a friendly, yet competitive voice. These card games used to be famous for two things, competition and talking some sure enough trash.

"Bitch y'all ain't done nothing. 'Cause me and Margarie fixin' to come back on your sorry ass like polio. Watch us run at least a eight on y'all non playing ass. You ready Marguerite?"

"I was born ready and been ready ever since".

It seems the girls have got themselves a serious spade game going on. It wasn't too long ago that I'd be right in there with them. That is of course before Jamie became such a big part of my life. Caressa and I used to be hard and heavy running partners. Janetta was a lot different than Caressa and me. She was always the quiet type. In some ways she's like the odd man in this crew.

She and I used to be real tight. Not like me and Caressa but we had been friends since junior high. It might be said that Caressa and I were kind of boy crazy. Janetta wasn't as well-known as we were for spreading our loving around town.

For years I didn't think she was doing nothing. She wasn't the type to go out and party or chase after men. Then the next thing I know, she done turned up pregnant. She ended up shacking with the baby's daddy, Myles Graham. I used to go with Myles for a short time, years ago. In a town as small as this one, it's not unusual for everybody to end up going with everybody else. You can't let that mess up any real friendship. Still, she and I were friends until Jamie moved in with me. After that she'd quit sitting with me at work on our breaks. Then she stopped calling and would barely speak. I should have been able to guess what was going on, by the way Myles started acting towards me.

Even though he's been with Janetta for years, and knew that we are tight, he'd still bet trying to hit on me. He'd say for "old time sake." I never did once they moved in together. It would've broken homegirl's heart. After it became known about Jamie and me Myles was one of the first people to curse me out. His pet phrase was "nothing but a House bitch." He couldn't deal with the fact that a white man was getting something he couldn't get anymore. Janetta finally told me that he didn't want her dealing with a "Cracker loving bitch." I guess he thought it was contagious.

Marguerite was always Tanesha's friend. They'd shop together, eat lunch together, go to Greenville and catch movies together. They were the best of friends. She never would get too close to me because of her husband. She never said anything to me about it but I could tell. I think she just puts up with me to please Tanesha.

Of course if I looked like Marguerite, I'd be worried about my man too. If I was a man I'd have to have a whole lot of liquor in me to screw Marguerite. To say it kindly, she is rather plain. It's not like I'm hung up on looks or anything, but she's just looks like a board. I guess her man like it. He definitely liked it enough to put two babies up in her. So I reckon the liquor store made some business those two nights.

I also believe she thinks she better than me. At times it just seems like she doesn't want me around. Since she's always been my sister's number one partner, I put up with her. It's because of her I don't want to join them. I don't want her to know my business. Janetta and Caressa would understand. I don't want Marguerite to see my shame.

I think to myself they've probably already seen Ant. Besides that I'm sure Tanesha has already told Marguerite about last night. I continue to listen from the safety of the bedroom, undecided if I'll join in, or wait until they leave.

"Alrighty Janetta it's your deal, so shuffle them cards and we'll finish putting this ass whipping on these bitches"

That's my girl Caressa. I guess she is partners with Janetta, so they are going up against Tanesha and Marguerite.

"The only person who's gonna be gettin' their ass whipped is you two whores."

As I hear my sister's reply, I realize how lonely and isolated I feel. I recognize how badly I want to join in. A hell of a realization. I shouldn't have to give up all my friends and love ones simply because the man I'm sleeping with is white. I decide at this point in time, I'm tired of hiding and holding unto shame that's not mine. I boldly enter the room just in time to hear Janetta announce the next game.

"Alright y'all listen up. Here come the cards down and dirty"

On the table are several empty bottles of Pink Champale, Schlitz Malt liquor, Budweiser and Orange soda. As always, Janetta is a bit different. These card games are about socializing and escaping. So everyone drinks, talks trash, drink, tell lies and drink some more.

One of the things Tanesha got from Mama is her love of drinking. She can put down some liquor. Everybody except Janetta looks like they've already had a few of their favorite alcoholic beverage. Caressa is the first to speak to me.

"Well I be damned! If it ain't my long lost homie. Home Girl, I didn't know you was still living. I thought you had left town or something. C'mon over here. Go 'head and pull up a chair, and slide on over next to your used to be partner. I ain't mad at you 'cause you put me down for that fine ass white boy. I'm just ain't sure why you had to put me down.

"C'mon over here and brang me some good luck, even though I don't need it to whip up on these pitiful whores. And while you at it, you might as well give me the 411 on what's going down."

I'm think to myself, I'm pretty sure she already knows what's going down. Even though my head is splitting I fake a smile and play along with the game.

"Now it not like all that. I ain't put you down."

I drag a chair over between Caressa and Tanesha. This location is better than being next to that bitch Marguerite. Caressa picks up her Bull and takes a big swallow.

"You know you fired me sister, but like I said, I ain't mad at you. If I had a man as fine as Jamie I'd stay at home gettin' me some everyday. Ain't that right Janetta?"

Her response is a little more enthusiastic than Strom Thurmond, to an invitation by the NAACP to be their keynote speaker.

"I reckon."

"Reckon my ass! That son of a bitch ain't worth the dirt on my shoe. If Maya had a bit of sense she'd been done left his sorry ass. But that's my. Sister. A damn scum magnet."

I look at Tanesha. It's obvious from the three Bud cans sitting in front of her that they haven't mellowed her out. We all exchange our hellos and complimentary introductions. I try my best to be upbeat. Caressa and I chat as Janetta begins shuffling the cards.

"So Maya, I hear tell things ain't going too good on the home front."

I look at Tanesha in disbelief. She in turns shoots a glance at Marguerite, who simply looks away.

"Well they was gonna find out anyway, and it no use in trying to keep nothing a secret in this damn town no how."

"I still didn't want you tellin' everybody my business."

"I just told your friends. Besides it wasn't like you did nothing wrong. You the one who got your ass beat."

"Don't worry about Jamie, Maya. Everything gonna work out just find. You and him gonna be back together in no time at all."

"No they ain't! My sister ain't stayin' with no man who gonna be beating her ass like she some kinda drum."

"What's a lil' ass whipping? Shoot I'd trade a ass whipping for a fine man any day. You won't be sore but a day or two. Besides ya'll forget all 'bout that when you and him get to making up."

As Janetta deals the first round and second round of cards, Caressa starts examining her hand and talking trash.She announces, "Aw hell, y'all in trouble this time. I ain't seen nothing but trumps. Partner you dealing me a hand over here".

Tanesha examining her own cards and counters Caressa claim

"She lying, Marguerite, she ain't got nothing. I got some good cards myself".

Marguerite looks at her own cards and can't even muster a smile.

"I hope so partner cause I ain't seeing nothing"

Janetta continues dealing until all of the cards have been dealt. Everybody takes a moment to study their individual hands.Caressa is the first to speak.

"'Netta I see 3, 4 and a good possible. I think I can get us 5 books" Janetta the ever cautious one informs Carssa,

"Now all we need is six books to win the game, so don't be over bidding".

"I ain't overbidding, I can see at least four and a good shot at five books. How many you see?"

"I can get three and I got a good possible"

"Well that can be nine books".

"We don't need to bid that high and get set".

"I know that, let's just go a seven".

"All we need is six".

Tanesha tries to goat them,

"What y'all scare of your hand? Y'all been underbidding all damn day".

"Sho' is"

"Y'all bid y'all's own sorry ass hand and me 'Netta will take care of ourselves. Alright 'Netta lets go six. But you know if they mess around and win the second game by more than us they gonna be talkin 'bout how they beat us whores."

"I ain't worried 'bout that. Let's win the first game, get that moneyand then we'll worry about taking care of the second one, Alright?"

"Alright"

"Alright Tanesha, Marguerite what y'all bidding?"

Tanesha inquires, "What you see Marguerite"

"I don't see much of nothing. I got two books and one possible"

"What? That's it?"

"You asked me what I see and I told you. I got two books and maybe two possibles. What you got?"

"Damn, I got about the same. Well let's go seven."

"We can't make no seven."

"It don't matter. If they get seven books they win anyway. If we get seven we set them and we are back up."

"Alright I guess we'll go seven then. On you Marguerite."

Marguerite plays her first card, as she wins the first book, Carssa immediately starts talking junk.

"That's about all y'all gonna win. Soon as you play that next card it is all over".

The game progresses onward and goes pretty much in the favor of Caressa and Janetta. With each book that they win Carssa seeks to irritate and distract Tanesha more. She whether realizing it or not returns the conversation to my situation, thus further upset my sister.

"So Maya when you headed back home to your man, cause I 'm here to tell you, if you stay away too long I might have to do a little tipping myself. I'm kinda curious about things on the other side."

This cause myself and Janetta to chuckle at Caressa attitude and being totally unaware how Tanesha is feeling about the matter.

Tanesha in a stern voice answers for me.

"She ain't going back to that motherfucker. I done already called the Sheriff office. On Monday morning we going down town to get that sorry bastard put out of that house."

"For what? A lil' slap on the face? Maya you listen to your homegirl on this one. Don't you let that fine ass man go over one mistake. If a woman left a man every time he got drunk and rough her up a lil' bit then there wouldn't be any married couples in this sorry ass town, and that's black and white."

She takes another drink from her beer. Janetta knowing my sister, attempts to redirect this conversation.

"Caressa this sound like a personal family matter. You need to let them settle it."

"Them, them who? This is Maya's business and Maya's decision and I'm telling her that a man like Jamie deserves a second chance. Shoot her girl Marguerite no damn well her man done went up side that head many a time."

This gets the expected reply from Marguerite.

"Caressa you don't know a damn thang 'bout me and my man. So you need to keep my name outta your mouth!"

"And she still with his ass. Ain't going nowhere. And your sister Miss thang, over there ain't even got no man. Her pussy gonna lock up on her if she don't get some dick in it soon. You wanna be like her?" I laugh at Caressa. My girl is always going to act a fool.

"It sure as hell will dry up 'fore I put up with somebody like that sorry cracker."

"Are we still playing? Then lets get back to the game" inquires Janetta.

"Damn right I'm still playing, I ain't through spanking that ass yet. Not with them about to owe us ten dollars. Who's play is it?"

Janetta replies. "It's on you."

Caressa slaps the table with an Ace of diamonds, which can't be beat. She screams out at Marguerite and Tanesha.

"Bam. I am getting ready to run this motherfucker slam out. You here me homegirl. I am getting ready to ride this train, just like I am gonna ride your man if you stupid enough not to go back to him".

Caressa is too busy talking trash, having too much fun and her head's too bad to pay attention to what's going on. She doesn't respond to the fact that having won the last book, it's on her to continue play. Tanesha attempts to get her refocused.

"Caressa, what you gonna do?"

"Bout what?"

"Bout it's your play? You runnin' off at the mouth and not payin' attention to the damn game."

"Heifer I'm talking to my partner and you just mad 'cause we kickin y'all ass. Alright you wanna see me play. Bam!" She slaps the table with the King of Diamond, another unbeatable card. Unless Tanesha or Marguerite have a trump to cut it with. They do not which this time irritates Marguerite. Marguerite comments.

"You sittin' your ass over there talking to Maya, she ain't got a penny on this table. I've got five dollars on this game, so you need to pay attention and play."

"Damn you. Ain't nobody asked you a damn thing 'bout nothing, Miss thang."

She flings the Ace of club across the table. Still another unbeatable card. She looks at my sister and laughs. She turns back to me and states.

"You know if Jamie mess 'round and get horny I'm gonna go over there and get me some of that stuff."

I laugh along with Janetta. As she does you can see the irritated look on both Tanesha and Marguerite's faces."

"Yeah I figger a good lookin' man like him ain't used to goin' too long without a some pussy. You go 'head and listen to Miss Tight Ass over there and in a week's time I'm gonna slip over there late at night. I'm gonna grab hold of that tight butt of his and ride 'em like its the Kentucky Derby. I'll put this pussy on him so good he gonna say Maya who?"

Janetta and I continue to laugh at Caressa's foolishness. But even as I laugh, a part of me wonders if what she is saying turns out to be true. Not about her but about maybe another woman. She proceeds to takes another swallow from the can.

"Sister Girl, I just wanna know one thing fore I sneak on over there in your bed, with your stuff."

"What's that?"

"Fore I ease on over there, I wanna know is it true what they say 'bout them white boys?"

"On Lord" replies Tanesha

"Is what true?" "Is it true 'bout they peckers I don't wanna go over there lookin' for no dick and ending up with a peewee"

Janetta and I bust out laughing, and even Marguerite has to smile. This of course annoys Tanesha to no end . She simply can hold back her fury no longer.

"The bastard a probably ain't got no dick. He damn sho ain't no man. What kind of man go 'round beating a woman?"

"Damn near all of 'em I know, besides I ain't askin' you nothing Miss Dry Box. Damn pussy dry as a sidewalk on the Fourth of July. Sister Girl I gotta know if it's gonna be worth while 'fore I go tipping. Does the white boy got enough pecker to play at the bottom?" I laugh and smile at the same time.

"I don't know if it's true what they say 'bout them other white boys, but mine can hit bottom"

"Are you gonna play or what?" Demands a more irritated Tanesha.

This causes Caressa to rise up from her seat at the table and do a little nasty dance.

"Hot damn! That's what I'm talking 'bout. I'm gonna go get me some white meat. I don't need no man who can't do nothing but play 'round at the top. Now that you done told me he can go deep, I'm gonna have to cross over too."

"Go 'head and cross over sister" shouts Marguerite as if she was at a church revival, "but before you do finish the damn game."

Caressa sits back down but instead of immediately resuming play ask me an additional question.

"Sister Gal, lemme ask you one mo' thing 'bout that white meat."

"Are we gonna finish this game or you two gonna keep on talking 'bout a white boy's pecker?"

"Now hold on Marguerite, this game ain't going nowhere. I just need to know one mo' thing and it don't have nothing to do with his pecker. Home Gal, I got to know 'bout what they say. You know 'bout them white boys and they tongue. I mean give it to me straight now. Can the boy eat a pussy like a hungry brother goin' after a cold watermelon on a hot Summer day? I need to know now!"

That's it. Tanesha realizes that this is one situation that she has absolutely no control over. She tosses all of her cards into the air and knocks the remaining cards off the table. Everybody, drunk or sober, has to laugh at the contrast between Caressa and Tanesha.

"Damn gal. What you throwing them cards all over the place for?"

"Cause this game is over. You runnin' off at the mouth 'bout a white boys pecker and a white boys tongue. Don't nobody wanna hear all that nonsense."

Caressa looks at me smiling as big as a Cheshire cat. She's on a roll now. As the others at the table toss in their cards to her unbeatable hand, she continues.

"Maya I don't know how you put up with that bossy ass sister of yours. Can't even talk 'bout a lil' bit of nookie without her throwin' stuff every damn place. But I hope she got a maid 'cause I ain't 'bout to help clean up this mess."

"Did I ask your horny ass to help me clean up?"

"And you better not."

For the first time in the last twenty-four hours I actually feel good enough to laugh. That's my girl, Caressa, she always could pick me up like nobody else. Even though I feel better I realize that my headache is still with me and I need something for the pain. I get up from the table and head to the bathroom.

"Where you going heifer"

"I gotta use the bathroom. I'll be right back."

As I walk down the hall into the bathroom, I hear the conversation turn back to the card game.

"Well are we finished?"

"Hell no, me and Janetta gonna take some more cash from y'alls sorry non spade playing behind. As soon as Tanesha picks up these cards and Maya gets outta the bathroom, I'm gonna take a potty break."

I open the medicine cabinet and find some Tylenol. My sister is a human pharmacy. She's got Tylenol and Aspirin, and Advil. She's got Pamprin and some prescription meds I don't know anything about. The one thing she doesn't have is cups. Tanesha forgot to put some cups in the bathroom, so I pour a few of the tablets into my hand and walk back to the kitchen. I pass Caressa in the hallway. She is moving fast and instructs me to,

"Girl you better get outta the way."

I side step her in the narrow hall, I walk past the other three in the room where the card game is getting ready to resume. I glance in at the membership. No one from the really pays me any attention as I head into the kitchen. Marguerite and Tanesha are picking up cards and Janetta is trying to find a jam on the box.

I look into the cabinet and get a glass and fill it with water from the sink. Through the kitchen window I look out and see Ant playing basketball on the playground hoop. He's decked out in his number 23 Chicago Bulls jersey.

I walk out the back door to get a bit of fresh air. It might just help with my headache.

As I watch him play I feel joy. I can't keep on putting him through this ordeal with Jamie. How could I justify putting him back into that situation? How many times can I ask him to put up with stuff no child should ever have to put up with?

Ant catches a pass from one of his teammates, he half shoots and half slings the ball skyward. It misses the hoop but does manage to clang off the backboard. I laugh. I step out onto the patio to watch my son. It all seems clear to me now. For the first time in a long time, I know exactly what I must do.

As I turn to walk back into the house, the kitchen door opens and in walks Tanesha and Marguerite. They are holding beer cans and trash to be dumped. I'm still angry with Tanesha about putting my business in the street, especially for telling Marguerite. I decide it'll be best if I stay outside until they finish up in the kitchen.

I turn around, take a few steps away, and look back out to the playground. There I see my boy Ant, gunning up another shot. One thing that's for sure, he's not shy about shooting. He fires up another brick. As I turn back around to the kitchen, I look in to see if they're finished. They are not. I nearly drop my water glass as I see my Sister and that bitch looking longingly into each other eyes. I think what the hell?

Then only as lovers can do, they embrace tightly. I'm not really sure what's going on in my mind. It's like looking at something, but you know it can't be happening. And if this wasn't hard enough to believe, Marguerite's right hand slide slowy and gently down her back, massaging and rubbing on Tanesha's ass.

I am paralyzed. I don't know whether to make a noise or remain silent. I kneel down to avoid being detected. This cannot be real. I must be dreaming. That's it, its, another bad dream. I pray for someone to wake me up, but there is no alarm going off. With her free hand Marguerite's rubs up and down Tanesha's back. Tanesha's gently caresses Marguerite's face. that plain dull face closer to her own beautiful one. As she does their lips move closer and closer until there is no longer any room between the two of them. I see their mouths open. Their tongues intertwined, probing deeply, exploring each other. They separate and look at the close door then giggle like two schoolgirls who are passing notes. Marguerite's mouth slides down from Tanesha's lips to her beautiful, flawless neck. I find my eyes fixed on this perversion. I cannot look away.

Marguerite moves from Tanesha's neck back up to her mouth. They again merge in a long soulful kiss. They release their embrace, while still holding hands. They look at each other. They can see nothing or no one else. In their eyes is a look that I've spent my entire adult life searching for, the look is devotion. They love each other. No mistake about it, their passion is unmistakable. Theirs is the ultimate bond. They love each other. Caressa bellows out.

"Is one of y'all gonna bring me damn Bull or what?"

They exchange a quick peck on the lips. Marguerite kisses Tanesha's breast through her clothes and pats her on the behind. She grabs a beer and a soda from the refrigerator and walks back through the door. Tanesha adjusts her shirt, grabs two more drinks from the fridge and enters the room.

I straighten back up and stand in the same spot for at least a minute. I don't have a clue as to what to say or what to do. I am stunned. I guess I should have suspected it, but I didn't. It sounds stupid but I don't ever remember any lesbians being in Tylerville. People just can't be gay, it's not allowed. Now that I come face to face with it, everything now makes sense. Hell Marguerite didn't fear me taking her husband. She didn't want me having my sister.

I finally compose myself enough to walk back into the apartment and through the living room. As I enter from the kitchen both Marguerite and Tanesha look at me and then at each other. Their eyes say I shouldn't be coming from in there.

"Sis what you doing in the kitchen?"

I stagger through a half-truth.

"I wasn't coming from the kitchen. I was outside watching Ant play basketball."

A look of relief comes onto Marguerite face.

"Oh. How is the future NBA player doing?"

"Well he likes to shoot, that's for sure."

"Did you walk all the way down and see the new rims?"

"Them damn rims ain't all that new. What you talking 'bout Tanesha? They been out there since the beginning of last Summer."

"No I didn't go all the way down." I lie. "Just 'bout halfway."

You can sense the tension leave Marguerite.

"Its good he can play while you're here. Lil' boys should be able to have some fun."

The uneasiness hangs over this conversation. Caressa drunken impatience terminates the anxiety.

"Damn where Maya been, it's your deal Marguerite."

She picks up the cards. I look at Tanesha who's attempting to stare straight through me. I turn and to walk toward the bedroom.

"Where you going partner, we ain't had enough time to catch up on everything."

I think to myself, I've caught up on everything I need to catch up on.

"I'm gonna lay down for a while, I got this terrible headache."

Another Chance

Looking through a window that is crystal clear, with eyes that see a life as murky, as the Catawba River following a rainstorm. I can't see my way out. I look to my sister and things only get more clouded. Tanesha is gay. My baby sister is a dyke. I search for a plausible reason. It's got to be that man looking Marguerite who turned her out. Tanesha hasn't always been that way. She couldn't have been.

When you grow up with somebody you think you know her in and out. My Sister was never what you'd call man crazy but she always used to appreciate them, a little bit anyway. No doubt in my mind, it's that bitch Marguerite's fault. I just wonder how long this thing has been going on. Damn! I guess I wasn't the only one who crossed over.

"Mama I'm hungry."

"Huh."

I turn around and see Ant standing in the doorway. With all that has been going on in the past twenty-four hours, I keep forgetting about my baby. That seems to be happening a lot these days.

"Mama when is Auntie coming back. I'm hungry."

I stand and walk over to him.

"I'm not sure when Auntie will be back, but I'm sure we'll be able to find something to eat."

"Where did Auntie and them ladies go anyway?"

"I'm not sure. I guess they went out somewhere."

"I know what would be good for dinner Mama?" I smile as we walk arm in arm into the living room.

"And what would that be?"

"First we'd go to McDonald and get a Hamburger, and then we can ride to the 7-11 and get some red Slushie. Then we can come back home."

I laugh.

"Boy we ain't driving all the way to no McDonald's."

"Well how 'bout Hardees?"

"We ain't going to no Hardees neither. I'm not driving all the way to Greenville for no ice cream. What we gonna do is go in the kitchen and see what your Auntie brought from the grocery store this morning. Then we gonna fix some supper."

"All Mama that don't sound like no fun."

"Supper don't have to be fun, it's suppose to fill up that stomach of yours."

We enter the kitchen and I immediately head for the cabinets, as Ant flops down dejectedly unto a chair. I search through the cabinets hoping to find something that Ant will eat. He s like most children his age, picky, picky, picky. If I allowed him to, he'd eat hamburgers and French fries seven days a week.

"How about some Salmon Croquette and Cream corn?"

"Nope."

"Well, how 'bout some Vienna sausages and Macaroni and cheese?"

"Gettin' warm."

"Well boy what you want to eat?"

"I want a Happy Meal, and then a slushie."

"Well you're not too old for your wants to..."

Ringggg, ringggg, ringggg. The phone startles me. It rings a second time.

"I'll get it Mama." He bolts to the phone and picks it up.

"Hello."

A frown comes over his face. His eyes say it all. It's somebody he doesn't want to hear from. In a dejected voice he announces.

"It's for you Mama."

I walk over and he hands me the phone. He walks back to the table and looks at me with those big sad eyes. The pained expression on his face indicates who's on the other end of this phone. I clear my throat.

"Hello this is Maya."

"Baby, it's me. It's Jamie."

This is the call I've been waiting for. Now that I've gotten it I don't know what to say or do, My mind goes blank.

"Did you hear baby, it's me Jamie?"

"Hello Jamie. What do you want."

A pause.

"I was, I was just calling to say, to say how sorry I was 'bout last night." I continue to listen.

"I don't know what gets into me sometimes. Baby it's that damn liquor. It's the liquor. You know I'd never do anything to hurt you if I wasn't drunk. You know how much I love you. You know how much you mean to me." I remain silent.

"Baby without you my life means nothing. If I drove you off, if I made you leave me for good then my life ain't worth living. I mean it. I'd just get me a pistol and blow my damn worthless brains out. Baby you gotta give me a second chance, you gotta come back to me. Maya I'll make it right. I promise to you, I'll make everything perfect."

For the first time I open my mouth to speak. Before any words come out I look over to Ant. Those eyes of his are fixed on me. They are both hopeful and fearful.

"Jamie I can't go on living like we been living. I can't go on with the drinking and the fighting. I love you with all my heart but I just can't put up with anymore of it."

"I know baby, I know. But this time I promise with all my heart and all of my soul, things are gonna change. I'm gonna change. No more excuses no more lying. I'll do anything baby but please come back home. Come back today Maya. Please!"

"Anybody can say they gonna change, but how do I know you gonna change? How do I know once I come back things want be 'xactly like they was before? How do I know that next weekend you want go out and get drunk, come home and beat the hell out of me? How do I know that the next time you want stop at punching Ant one or twice? What if you lose control on him like you did with me?

How do I know Jamie? Promises don't mean nothing. Promises ain't nothing but words. I need more than words."

"And I'm gonna give you more than words. I'm gonna show you baby. I'm gonna prove it to you. It's gonna be better'n it ever was before between us. It's gonna be better'n it was when we first started out."

This statement brings back memories. Memories of the roses and the bracelet and the attention and how special he made me feel. Memories of the Jamie I'd fell in love with and not this mean spirited impostor who had taken over his body and our home the past month.

"Do you hear me baby? It's gonna be better'n it ever was before. I swear on my Mama's grave. I swear to Goodness. I'm gonna make it right."

"How Jamie? How you gonna do that?"

"Well I'm gonna start off by stopping the drinking. No more liquor, and no more getting drunk. Them days are over with."

"Jamie you tried that before and it never lasts. What's gonna make this time any different?"

"This time I'll go get some help. I'll go get some counseling. That's right I done already made up my mind. I been thinking 'bout it all day long. I'm gonna go to the clinic and get myself a counselor, and I'm gonna go to some of them AA meetings too. And I want you to go with me baby. I want you right in there with me too, so you can see how serious I am 'bout making some changes. And after we get the drinking problem whipped, I figure we can open up a joint bank account and start paying the bills together. I'm gonna let you handle all the money. That's right. Come payday I'll deposit all of my paycheck except for maybe twenty or thirty dollars. Then I'll let you make out all the bills and pay them on time. No more of that crap where I go out and mess up my whole check and leave everything on you. That's gonna change."

All of this sounds too good to be true. I hesitate for a second in thoughtful bliss. What if he really does change? I mean people can change, people do change. I briefly allow myself to feel optimistic. I actually feel more than optimism, I feel hopeful. But hope proves to be a peculiar item. It vanishes with the sound of a car pulling up. It must be Tanesha.

"Jamie you gonna need to give me time to think this thing over."

"Baby I need you here with me. Can't you think it over at home? Il'l give you plenty of space. I want bother you at all and that's a promise.I just need to know that you are here with me, in this house. That I'm not all alone. I feel so lonely when you're not here. I feel like I been abandoned."

Loneliness, that is a feeling I know about all to well. The sound of key heard in the lock. Tanesha is singing some song. She sounds quite happy. That is a feeling I only wish to know.

"I'd never never leave you Jamie. I love you as much as I can love any human being."

As the words exit my mouth Ant looks at me and walks over to meet his Auntie. Tanesha is entering the house. The cheerfulness of the song is now gone. On her face is an expression that asks the question, what's going on here?

"And I love you just as much. I just been messing up here lately, taking you for granted. But all that's gonna stop. I realize how much you mean to me. I know I can't make it without you."

I glance over at Tanesha. It's obvious that she has figured out what's going on. The look on her face has gone from curiosity to disgust and anger. I in turn feel pressured. The only thing I'm sure of is that I want to be loved. I need to be loved. I want the love and understanding of my Sister. I want the love and acceptance of my son. But I also need the love and passion of my man. I want to be loved.

"I just need some time to think things out. Can you understand that?"

"I'II try to. Just don't let nobody else talk you into doing nothing. I'm not trying to put Tanesha down, but you know she don't like me. Don't let her come between us. Nothing s' pose to come between us. We done went through too, much already. If we can make it through all that other stuff you know we can make it through this. We can make it 'cause we love each other, and that's all that matters. So you take all the time you need 'cause I ain't going nowhere. I'II be here in the morning and the day after that and for however long it takes. Just don't let nothing or nobody come between us."

Momentarily I forget about Tanesha. I listen intently to the words of my man. We have been through a lot. We owe it to ourselves to give it another try. We you shouldn't give up on love.

"I won't let that happen. If you go to counseling and stop the drinking I'll give it another chance."

"I'll will baby. I'll call the Drug place on Monday morning. As soon as you walk in the door you gonna see the change in me. I'm gonna be everything you want in a man. I'm gonna do everything in my power to make you the happiest woman in the world."

I smile. This is all I ever wanted.

"I love you baby."

"I love you to Jamie. And I'll be home soon." Tanesha just frowns.

"Thank you Lord, thank you Jesus."

"Bye, bye."

"Bye."

I hang up the phone. For at least one brief moment I'm happy.

Loneliness is gone and love is back in my life.

"What in the hell was that! I leave here and we talking 'bout getting the son of a bitch evicted. I come back and you telling 'em how much you love him. What's wrong with you Maya?"

"Ain't nothing wrong with me. I just feel like maybe Jamie deserves another chance."

"Another chance? Another chance to do what? To beat the hell outta you? Maybe he needs another chance to beat the hell outta you and Ant."

I look over to Ant who is in the unenviable position of watching the two people he loves the most fight.

"Ant I need you to go back in the bedroom and watch TV while Auntie and me discuss some things."

"Okay Mama."

He proceeds to obediently leave the room.

"That's not fair Sis. You know Jamie didn't hurt Ant."

"Not yet. Maybe he ain't been drunk enough. Maybe the bastard ain't been mad enough. All I know is it's just a matter of time before he does."

"You don't know that."

"And you don't know that he want. How many times has he told you he's gonna change?"

"He really means it this time Sis, I can tell the difference."

"You can tell the difference? What difference? That son of a bitch would tell you with a Bible in both hands that water ain't wet. How you gonna stand here before me and say you can tell he's changed?"

"He's gonna stop drinking. He promised me that he'd stop drinking. He never promised that before. All the rest of the time he'd say he didn't even have a drinking problem. This time he says he'll go get some counseling, and he wants me to go with him. He's talking 'bout going to AA and all kinds of things. He loves me Sis. He loves me."

"Okay Sis. If he loves you so much, and he's gonna make all these changes, why don't you do this. Let Ant stay here with me til you and him get y'all stuff together. Then later on he can come back and be with you."

This catches me by surprise. I know Ant would be in good hands with Tanesha, but I can't imagine him being away from me for any extended period of time. Over the last eight plus years he has been one of a few constants in my screwed-up life. In spite of anything else I love Ant immensely. I cant conceive of giving him up to Tanesha. I can't abandon him. I won't.

"What you mean give up Ant. He's my child and he needs to be with me. I'm not giving him up."

"I'm not asking you give him up . I'm asking you to let him stay with me like you've done fifty times before. Then you can see how much your so called lover has really changed."

"He don't have to be with you for me to see how much Jamie done changed. As a matter of fact, it makes more sense for Ant to be with me. That way he and Jamie can keep on getting to know each other."

"I think he already knows Jamie just fine!"

"Well he's my son and I think he needs to be with me."

"Son or no son, I love that boy as much as anybody can love a child. And I'm tired of his catching hell 'cause of you and your sorry ass men. And he done told me that the cracker bastard hit him last night."

I minimize.

"He just lost control this time that's all. Jamie likes Ant a whole lot. He just snapped this time."

"And what about the way he talks to Ant. I know all about it Sis. I know how he treats him. And you gotta know how this makes Ant feel. All I'm saying is until he proves he's changed then let me keep Ant. I'm not talking 'bout forever. I'm not even talking 'bout a long time, just long enough to make sure Jamie's has really changed."

"I don't think so Sis. I think Ant needs to be with me wherever I am."

One thing about my sister, she is not used to losing, not to me. She is used to me giving in to her. I don't know if it was the liquor or the fact that she really hates Jamie, but her next statement had to be motivated by something powerful.

"I didn't want to put it to you like this Maya, but I'm not gonna see you take this boy into that situation. I'm tired, Lord knows I'm tired of it. If you go back to that bastard, then you're a grown woman. But somebody's gotta look out for that child. Somebody's gotta look out for my baby."

"What you saying Tanesha?"

"I'm saying if you don't let me take care of him 'til you get yourself together, then I'm gonna call Social Services. I'm gonna report his drinking and y'alls fighting, and him hitting Ant. I don't wanna do it, but I mean it this time. I'm gonna ask for custody of him."

Although I have been angry with Tanesha many times in our lives, I can never remember the simmering hatred I feel right now. I'm not used to doing anything except going along with her, but not today. Right now, all I feel is rage. Who in the hell does she think she is? Threatening to take my child away from me. Hell no.

"You gonna stand there and talk 'bout taking my child away from me! That's my flesh and blood."

"That's my flesh and blood too, and I'll be damned if I'm gonna let him be knocked around just because you happen to like bouncing your ass on that cracker's dick!"

"Well at least I'm getting some dick. You sneaking 'round here letting another woman screw you!

Have mercy! If the slightest breeze were to blow, it would knock her over Her mouth falls open and her eyes are big enough to see into the next county. The realization hits her. The secret is out.

"What you mean by that?"

"I mean I know 'bout you and Marguerite. I know all about y'alls little secret."

"Marguerite is a happily married woman."

"I guess that's y'all way of fooling people. Well you ain't fooling me. I saw y'all today."

"Saw what?"

"I saw the hugging, and the kissing in the kitchen."

"That wasn't nothing. That wasn't nothing but a friendly hug and a small peck."

"I saw her tongue in your mouth Tanesha. I saw her squeeze your ass like she was your man. Like only a man should be doing. You think I'm gonna let my son stay here with you and that pussy licking dyke! You wanna tell Social Services something. I'll tell 'em something. I'll tell them and then I'll tell Margurite's husband and if I have to I'll tell the whole damn town, but you ain't taking my boy!"

"I wasn't trying to take him away from you."

"The hell you wasn't. If I hadn't found out 'bout y'all you would be talking to them social workers now. I know you. Always got to get your way. Well not this time. Tomorrow morning I'm gonna get my boy and my stuff and we are heading back home to my man. And I mean a real man."

She looks at me with the most heated, hateful expression I'd ever seen from her. I didn't mean for things to be so hurtful. It's just that I can't imagine my life without Ant. As scalding hot tears flow from both of our eyes, there's and understanding that our relationship has forever been changed. We'll continue to love each other but things will never be the same. All my life the only person I could totally depend on was my sister. Regardless of what problem life has brought me, I could count on Tanesha. I can't recall any time when I purposely tried to hurt her. Tonight all that has changed. There will be no undoing what has been said and done.

"I wasn't trying to take him away from you. If you don't know it by now, I love you and that boy more than I love myself. I just want what's best for y'all."

I look away from my adversary, who happens to be my sister, who happens to love me. Although I have won, there is no joy in this victory. The salted tears testify to that. Ashamedly I steal a glance in Tanesha's direction. I think to myself, why should I be feeling ashamed? She turns and walks away, exiting down the hall and into the bathroom. I sit down on the couch and think to myself once again. Although well still love one another, and we will find it in our hearts to continue loving each other. There is also absolutely no doubt in my mind, that things will never be the same

Directions

One of these days I'm going to have a restful night. One of these days I'm going to wake up from a peaceful sleep. I'm going to lie my head down on that pillow and just drift off into undisturbed bliss. I just don't know when that night will occur. It sure as hell wasn't last night. Too much going on. When everything you got in life, no matter how screwed up that life happens to be, is slipping away then it's hard to rest. So you wrestle with the things that are taking away your potential happiness. You fight to hold unto that which you hope will bring you love.

Love has been called wonderful, beautiful, special, blind and even strange. I don't recall anybody ever describing it as tiring. I love three people. That's simple enough. Right now Ant and Tanesha hate Jamie. Jamie dislikes Tanesha and emotionally abuses Ant and me. Right now the word that describes love is bitch. Love is a bitch.

I've never been a person who was a big church participant, especially after I took up with Jamie, but this morning I find myself longing for something that may point me in the right direction. I don't know what good going to church will do, but as the saying goes, it can't hurt. I need to turn my life around. I need to make the right decisions. God's house seems to be the logical starting place.

From my bedroom I make my way to the kitchen. Sitting at the kitchen table with the coffee already brewed is Tanesha. I look at her and she at me. If there has ever been a more awkward moment, then I can't imagine it. This has always been the time in our history when I would apologize. This time there will be none forthcoming.

I make my way around her and secure a cup from the cabinet. I locate the sugar and a spoon. I count too myself, one, two, and three spoonful. I pour the coffee from the pot and stir it. The entire time I'm trying to avoid eye contact. I don't know what to say. It should be easy, after all this is my sister. It should be easy when you love each other, but at this time it is not. Neither of us knows what to say.

"I don't feel guilty about it."

"What?"

For a few seconds I wonder what she's talking about, then it comes to me.

"I said I don't feel guilty about it. I don't feel guilty about loving Marguerite. don't feel guilty about loving another woman. For years now, since I realized I was gay, I'd always felt guilty. I was like why me?"

I sit down at the table, across from my Sister. In a way I'm sitting here with a stranger. There is so much of her that I've been in the dark about. Or at least I'd wanted to be in the dark about.

"No Sis, I'm not ashamed. And I'll tell you another thing, believe it or not, for the longest time I was proud of you and that peckerwood."

"Of me and Jamie?"

"Yep. Even though I'd never would'a said it, I just thought it was great the way you and him love and cared about each other in spite of what everybody thought. Including me a li'l bit. Me and Marguerite used to talk 'bout how brave y'all was. To show y'all's love in spite of all the hate, that was just so fantastic. Of course he turns out to be a total asshole.

We talked 'bout how one day we could be that brave, but we never did. So we just kept everything a secret. Secrets can be fun for a while. Then they become a heavy load. As time goes by secrets just tend to become an unbearable burden that weighs you down. Lately that burden has gotten bigger and bigger. It's so hard to live a lie. The times I'd go out with men just to keep that secret. The times I tried to make love to them just to prove that I was normal. In a way I was glad that you found out. For the longest time I've felt like the biggest liar in the world. I couldn't even tell my Sister that I was in love.

When you found out, it was like part of that burden had been lifted. Last night I cried. I cried 'cause I had been set free. I was no longer a slave to who I really was, the chains had been unfastened. For the longest time all that would come out of me was anger and resentment. But last night I cried out of relief. Them tears they washed away my burden. Them tears loosened me. Do you understand what I'm saying?" I nod my head, in silent agreement.

"This morning I woke up and I'm slowly tearing down the prison that's been my entire life. I don't know how long it's gonna take. I don't know how many more barriers I got to tear down, but this morning I do know why so many people have died to be loved and to be free.

All my life, and I guest yours too, we been feeling guilt. Guilt about one thing or 'nother. Guilt that wasn't even ours. But starting today I'm through feeling guilt or shame 'bout nothing. I love a wonderful person and she loves me. I'm in love and that's all there is to it."

Amen Sister! Amen. I want to scream. The way she feels about Marguerite, that's how I feel about Jamie. I want to shout to her that I know how she feels. When things are going good between us, I feel the same way. But the problem is when things are going bad, then I feel like the prisoner. It's really quite ironic. Love and discovery have freed her. That same love and discovery at times it imprisons me.

"That's all there should be. It will take a while for me to get used to it, but if you love her and she loves you, then the rest don't matter none. If you're happy then I'm gonna find a way to be happy for you."

"Thank you Sis. It makes me feel good to know you feel that way."

"The only thing I ask is that you be happy for Jamie and me. We gonna work this thing out. I know you don't believe that, but we're gonna make it work." She pauses to make certain her words are what they should be.

"You know I wish nothing but the best for you. And nothing would please me more than if what you're saying turned out to be true. But I just don't think it is Sis. Jamie ain't nothing but a white version of what you been going out with the last few years. For him to beat on you and act the way he does, I can't be happy for you. If he straightens up I guarantee nobody's gonna be happier for you. If he decides he wants to be a father to Ant, then I'm gonna be the first to hug his neck. But I just don't think it's ever gonna happen. He done showed his true colors and it's a bad hue. He just ain't no good. I hope I'm wrong, but I don't think so."

"But if he straightens up, then ya'll be happy for us?"

"If he straightens up I'll kiss his pale white ass." I laugh.

"That's all I wanna hear Sis. I don't want no limit on my love. As much as I love Jamie, without you and Ant being happy for me, I can't be totally happy. Love is not love with a ceiling on it. This time I want a love that reaches to the sky. This time I want a love that when the angels sing, their voices echo off of it. I want all the people who I love to love one another."

She looks down at the floor. I talk about a love that reaches the heavens and she looks down at the floor. I strive for a love that extends beyond the clouds, and my Sister is unable to believe it'll ever get off the ground. In spite of everything else, Tanesha is basically an honest person. She smiles wishfully.

"One thing for sure, it can't get any worse."

This time I smile with her. No it can't get any worse. I sip on my coffee as I announce to her.

"Well, guess where I'm going this morning?"

"Where?"

"I think I'm gonna get ready for church."

"Church?"

"Yeah church."

"You going to church?" "Yep."

"Flint Hill Baptist?"

"Flint Hill Baptist."

"Why on earth would you wanna do that?"

"Cause it's my church, it's your church, and before Mama died, when she went, it was her church."

"I'm glad you decided to go back to church and all but you haven't set foot in that church since a bit after you and Jamie been together. Them church folk, them good Ol' Baptist may act like they accept you on Sunday, but I still know that they'll be talkin' 'bout you like a dog on Monday. and so I don't see why you wanna be sitting up with them in no church."

"It's not about them. It's 'bout me. It's about me and the Lord. It's 'bout starting over and doing the right thing for the right reason. I done heard everything them good church folk done had to say 'bout me and Jamie. What else can they say? I'm kinda like you today Sis. I'm tired of running, tired of having to be worrying 'bout who's thinking what. This is the day I quit carrying other folk's burden. If they don't like me 'cause of who I love, then that's on them. If you wanna join me I certainly welcome you."

She looks at me with an expression that says, no way in hell.

"Do you mind watching Ant for a few hours, I'm going to serve and praise the Lord."

As I get ready for church all kinds of thoughts go through my mind. I keep telling myself that I can do this. I can't let other people keep me from doing what I know is right. I can't let them keep me out of the house of the Lord. Furthermore, since I made that big announcement to Tanesha, I'd feel like a fool if I change my mind now.

After I check my make up for the fifth time. I make sure the dress I borrowed from Tanesha is okay. I make sure it's not too revealing but not too prim and proper. That's easy with her. Tanesha has never been one to go in for too much flash.

Driving down the road, a road that allows you to either go on or turn around. I think how easy it would be to again alter my direction. I think Tanesha would understand, but I'm not sure if I would. Anyway, something keeps me going. Hopefully on the correct path. After all, what I'm doing is the right thing. If I keep doing the right things my life can and will turn around. As I pull up onto the gravel parking lot, I get out of the car and look toward the building that is the Flint Hill Baptist Church.

Tylerville can be described as a one horse and, four church town. The white folk will belong to the other three. The only thing more segregated than our schools are our houses of the Lord. If you are black and attend church here in town, you go to Flint Hill Baptist Church. You get baptizes here, you married here, and when you die, you get buried here, as long as you have paid for your burial plot. Speaking of burials, if any dirt is to be thrown upon living soul, you can bet it'll get started at the mill or the church. It's not officially gossip until the usher board done stamped its approval on it.

It's a lonely walk up to the church doors. The service always concludes with the doors of the church being open. Most of my life these door have been slightly closed. With Mama running a semi-liquor house, and all the dirt the town folk shoveled on her, church wasn't always the place we choose to be. Things didn't get any better after Mama died. By the time I was fifteen I had picked up on some of Mama's reputation. Soon after I got pregnant with Ant. Since nobody thought it was an Immaculate Conception, the good church folk had another reason to look down on the Baxter clan. Finally, I topped all that history of by falling in love with a white boy. These thoughts and more crossed my mind as I slunk toward that door.

As I approached the Usher, my intention is to proudly walk to the very front of the church. My intentions are to let them know that this is the new Maya. I'm not going to let anybody or anything turn me around. That is except myself. As the Usher hands me the program, I do, my best to not draw any attention to myself. I ease into the next to the last pew, feeling like a whore on revival. I guess old habits die hard.

Inside the church the Senior choir is singing a hymn in preparation of the message. I've always preferred the Seniors to the Regular choir. Their songs are always in Rhyme and Repeat style, that way I always know the words. For as long as I can remember Ol' Pete Josephs been leading that choir. He has been old Pete since I was a child, so I guess he must be about 100 years old. He has this really distinctive bass voice that sounds as if you're surely going to hell if you don't repent. His voice is kind of what you'd expect God's to sound like. That glorious voice explodes into sound.

"Nearrr the Cross, O' nearrr the Cross, be my glory ever."

A chorus is echoed by the Senior Choir.

"Nearrr the Cross, nearrr the Cross, be my glory ever"

As they do this the entire church keeps in rhythm with the steady clapping of hands and patting of feet. The entire event could not have been choreographed any better. It is a thing of continued beauty when Ol' Pete falls into the next verse. As is his usual he begins to get a bit more animated as he feels the inspiration of the Lord. This kind of gives permission to the others on the choir and in the congregation to cut loose.

When an entire church, well not really an entire church, feels the spirit of the Holy Ghost it is a wonder and an amazement. It will not be long before Sister Althea starts lifting up hands to the Lord. Most of the folks around her know to give her a little elbow room or else risk catching one in the mouth. Once Sister Althea gets going the only thing anybody can remember slowing her down was the time she knocked off her black flowered hat and the gray wig she wears. She's also been known to do a mean strut down the aisle, gimpy leg, bad hip and all.

Soon after Sister Althea gets going good, Sister Minnie Lee starts talking in tongues. I don't know if anything in my life scared me more, than the first time I heard her doing that. I didn't know if she was having a spell where she was back in Africa or what. I didn't know what that talking in tongues was about, but I knew it wasn't for me. I mean I couldn't make out hide nor hair of what she was saying and neither could anybody else, but she just kept right on. You would think one day she'd let us all in on what in the heck she's saying.

"Ay ayor rama tata dom mamor ay yor ayrama tadomma."

On a good day Sister Minnie Lee can have a pretty good speaking in tongues conversation with herself. Today she cut it a little short.

I look around a half empty church. I see a few people my age. Unless it's funeral, only the older people come out on a regular basis. The majority of the church is elderly and also more women than men. The younger men spend too much time on Saturday nights to be bothered with Sunday morning. Today is no exception. There are maybe five men between the age of twenty and thirty years old.

One of the people I do see is Marguerite. She's sitting with some of her kinfolk and her two children about five or sixpews in front of me. I doubt if her children know that their mama prefers my sister to their daddy in the bedroom. Hell, that's really not a bad choice. Any breathing creature, male or female, would prefer anything to her man. I bet Tanesha has told her that I know. I bet she knows that I know that she's nothing but a lying, pussy licking dyke. All those times she would look down at me. I'd like to see her face now. I like to look her right in the eye and just smile. Bitch, and I bet she turned my Sister out.

The congregation settles down as Ol' Pete finishes up. Sister Althea falls back into her seat exhausted having unleashed the Holy Ghost.

Right on cue, up bounces the smiling Reverend Clifford Albert Dubois. Word around here was he was kin to W.E.B Dubois, but nobody ever confirmed that rumor. Of course, a good juicy rumor doesn't need to be confirmed, it doesn't even need to be the truth. It just needs to be good and juicy.

Reverend Dubois has been pastor here for the last twelve years. That in itself says a lot. The minister before him was run off after he was caught at the Motel 6 in Spartanburg with the Sunday school teacher. That was part of the reason they run him off. Once the rumor got started that he'd bought her new-used car with church money, then he had to move on. If you a preacher you can get a little stuff on the side, just don't mess with the money. Small town preachers either become an institution or they better get a moving van.

Revered Dubois is an old school minister. When he spoke of sin, he knew about it from a first-hand perspective. That was all right by me, I always liked a preacher who had some sinning in his background. Often times he'd talk about how the Lord saved him from liquor and the other evils of the world. His only overindulgence these days was his fondness for fried chicken and macaroni and cheese casserole. It didn't really take twenty-twenty vision to see that Reverend Dubois enjoyed a good meal.

Another thing I liked about Reverend Dubois was his forgiving nature. When he preached Mama's funeral, he humbly and nimblytip toed around her little indiscretions, and that was no easy thing to be able to do. He is more of a New Testament preacher. By that I mean he would more times than not, speak of the goodness of God and the New Covenant Jesus.

One time he actually got into trouble with the church old timers because he didn't speak enough about sin and punishment. I guess since they were too old to get into most kinds of trouble, they just assumed that the hammer needed to be brought down on the rest of us.

"Praise be to God."

A pause allows for a chorus of Amens.

"I said praise be to Gawd!"

Again, the Amen chorus ensues. The crowd is getting more enthusiastic because they know the word is about to be preached. Rev is going to jump right into it this morning. When Rev gets really fired up God becomes Gawd. The tone in his voice becomes one of excitement. When those feet, like David dancing, start to move it's time to cut loose. Usually, it takes a little while for God to become Gawd, but not today.

"How many of y'all this morning feel that Gawd is worthy to be praised."

"Amen brother, hallelujah."

"I tell ya he's an awesome Gawd! He's a mighty Gawd! A doing God and an undoing God. He's a can do Gawd!"

The entire time Rev is going the chorus of amen and hallelujah are becoming louder and rising closer to Heaven.

"If he woke you up this morning you ought to praise him! You ought to stand up and shout out thank you Lord, thank you for simply waking me up this morning. Psalm 150 and the sixth verse tell us, that everything that has breath ought to praise the Lord"

By now people are getting up out of those seats. Those pews can't hold them. I remain seated.

"Everybody who can stand ought to stand and thank Gawd for your health and strength. I tell ya that there are some people, somewhere who wish to Gawd that they could stand."

He pauses for a brief second. Then refocuses on the audience.

"I mean it. If you was watching Michael Jordan going in for a slam dunk, I betcha all the rope in this county couldn't hold you down, but when it comes to praising the Lord, ya wanna sit there with your arms crossed."

He demonstrates.

"Sitting there tryin' to act cool. Well all the ice on the North Pole won't keep you cool enough when you're chillin' in hell! I'm gonna tell you here and now, and I don't care who knows it. I will make a joyful noise unto the Lord. If I could, and y'all ought to do the same, we should make a noise unto the Lord that is so loud that the gates of hell are rattling on their hinges. We ought to praise the Lord so loud and so hard that the Devil will have to find his self a new home."

By now almost everyone is up and praising the Lord. The merging of salutations and praises unto the Lord while maybe not shaking hell's gates are surely working on the foundation of this old building.

Reverend Dubois has a way of getting those feet patting, hands clapping, and voices shouting. The spirit of the Lord is within this place.

"How many of y'all wanna get closer to the Lord? You know, Jesus, he died for you up on Calvary's Hill. Jesus the Great Preparer got a place ready for you. Our Lord and Savior Jesus Christ wants you and everybody in here, and every sinner on the face of this earth, he wants us with him. He loves us so much that he gave his life so that we could be with him. He wants all of us sitting there on the right hand of his Father's glorious throne. How do I know it? I know it 'cause the Bible tells me so!"

He raises a Bible in his right hand and proceeds.

"It says so in here and that's good enough for me. Folks going 'round talking 'bout they ain't Fundamentalist. They don't believe the Bible is applicable today. That's just fine by me, 'cause them same folk gonna find out that Hell is totally applicable for them. I'm here to tell ya that his word is as solid as a rock. It was good yesterday, good today, and good tomorrow. Glory be to Gawd! Glory to his word, his most wonderful word. How many of y'all got your Bible with you this morning?"

A show of hands as people lift up those King James. I look to both sides of me and try not to be noticed. Needless to say I don't have my Bible.

"In order to know the Lord, you gotta know his word. To know his word, you gotta know this book. Speaking of which, Wednesday night around here done been mighty slim, 'specially y'all men. If you didn't know any better you'd think Wednesday was ladies night up in here. And Lord knows Sunday morning Bible Study ain't no better."

He pauses for affect.

"I'm gonna tell it like it is today. And if I step on your toes then you either get some harder shoes or preferably get right with the Lord. How you gonna get closer to the Lord if you don't know him? Huh? And how you gonna know him if don't know his word? Huh? C'mon on now. You gotta know his word! You gotta live his word. Some or y'all act like you never even heard of Bible Study."

As Rev gets a little up close and personal the enthusiasm wanes a bit. It would appear that I'm not the only one missing service.

"I want to continue on last week's theme. Y'all that was in the house know what I'm talking 'bout. The rest of y'all just grab on and ya'll get the drift. Today's theme is concerning those of us who are called to serve. Saints lemme make sure you understand this. God is gonna call on you. I said Gawd is gonna call on you. Ain't no ifs, ands, nor buts about it. Gawd is gonna speak to you. Today I want you to consider what your answer's gonna be."

A pause.

"How will you, Gawd's chosen people, answer when he calls? What is your answer gonna be? If you have your Bible, I want you to turn with me to First Corinthians, First chapter verses one through three. If you don't have a Bible either look on with someone they don't mind, just follow alone with us."

He proceeds onward with the chosen subject matter.

"Saul, Who became Paul, was called to be an Apostle. He was to be an Apostle of the savior, Jesus Christ. When he came upon Jesus he was knocked to the ground. The light of our savior overwhelmed him. This is the manner in which he was called. Well just like Paul was chosen, you are gonna be called. Well just like Paul was chosen you are gonna be called. You may or may not be called to preach the Gospel of Jesus Christ. Or you may be called to fulfill another role. It is written that each Christian has a role, a job to do. My question to you is are you prepared to do your part? If the Lord calls on you today, are you willing to answer that call?"

A chorus of Amen.

"Are you ready when times are hard? Are you ready when your back is against the wall? Are you gonna be ready when all your friends tell you otherwise? When the people that you love, when they turn their back on you? Will you answer his call? 'Cause I'm here to tell you that there is one who has never turned his back on you. He didn't turn his back on the Cross of Calvary. He didn't turn his back when they placed on his head a crown of thorns. He didn't turn his back when they spat on him, when they laugh at him. He sacrificed for you. The perfect sacrifice for you. He fulfilled his role!"

Once again the masses are getting stirred up. The Amen's, praise the Lord, and Hallelujahs are coming fast and free.

"Some of us, if it requires a lil' more effort, then we don't want to do our part. We wanna serve the Lord only when the task is acceptable to us. Lemme tell ya church. I don't know if carrying that cross was the easiest task. It was a necessary task. The Bible says it was necessary so that you and I might be forgiven. Washed in his blood. Gawd, so love us, the sinners, that he wanted us to be with him. And since nothing we could do was good enough, was perfect enough to wash away our sins, Gawd made the perfect sacrifice. Gawd did his part for us. I'm so glad we got a second chance Gawd. I'm just as happy as a starving man sitting before a plate of pintos and collards with a lil' bit of neck bone in there, that we got a third chance, and a fourth chance Gawd."

He pauses to laugh.

"I'm happy to have a third chance and a fourth chance and a how many chance Gawd I need, so that I can do my part."

"Of course, and I hate to say it but I'm gonna walk heavy today. Well you got what I like to call the out-front type of Christian. You know the type. They willing to do their part if they can be seen. If they can get some credit. Unless we have the lead part, you know the part where you all out there in the front, we don't want no parts of nothing else. A lot of folks like that in the church. One of the biggest problems in the church today is to get everybody working. On any Sunday morning we don't have people for the nursery, we don't have people to teach Bible School, we don't have Ushers and the list goes on and on."

He pauses.

"Paul was the one who was out front, that was the role God had called him for. But he had an assistant, possibly a secretary by the name of Sosthenes. Sosthenes may have written down Paul's letters to the Corinthian as Paul dictated them to him. He gladly fulfilled his role. He answered when he was called. He didn't say I wanna be the leader. I wanna be Paul. He fulfilled the role of secretary just like Gawd had planned, and he did it gladly."

Another pause.

"I wanna ask you today, if you ain't active in the church, if you ain't working in the church, if you are not serving and doing your part, then you are indeed blessed. 'Cause Today is the day you can get turned around."

He spins and does a three hundred and sixty-degree turn to emphasize his point.

"Everybody, I don't care who you are, at some point in time needs to stop and turn his or herself around. To stop and answer the call of Gawd. In life sometimes we get headed in the wrong direction. It's no shame church, to stop and get turned around."

He spins a second time.

"Right now the Lord is speaking to you. He's calling out to you, the sinner. Gawd uses sinners. He washes them clean through the blood of our savior Jesus Christ. He washes them and calls upon them to serve as saints."

I find myself totally inspired.

"He's calling on the dope dealers to turn around and do your part. He's calling on the liars, to turn around and do your part. He's calling on the thieves, the fornicators, the adulterers, the gossipers, and the alcoholics all the sinners to hear his message, to stop and turn yourself around, and find your role, here in Gawd's house."

As Reverend Dubois continues, I find myself profoundly moved, an agonized soul must surely lament. I came here for hope and guidance. I think to myself, yes I do hear God calling me. It's unmistakable. God is telling me to stop and turn myself around. The words are so very clear. Yet there are now tears in my eyes and they simply will not stop. They won't stop because in spite of God telling me to change, in spite of God's infinite wisdom, in spite of those things and more, I just don't know if I can change. I've tried so many times before. It's a sad, pathetic pitiful thing to say, but I'm not sure if my life can be changed. It sounds terrible, but I don't know if God is God enough to change my life.

Still I look upward toward the heavens, searching for some divine sign. For the briefest moment, through my blurred tear stained vision I see what looks like a face. I swear it's a face! Can it be? Can it be? No, It is not the face of God. It appears to be the face of a woman. She's trying to tell me something. I hear her just as clear as I hear Reverend Du'bois. She's saying to me.

"You won't change. You won't ever change. You ain't never been nothing and you never will be nothing."

Why won't you believe in me Mama?

Homecoming

It's a good thing this old car knows the direction. It's wonderful that it knows the way home. I look up at the various sights. These are sights that I've seen over a thousand times before. But this time it's different. Even though I know the destination, I'm still searching for direction.

This time I've actually prayed about it. I've prayed before but this time it seems to be different. I asked God for guidance. I've argued with my Sister about it. I considered and reconsidered so many times Ant's feelings. The problem is I'm still guessing on which way I should turn. Or maybe the problem is I do know which way I should turn. Perhaps God is guiding me, after all I've heard it said a thousand times that he is a forgiving God. If anybody needs a little forgiveness, it's Jaime.

Maybe I'm asking for too much? Why should I expect to be happy? A part of me feels that it's my destiny to never find love and happiness. Isn't a person who keeps screwing up over and over again deserving of what happens to her? On balance, if you make a bad decision shouldn't you expect a negative consequence? God gave you a brain, use it. If you get burned by a bad decision, then that's the way life happens to be. How many times does a person have to get burned by love before she realizes the safe thing to do is move back from the fire? I don't know how many times, but I do know I've met the quota. I do know that I've been fried to a crisp. So driving home I find myself with definite feelings. I would have to say that I'm very negative about the way things have been, but with a high amount of hope about the way things can be. In other words nothing has changed. I am scared. Hope will take care of many things. Fear is not necessarily one of them.

The car pulls into the driveway practically driving itself. It's not fair. This is my home. Why should I be afraid to enter my own home? What in the hell does love have to do with fear? Why does, with me any way, the two have to go together?

I turn off the motor in the car. It tries to keep going, then there is a temporarily silence. I notice a pounding sensation. It comes from my heart and from my head. I begin to have difficulty breathing. I pause in the car for a moment to catch my breath. Is this the road that will lead me to happiness? If it is, then why am I so troubled? Damn this car. Why did you bring me here?

As I reach the porch, I fumble with the keys. It seems that my hands don't work exactly right. My palms feel sweaty and slightly moist. My fingers tremble. It's amazing to me that the keys still open this door. Why I don't know? This is still the same house, but it hardly feels like my home. I push the door open, I'm unsure if I should knock first. Even more unsure if I should enter. The future has always caused me to be most unsure. I reflect, actually it's the future, the present and the past that seems to cause me problems.

I walk in. As I do I immediately look around. The room is familiar. I mean there is the same old couch, the same tables, and the same old everything. The room looks very familiar. Except for one thing. Where is Jamie? Should I call him? Or should I look around the house for him? I ask myself what different does it really makes?

Before I can make a decision, he appears standing in the doorway. There he is. Even in a rumpled old sweat suit he looks gorgeous. He looks tired but gorgeous. I look at him and he at me. He then directs his fatigued eyes down to a floor that can't look back. He looks back up at me. This time there's the slightest hint of moisture in the corner of his eyes. This of course is very unusual for him. I have never seen Jamie care enough about anything to actually cry. Is that a good sign?

So here we stand, a room apart physically, but emotionally I'm not sure if that distance can be measured. I love him and I desperately believe he loves me. So why is everything so damn hard? So here we stand both of us trying to make sense of what should be easiest thing in the world.

I look at him and the negative feelings and the doubts are at least minimized. I know he's hurting. I feel bad for him. His heartache is obvious. At this moment I just want his pain to cease. He moves toward me and I instinctively walk over to meet him. We embrace. For the longest moment his arms are my comforter and my sanctuary. I don't know if there is a better place in the entire world for me. At this moment in time I know what I think to be the security of love. If it doesn't last, if it ends too soon, at least I know what it is that I covet. Damn you love! I just wish you weren't so wonderful. I look into those beautiful, slightly bloodshot eyes and I again know love. They are not the eyes from a few days ago. In these eyes there is no rage. These eyes speak the truth. These eyes do not lie. He babbles.

"I'm so sorry. I'm sorry baby, I'm sorry, I'm sorry, I'm sorry."

"It's okay Jamie. Everything is gonna be alright."

I immediately think to myself one simple thought, why am I comforting him?"

"Im so sorry."

Again, I notice the tears in what looks to be loving eyes. I can't stand it. I know that it's human nature, but why does it pain me so much to see someone else hurting? Shouldn't he be the one comforting me? Yet it is I who pulls his face closer to mine and kisses him gently right above those beautiful eyes. I then kiss him on his forehead. As I do he again whispers.

"I'm so sorry Maya. I know I've said it before, but this time it's gonna be different. This time I learned my lesson."

I don't know why I believe him. Other than deep inside of me there is a part of my heart that sincerely wants to believe him. So, because of a thing called Hope, I whisper to him.

"I know it Jamie."

"When you left me, I thought I was gonna go crazy. At first I was mad. Then I was depressed. The next thing I know I'm feeling lonely and afraid. Hell I knew I was going crazy. That's when I realized how much I love and need you. I mean if you ever leave me I don't know if I can make it. That's why I came to this conclusion. Maya I want you to be mine forever. I want us to get married and be a real family. Maya I want you to be my wife."

"I think to myself, that's funny, it sounds like he just asked me to be his wife. My ears confirm that the message was received. My brain takes a moment to process this information. It then sends a message to my legs. My legs respond by losing their ability to hold me up. The roles have again switched. It is again his turn to hold and comfort me. His words ring in my head over and over again. Marry me, marry me."

As he embraces me, and for all intent and purpose holds me up, I realize that someone loves me enough to ask me to marry them. All of the past men in my life wouldn't commit to the next weekend. Here was someone who wants me for the rest of my life. Here was this beautiful, wonderful yet troubled man saying he wants to spend the rest of his life with me. The multitude of feelings I can't explain. He whispers softly to me.

"I know I don't have no ring right now, but as soon as I get a few dollars saved up, I'm gonna go straight down to Brendles and put you the most gorgeous diamond ring you can imagine on lay away. You don't have to answer me right away, just think about it. I know you got a lot on your mind with the way I been acting. But if you will marry me I promise you that I'll straighten up and that I'm gonna love you for the rest of our lives."

Besides Tanesha and Ant, I'm not even sure if anybody else has ever truly loved me. This is the first and only person, outside of family who loves me enough to say I want to be with you forever and ever. He really loves me! I reach up on my tiptoes and kiss him deeply. He begins kissing my lips with the passion of lovers who have been separated for way too long. He moves down to the nape of my neck. It's a good thing he's already holding me up, because the feeling of his lips on my neck has taken all the strength from my body. He begins to move downward. He nudges the material of my dress down off my shoulder. His lips gently slide over my right shoulder, caressing it with his wonderful tongue. I feel a tingling sensation throughout my entire body. He rubs my back softly and so, so gently. He continues until that doggone dress has just slipped off the other shoulder. It isn't long before the combination of the back rubbing and the tongue gliding has that dress down below my waist. It drops silently down to the floor.

My body is alive with anticipation. Every fiber is screaming for this feeling to continue. Love is an emotion, but when it's right there is nothing wrong with just the physical part. He steps away for a second and effortlessly slips out of the sweat suit. I can't help but think how absolutely extraordinary it is to be back here with him.

He steps back up to me and slips off my bra and then my panties. We're both naked. He picks me up and carries me into the bedroom. Since my legs no longer work, extremely glad for the ride. I wrap my arms around his neck and cradle my head into his chest. He proceeds to lie me down on the bed as if I was a fragile treasure. At this moment, that is exactly how I feel. He slides down next to me and begins to kiss me on my stomach and my thighs. This continues for several wonderful minutes. The warmth of his lips and tongue are in contrast to the coolness of the air. I'm not sure how good Heaven feels but if it's this good, I've got to find way to get in.

Just as I think the pleasure can't reach any higher, my body jerks in a small way involuntary explosion. All of my senses become wholly alive. A small but glorious orgasm overwhelms me. If I could, I would shout out for all to hear. Thank you Lord! Thank you! But sometimes words just can't express how magnificent something feels. This happens to be one of those occasions. So I pant out in rapid breathes my approval of what he's doing for and too me.

As he prepares to continue it suddenly occurs to me that I didn't take my birth control pills yesterday or today. That would be all I need right now, to turn up pregnant.

"Stop Jamie." "Huh?"

"You have to stop for a minute. I forgot to take my pills."

"Your pills?"

"My birth control pills."

"Oh those pills."

He looks at me and smiles deliciously. I'm not sure what thought is going through his mind, until he announces.

"You know, you don't really have to take those. If something accidentally happened...well I want you to know I wouldn't mind."

I smile nervously. That's all I need right now. To turn up pregnant again, with no husband.

"We had better wait on that Jamie. After we're married."

He rolls over and allows me to rise from the bed. I head into the bathroom. On the counter he has some of his junk. I'm in too good a mood to get mad. I smile and repeat the phrase. "After we're married." I just remind myself that every man I've ever known has left a messy bathroom. I decide I'll just toss the stuff under the counter. I open the medicine cabinet. I easily locate the pills and from the holder. I turn on the faucet and fill the cup up.

I idly turn and accidentally knock a bottle unto the floor. I notice that it is part of a S Curl kit. think, this is not mine. I ask myself what in the world is Jamie doing with this? I examine the bottle. It is for curling and straightening hair.

I turn off the light and head back into the bedroom. "Jamie?"

He rolls over and answers.

"Yeah baby?"

"There's a bottle of relaxer in the bathroom. I didn't know you relaxed your hair."

"Yeah. Ah it's really the first time, ah baby."

"Why?"

He hesitates for a moment.

"Well it's like this, ah the men in my family, they all have this really curly hair. While you were gone, I ah was kinda bored. I had wondered how I'd look with straighter curls, so I was just kinda trying it out to see if you'd like it. I thought I'd surprise you."

I attempt to take a closer look at his handy work. He becomes noticeably defensive.

"What you doing?"

"I was just checking it out. I wanna see if I can tell the difference."

"You don't need to do that. The truth is I got scared that the stuff would make my hair too straight, so I washed it out before it was time. So I don't think you can see any difference."

"Well straight or curly, I'll still love you." He laughs defensively.

"Thank you baby. I appreciate you sayin' that."

I smile at him and basically agree.

"And I appreciate feeling that way."

"So since we both feeling that way, let's get back to where we were before my hair became so important."

I sheepishly smile.

"Right now I can think of a part that's more important."

I walk back to the bed and his waiting arms. We resume. It takes only a few moments, and even fewer caresses to revive our passion. And what amazing passion it happens to be. We spend the rest of the day making love as if we'd been apart for years. There's no doubt about it, the best part of breaking up is the making up. I Caressa is right about one thing. Who knows, maybe coming back home was a move in the right direction.

Schoolin'

When I opened the letter I knew it wasn't good news. My son doesn't bring home letters from the school saying he won the spelling bee or was the student of the month. No, I knew before I read the first word something was wrong.

To: Ms. Maya Baxter

Re: Antonio Jervario Baxter

Ms. Baxter,

According to the policy of the Tylerville Elementary School Disciplinary Codes, your child has been suspended pending a conference with his parent. This conference has been scheduled for Friday, April 4, at 10:00 AM. Please contact us at the school if this time is not acceptable, otherwise we expect to see you at the stated time.

Sincerely,

Mrs. Sarah Miles

Asst. Principal, Tylerville Elementary School

Sitting here waiting on these people I can feel the knots in my stomach. Ant is sitting there as if he's being led to slaughter. I tried to talk to him several times about what had happened. The only thing he'd tell me was he'd gotten into a fight. According to his version this boy had been picking on him and he'd gotten tired of it. I can't help but wonder how much of it is related to Jamie. I mean Ant never got in a fights before.

I look over at the secretary. She seems about as friendly as a copperhead that you just stepped on. I think to myself, she knows. She knows I got me a white boy and she doesn't like it one-bit, ugly bitch.

The phone rings and Miss Copperhead picks it up.

"Good morning, this is Strom Thurmond Elementary School"

A short pause as she listens. "Uh,huh. Uh huh. Yes ma'm,"

Another pause occurs as she searches for a notepad.

"Hold on one second please." She locates the pad.

"Go on ma'm. Uh, huh, uh huh, I see. No ma'm that want be a problem. We do it all the time."

I look briefly at the clock and then at my son. Ant instinctively, with his eyes, finds a spot on the wall in another direction. I look back at the secretary.

"Yes ma'm I got it. Jeff Davis Morgan is to be a car rider today. His mama's gonna pick him up, in front of the school. He's to eat in the cafeteria today and will bring a check tomorrow to cover the fee."

Just as she's finishing up this fascinating conversation on little Jeff Davis, out from an office walks a tall, bespectacled middle aged white woman. The lady smiles and looks to the secretary who is now hanging up the phone.

"Mrs. Miles that was Rebecca Morgan little Jeff's mama. He run off and left his lunch this morning. She wanted to know if it would be okay for him to eat in the cafeteria today and she'd pay for it tomorrow."

"Did you tell her that would be fine?"

"Yes'm I sure did."

"Good."

"And she also wanted to let us know she'd be picking him up today, and we shouldn't let him get on the bus."

"That's fine. You go ahead and take care of that with Jeff while I meet with Miss Baxter."

She turns and walks over to Ant and myself. We rise up from the chair and I cautiously shake her hand.

"Miss Baxter, Antonio I'm so glad you could make it. If you'd please follow me into my office. This shouldn't take more than a few minutes or so."

We walk behind her and turn down a short hallway. We proceed into her office. All this time Ant has his eyes focused on any and everything but a human being. It is obvious that he's totally dreading this meeting. He is not alone. I for the most part have always been fearful and distrustful of whites. That's why it still amazes me that I love Jamie so much. Deep down inside I don't have so many of those feelings toward him, but he hasn't made it any easier to trust white folks.

"Miss Baxter again I appreciate you making the time and effort to meet with me today. I'll get straight to the point. The reason I asked you in today is to discuss Antonio's recent behavior and progress. I'm very interested in seeing if we can help out in any way."

I nod my head in approval.

"First of all his attendance over the last two months has not been very good. To be perfectly honest, his attendance has actually been terrible. Out of the last 45 school days, he's been absent 12 times, tardy another eight, and suspended for another three."

I look over at Ant who reacquaints his self with that spot on the wall. He has to feel my eyes burning through his scalp. This is a total surprise to me.

"I had no idea he's been staying out of school that much. I mean I try, I really try. I get him up everyday and get him ready for school. I just got no idea why he hasn't been showing up."

I again look over to Ant who has the nerve to roll his eyes at me.

"I'm sure you do ma'm. Maybe he can help shed some light on this problem."

She kindly asks Ant.

"Antonio."

"Yes ma'm."

"Is there anything you'd like to tell us?"

I look on not exactly sure of what to say or do.

"No ma'm. I can't think of nothing."

"I see. Well is there anything we can talk about? Anything that's bothering you at school?"

"No ma'm. I don't believe so."

It's apparent from the look on Mrs. Miles face that she's slightly annoyed by her powerlessness. She looks to me for some type of assistance but I'm a bit unsure of what to say and I'm also unsure of what Ant's response will be. I don't want him saying too much about what's been going on at home.

"I guess what I'm asking Antonio is what happens that you don't make it to school? Your mother has said she gets you up and ready to go."

A heavy delay hangs in the air. This causes me to feel anxious. As the pause continues I feel compelled to break the silence. I instruct Ant to respond.

"Go ahead son. Answer Mrs. Miles." He shrugs his shoulders and responds.

"I dunno."

This frustrates me. I now share Mrs. Miles feeling of powerlessness and right here in front of this stranger. A white stranger at that. A transition occurs, as frustration becomes anger.

"Well Ant that's just not good enough! Here you been skipping school left and right with me not having a clue 'bout where you been or what you been doing. Now you tell me and Mrs. Miles why you haven't been going to school. And I mean right now!"

Mrs. Miles is slightly stunned by my sudden change in temperament. I am in a fact a bit surprised by the tone of my voice. Ant looks shocked. It's rare for me to so demanding of him. Mrs. Miles attempts to soften the roughness of my tone.

"Antonio, please don't misunderstand, we just want to help. We want to try and find a solution to anything that might be bothering you."

I find myself like so many other times in my life, torn. One part of me wants to take my fist and knock the little rascal into next week.

The other part wants to rescue him. Either way I have to consider my role in this mess. He stares at me with those eyes that look like Bambi.

"Sometimes ma'm, sometimes I might miss the school bus."

"Okay Antonio that's a start. And how often would you guess that might happen?"

"I dunno exactly. I guess ever now and again."

"Okay, And what happens on the other occasions, when your mother gets you ready for school?"

You can see him racking his brain searching for a plausible excuse.

It's obvious that he wishes this lady would just leave him alone.

"Antonio, please understand my point of view. At this point in time, I'm not here to criticize you or anything remotely like that. The reason I'm here is because the school is very much interested in your well-being. We. want very much to see you do as well as possible in school and later on in life. Do you understand that?"

"Yes'm, I think so."

I look on at the two of them. I think to myself this is the only kind white person I've come across in the past six months. She seems to really care about my son. She looks over to me.

"Mrs. Baxter I really must express to you and Antonio the importance of his attending school everyday, unless he's sick or there's some type of emergency. The State of South Carolina mandates that certain attendance requirements be met. If he continues to miss school at his current rate then he could be taken into Family Court for truancy. Also the Department of Social Services could be called in for an investigation of the home."

"What do you mean Social Services being called in?"

"Miss Baxter because of the Attendance and Truancy laws, it's possible for you to be considered a neglectful parent. You could be fined or Heaven forbid, you could be taken to Family Court and Antonio could be removed from the home. So, I hope both of you realize the severity of this situation."

I am stunned by these words. My first reaction is really defensive. I think, nobody is going to take my son from me. Nobody. I don't care what the law says. This bitch better just shut her mouth. Who in the hell does she think she is? This is not Master's damn plantation and we're not her damn slaves to be sold down the river. I've never really stood up to white folks, especially those in positions of power. But she talking to the wrong sister. My boy is my heart, and no one is going to cut out my heart.

"Now you better just hold on for a minute, ma'm. I don't know nothing 'bout no Family Court or no Social Services, but I can tell you one thing, ain't nobody gonna take my baby from me."

"Don't get me wrong Miss Baxter, that's not what I had in mind."

"Well that's sure the way it sounded to me."

"No ma'm. What I wanted to convey to you and him was that unless he does better in school, then all kind of things are possible. No ma'm, I assure you that neither myself nor anyone else has any intentions of removing your child. It is our most sincere wish that Antonio does well in school and remain in the home. But in order for those outcomes to occur then he must do better in school."

"Nobody need not worry 'bout that anymore. I'm personally gonna see that he has himself in school every single day."

I look at Ant who is presently trying to stare a hole through the tile floor. He seems lost. I remind myself that he's only a child. A child who is having to put up with too many unnecessary burdens. But I need him. I need him so very much.

"I certainly appreciate any and all of your assistance in this matter."

"Bitch!,I say to myself. She appreciates my assistance. This is my flesh and blood child. She sounds like she just thanked me for bringing the potato salad to the church picnic. I don't need her appreciation. I'm sick and tired of the Tylerville School System. No matter what happens with my baby, they got to blow it all out of proportions.

"You welcome ma'm!"

I sure didn't mean that. As soon as the words left my mouth, I had already regretted them. White folks in offices always have a way of getting me to talk up to them. Here I am thanking this bitch after she done talked about putting Social Services on me.

"Miss Baxter, I really hate to bring this matter up at this time."

I think to myself, then don't bring it up. Although somehow or another I know she is going to bring it up.

"Antonio please don't feel like we're picking on you, 'cause that's really not the case. It's just that your mama needs to know everything."

"What else is there, ma'm?"

"There is this little matter of his getting into fights. The past month he's gotten into two fights with other boys. Both of the boys, I was told, happen to be friends of his."

Ant looks up long enough to disagree.

"They ain't no friends of mine. Besides that, they started the fight. And my Aunt Tanesha says don't let nobody take 'vantage of me."

I think to myself that sounds exactly like my sister. Tanesha always would fight the world. Regardless, win, lose, or draw if you did something to her, she'd be right back tomorrow to go at it again. My sister is a fighter.

"Fighting with friends? This is the first I've hear tell of that. Ant who you been fighting with?"

"Antonio please tell your mama your version of what happened and how it happened."

She looks at me as if to say let's form a union. I perceive pressure. I'm his mother but she sounds more like a damn lawyer. He should be able to talk to me about anything. Still I decide to join in with her.

"Ant, baby tell Mama 'bout the fight. Tell me 'bout them boys picking on you."

"Antonio don't be afraid. We want you to feel free to tell us anything and everything about those fights."

Still no answer is forthcoming.

"Ant talk to Mama. What happen that you been fighting with your friends?"

He looks up at me. Those eyes, those eyes talk without his mouth saying a single word. Those eyes don't really know what the mouth should say. In those eyes I see anger, shame, and confusion all contained within two little brown eyes. In those eyes I see pain, anxiety, and desertion. For moment I'm not sure whether I was looking into his eyes or into my own.

There is something about seeing a child struggle. Right now my child is struggling with everything. His life is too complicated. A child shouldn't have to suffer. But right now my son has no refuge. He catches hell at home and he catches hell at school, and to him there must seem as if there is no escape. So I look into his eyes and see torment when there should be happiness. I see him and I see myself.

"The reason I got in those fights was 'cause they talked bad 'bout my Mama."

"Good Antonio, now we're getting somewhere. Now what type of things would they say about your mama?"

He pauses. Again he isn't sure of what he should say.

"C'mon Ant tell Mama."

"They say my Mama fucks white boys. They say she a cracker loving whore. So that's why I been getting in fights."

Promises to keep

It took a week or two before Jamie followed up on his promise to get counseling for his drinking. Then it took over a month before the Greenville County Commission on Alcohol and Drug Abuse was able to see him. Of course by this time he was insisting that he didn't need to go, and that the whole thing was a complete waste of time. But this time I continued to hold my ground. Each time he'd say those words, I'd remind him that he'd promised.

I have to give him credit. The last five weeks he'd done his best. He had not drank anything what so ever, at least I didn't think he had. He had also gone to at least two AA meetings, even though he said those meetings made him feel like drinking. He'd brought his check home and had been helping with all the bills. He would only take out forty or fifty dollars and hand over the rest of it to me. Most importantly he was trying to get along with Ant. I say trying because Ant wasn't trying very hard to get along with him. But I realized that would take time. I was just so happy to see him putting forth the effort.

I'd spoken to Tanesha a couple of times. We didn't talk about anything in particular. I guess in our own way, in the only way we knew how, we were saying to each other, I'm sorry. She even called me once to ask if I wanted to ride to the outlet mall in Gaffney. I wanted to go but she mentioned something about Margurite going. I still have a problem with that dyke bitch. Anyway, I reckon she was testing me to see if I was ready for that part of her life. I want my sister to be happy, but it's going to take a while to get used to this lesbian stuff. I know Tanesha loves her, I mean, but how in the hell can a woman lay down with another woman. It ought to be a commandment against that mess.

My life was genuinely getting better and I was going to do everything in my power to keep it going on the right track. This had been some of the best weeks of my life. In many ways it was better than when Jamie first started to love me. Most of that was a horny ass white boy trying to get him some black stuff. This was different. This was a man saying to me, and showing me that he loved me, Jamie was willing to do this for me. I am simply overflowing with that thing called love.

As we sat waiting for our appointment, the receptionist gave Jamie some papers to fill out. When she did this I noticed she brushed her hand up against his. I couldn't believe this little blonde whore was flirting with my man, right in front of me. I thought about cussing her ass out, but everything in my life seems to be going well. So I'll just ignored the trashy heifer.

While Jamie fills out the paperwork, I go back and forth between looking through at a magazine that's over two months old and scanning the waiting room area. Nobody in here really pays a whole lot of attention to us. I guess when you on coke, pot, or liquor you don't really give a damn about whom is sleeping with whom. Their number one concern is simply getting their life back s together.

I look over at Jamie. One time we made eye contact, his gaze remind me of just how much he loves me. I mean it's obvious that he doesn't want to be here. He pauses every few minutes, hesitating on some of the questions. I try not to stare at him. It's still pretty amazing to me that he's actually following through with his promises and he's doing it all for us.

"Well I'm all finished with this mess."

I smile, not really sure of what else I should be doing. I intend for my smile to be supportive and reassure him that he's doing the right thing.

"I still don't know why I'm here."

So much for a smile to communicate a message.

"I haven't had a drink in over a month. I been catching them AA meetings, been staying home on the weekends. Hell I been so good I've got to be the most boring son of a bitch in town."

This is the first time that I've noticed any displeasure in Jamie's voice. Even though it's not directed at me, I can't help but hope it's not a sign that he's drifting back into his old habits. I tell myself that maybe he's just feeling a bit anxious about all of this counseling stuff. I again smile nervously at him. I try to remain pleasant.

"Sweetheart the reason you're doing this is because we both love each other so much. Just remember how nice things have been the past couple of weeks."

This time he's the one who smiles. A very naughty smile at that.

"Yeah it has been real nice, 'specially last night."

The memories from last nights love session comes back to me. I can't help but join him with an ear to ear, thirty-two teeth, and bright, glistening grin. Our lovemaking has been blissful over this reconciliation time period. It had been a long, long time since Jamie had made love to me so delicately and so powerfully. Every kiss so soft and tender. Every caress so wonderfully gentle. Each time he penetrates me, I could feel the perfect length of his thrusts as they sink deeply into my warm, wet being. And the absolute best part of it all, was the cuddling afterward. I simply lay there in his arms feeling without a doubt that our two souls had indeed reunited. It has become more and more apparent to me how much he means to me. To say that I want, or need him just doesn't go far enough. He is my joy.

"So what you smiling 'bout?"

I just continue to smile. What else can I do? I'm happy. This is a feeling that has been a stranger to me for so long. This is so, so crazy. Here I sit in the Alcohol and Drug Rehab Center, and I dare to be content.

"Well since you won't tell me what you so glad 'bout, I'm gonna just take this paper up to that receptionist, since the mill's insurance plan covers everything, they should be pretty happy too."

He rises up and walks over to the blonde. She smiles at him again real friendly like, too damn friendly. She asks him something and he cuts loose with that crooked smile of his. They seem to be getting a bit too comfortable with one another. As hard as I done worked on this man, I'm not about to let any woman get too comfortable with him. I don't care if she black, white or in between. I assume he's forgotten his woman is over here. I call out to him and remind him who he came here with.

"Jamie."

He turns from the Barbie doll and addresses me.

"Yeah baby." that's right show Barbie that this is my stuff.

"Could you ask the nice secretary how much longer we're gonna have to wait?"

I put special emphasis on the we're. He then turns back to her and follows through with my request. She looks down on some piece of paper and responds. He walks back over to me and sits back down.

"She says it shouldn't be no more than five or ten minutes."

"I sure hope so. I'm tired of sitting here waiting."

"Well if you ask me, the best thing to do would be to just walk on outta here. I can take care of this thang all by myself."

"Jamie we done covered this territory before."

"Mr. Cook" Miss Barbie calls out.

"Mr. Cook, I can't make out this phone number and a couple of other things on this client information sheet. Can you step back over here for just one second?"

"Yes'm I'd be more than happy to."

He bounces up out of his chair and is back at that little window as fast as his legs can get him there. I think to myself, I'm nobody's fool when it comes to some bitch flirting with my man. I can't make out this phone number. She'll make out the number if she ever tries calling my house. I wish the hell this pale bitch would be calling my house for anything.

Just then they both laugh. What in the hell is so funny about a telephone number? If she doesn't quit this flirting mess, I'm going to grab Jamie by the hand and walk on out of here. maybe hes right. Maybe he doesn't need this place. After all he's been doing fine by just going to those AA meetings. I look over at her with my best, I'm watching you look. That's when Jamie decides to come back and join me.

"What as so funny over there?"

He recounts to me what just went on. The entire time he's doing this, he has trouble keeping a straight face.

"She was just joking with me 'bout my handwriting. Girl talking 'bout my writing bad enough to be a doctor. So I told her I was a doctor. So she says "what" kind of doctor are you?" Well I couldn't think of nothing but a heart surgeon. So she says to me "can you give me a new heart?" I say yeah but what's wrong with your old one? She says

"It just keeps getting broken." So I say to her,

"You don't need a new heart, you need a good man." By now he can barely contain his laughter.

"So she says "you're right, I don't need a heart surgeon. I need a brain surgeon."

Once again he laughs out loud. I simply look at him as if I don't get it. This is because I don't get it.

"What? Don't you see? She don't need a heart doctor, she needs a brain doctor."

"And that's s'pose to be funny?"

"Yeah it was funny. It was funny to me."

"What's funny 'bout it?"

"C'mon Maya. She don't need a heart doctor, she needs a brain doctor."

I look at him in disbelief.

"I repeat, and that was s'pose to be funny?"

"I guess you had to hear it first hand."

"I guess so."

While our conversation was finishing up, a lady walks up to us. She's about forty years old and maybe twenty pounds overweight, with dark black hair and some ugly glasses.

"James Cook?"

"Yes ma'm?"

"Hello I'm Debra Hurley, I'm a counselor here at the Greenville Center and I'll be working with you today. If you'll walk back with me we'll get started."

"That's fine Miss Hurley, but I want my girlfriend to come back with me."

She looks at me briefly, embarrassed by her oversight. I'm not sure if she's really concerned about me.

"I'm sorry. I didn't realize you two were together. Miss?"

"My name is Maya, Maya Baxter."

"Well Mr. Cook and Miss Baxter, usually we meet with the client alone for our first session."

"Mam, if it's okay, I'd really like for Maya to come on back with us. I ain't got nothing to hide."

"Well Ms. Baxter, if that's okay with you then we can do that and I can meet individually with Mr. Cook for the next appointment." I nod my head in agreement.

"Well if you both will follow me on back."

We stand and proceed to follow her down a concrete wall that's painted beige. We past several other offices turn a corner and walk into her office. She allows us to sit. There are four chairs in the room. We choose two chairs that are across from her desk. On her desk are two pictures. One of the pictures has her, two children, and a man. This must be her family. They certainly look like her family. They are all wearing glasses that say we chose the cheapest frames we could possibly buy.

On the walls are pictures you find in K-Mart. There is one of horses, and another of a farm scene. Maybe she's a country girl.

Now that I think of it she looks a bit like a country girl. I wonder if country girl is going to be able to help Jamie. She walks around to her desk and sits her country ass down.

"Mr. Cook today we want to begin the assessment phase of our program. During the initial assessment we basically want to look at what problem might exist. Then later on we'll look at what services we can offer. From there we'll probably make some suggestions to you and allow you to decide on which direction you want to go. Any questions so far?"

I look at Jamie, who gives me a what the hell is this look.

"How about you Miss Baxter?"

"No ma'm, I don't have no questions."

"You don't have to be so formal. You both can call me Debra."

This seems to be acceptable to Jamie and seemingly puts him at ease.

"Alright we'll call you Debra, and you call us Jamie and Maya."

"Jamie and Maya it is. I hope you don't mind if I take notes as we go along. My memory isn't what it used to be"

"That's fine. So Debra let's get started. What do you wanna ask me?"

"Maya I'll start off by asking Jamie some questions then later on, if necessary, I'll get to you."

I just nod my head in agreement.

"Let's just start off with an easy one. I see you're from Tylerville. Have you lived there very long?"

"Maya has lived there all her life. I just moved there about a year ago."

"Do you like living there Jamie?'

"It's okay I guess, nothing much too brag about."

"How about you Maya? Do you enjoy living in Tylerville?"

I hesitate. I didn't expect she'd be asking me any questions so soon.

"I reckon it's okay. I mean I never lived anywhere else. So I don't really have nothing else to compare it to."

She leans forward and nods her head as if to agree with me.

"Let me just ask you Jamie, what brings you here today?"

Jamie pauses for a split second. He looks at me as if he needs to decide how much he should be telling Debra.

"Well Debra I s'pose it has to do with the way I was drinking."

"Was drinking?"

"Yeah, you see I quit about 5 weeks ago. Hadn't touched a drop in over a month. And even when I was drinking, it wasn't like it was everyday."

I look at him and then her trying to convey to her that he's not telling the whole truth. He continues.

"I wasn't like a bunch of people who y'all see here. I mean I might drink a li'l too much on weekends or something like that. But it wasn't like I had a problem, problem. I mean I go to work every day, and never got into fights. No DUI's. I done seen people with DT's, I'm nothing like them. I ain't never even had the shakes."

"From what you're saying it doesn't really sound like you believe you have a problem with alcohol."

He looks at me and then answers.

"I don't believe so. I mean not a bad problem."

"So what brings you here?"

"Well it's kinda 'cause Maya thinks it might help us out."

"Help you out? Was the drinking possibly affecting the relationship and how so?"

He slowly rubs his hand across his face. He is trying to come ups with the right thing to say.

"Well I guess I'd find myself drinking a bit too much. Sometimes. It got to the point that Maya felt it might becausing me to neglect things."

"And how often would you say is sometimes?"

He begins to get uncomfortable at the nature of the questions.

"Sometimes is sometimes. I don't know exactly how often itwould be, just sometimes. Maybe I'd have a beer or two too many, on the weekend."

"A beer or two too many. Did you ever drink anything besides beer?"

"I'd drink liquor on some special occasions or sometimes just to relax a little."

"Did you ever find yourself drinking to deal with the relationship or any other stressful concerns?"

"Nah. Not of the relationship, but the pressure other people would put on us. It's hard enough for anybody to make it these days. But it's twice as hard when everybody you work with, and everybody who lives around you trying to screw things up. I'll tell you this, it's almost impossible for any couple like me and Maya to make it in a small

Southern town. Up North in a big city no problem, but in Tylerville it's hell."

I think to myself, Jamie never felt any pressure. If he did, he never told me about it. If he did he never showed it.

"So any pressure you might have felt came from the outside? From other people?"

"Yeah it came from the outside."

"Would it be a accurate statement to say that in order to deal with these outside pressures, you would sometimes drink a little too much?"

"Sometimes, yeah that sounds about right."

"I'm going to ask you a question. I want you to take a moment to think before you answer. Okay?"

He answers, but you can see that he is a bit concerned about where this conversation is going. He tries to remain calm.

"Okay, what's the question?"

"Let's say you were particularly stressed out, or maybe even celebrating or something like that. What is the absolute most beers you can remember drinking in an entire day?"

Again, he rubs his chin, looks at me and pauses to think of his answer.

"Well once and this was only 'cause of a big argument at home, I might have drank a twelve pack during the course of a day.

"Do you remember what the argument at home was about?"

"Nah, I can't say as I remember." She turns to me.

"Maya do you remember this particular occasion?"

This catches me by surprise. I become a bit anxious. I'm thinking what should I say? I don't want Jamie to come across as a liar, but I can remember a couple of times when Jamie supposedly got mad at me and went off drinking.

"I can't remember thatexact time."

She nods knowingly and turns back to Jamie.

"What does it say to you that you were able to drink 12 beers?"

He smiles slightly and half proudly announces.

"I guess it says I can hold my alcohol." She nods.

"Besides beer what is the most liquor you can recall drinking in one day?"

He pauses to consider which lie he'll tell.

"I guess a pint or a little more." She continues to take down notes on this paper.

"Besides alcohol, have you ever used or experimented with other drugs?'

"Before I answer that, lemme ask you one thing. Can any of this stuff get back to my boss at work? I mean I don't want any hassle 'bout what I do on my private time."

"I assure you that everything we talk about is totally confidential. It will never be released without your written permission, or a court order. I've been doing this almost fifteen years and I have never been called into court or asked to testify about a case unless it was about child custody situation."

This causes me to think about Ant. I reason that since Jamie is not his father that doesn't appear to be any type problem.

"Well I've like experimented around with pot and did some Soma and Darvocet once or twice, but that's been a long time ago."

"And how long is a long time ago?"

"Its been least a two years with both of them and probably closer to three."

"Would you say that either of those two drugs caused you any problems?"

"No not really. I would just do it to be doing something. To tell the truth I can't never remember buying any of the pills. I always thought the stuff was too expensive just to be giving you what a half-pint of liquor would do."

"What about your family? Did your mother or father have any problem with alcohol and or drugs?"

Jamie is slower than usual to answer. And even when he does answer there's a definite edge to his tone. It occurs to me that I know very little about Jamie's family. This is another of those areas he has always been very closed about. I have never talked to any of his family. He told me that both his parents were dead. He never gave any details, and I wouldn't pursue the issue.

If I asked about any other family member, he'd just make up some reason for me not to meet them or even talk with them. It got to the point that I asked him was he ashamed of me because of my color? He would only laugh about that and say of course not. He'd always tell me that he wasn't very close to any of them. To my knowledge, he had never even called any of them. The only thing he would really say was that they were all back in Atlanta.

"My parents are both dead."

"I sorry to hear that, but to your knowledge, did either of them have any substance abuse problems?"

"They both died when I was young, so I can't really say."

"No memories whatsoever?"

"None."

"No family member, grandparents, aunts or uncles ever mentioned anything about your parent's drug usage?"

"Look ma'm, nobody ever mentioned to me anything 'bout my parents drinking. I done told you I don't know nothing 'bout my mama or daddy's habits. I don't even remember them drinking at all. Besides what my parent's drinking got to do with me drinking a lil too much? I just don't see the connection!"

"Well Jamie alcoholism can have a genetic tie in. Your parent's drinking might be able to tell you something about your drinking."

"I done told you all I know. Okay?"

She continues writing, obviously noticing his mood and temperament. This reminds me of the old Jamie, especially when he was using. The one who got angry over any minor questions. I look at her, and realize she senses something. I look at him. I feel sorry for him. I want to say something to protect him from the questions, but I know that I shouldn't. So, I sit, on the outside looking in.

"Jamie please try not to take any of these questions personally. The only way I can get a clear picture, of who you are, is to get as much history as possible. Sometimes some of the questions may seem to be a bit off base but I assure you that there is a sound reason for every question. So, are you ready to go on?"

"For now I am."

"Have you are any family member ever had to be hospitalized due to depression, anxiety or any mental or emotional problem?"

"Excuse me?"

"Have you or a family member been hospitalized because of a mental or emotional problem?"

"What in the hell has that got to do with me drinking too much every now and again!"

"Again I'm just trying to get a good history. That's the only way we can develop a comprehensive treatment plan."

"I have never, and as far as I know, none of my family has ever been admitted into a psych ward."

The anger is etched Jamie's face as If it were a part of him. The expression on his face is one I haven't seen the past five weeks but it is still very familiar. The last time I saw it, was the night I got a size 13 shoe up against my ribs. She needs to move to another subject or this is going to turn out really bad. I instinctively reach out to Jamie and try to hold his hand. He pulls it away from me. I wonder if he's blaming me for the way things are going?

"What about sleep problems? Do you ever find yourself waking up during the night or maybe having a difficult time getting to sleep?"

"I sleep just find. No problems."

"What about problems remember things when you've been drinking or maybe somebody told you, you did something and you can't recall it."

"My memory is just fine. Never had any problem like that."

"That's good. Now Jamie what' about arrests? Have you ever been arrested related to alcohol and drugs?"

Although his mouth said nothing, the eyes screamed. Gone was any semblance of a smile. Also gone was any attempt to hide his true feelings. Etched in his face is both scorn and resentment. But instead of exploding he simply rises from the chair and walks to the door. He turns to me and simply informed us both that he needs to leave.

"I'm gettin' the hell outta here. You two can go on talking if you want to. I've had enough of this crap!"

He exits the room. I look at Mrs. Hurley in an apologetic manner. I feel like I need to explain to her why Jamie is behaving this way. Except I don't know why he's behaving this way. If I had known Jamie was going to pull a stunt like this, I wouldn't have wasted my time. After all he had promised me that he would come here and get counseling. Then he doesn't even make it through the first hour. I ask myself, should I go out and get him? Should I give him a few minutes to cool off? I'm just so unsure. And even if I go out and get him, what will I say to him? The past year I've come to know him all too well. He'll have a thousand excuses not to come back. He's going to blame any and everything but himself.

"Well this is not exactly what I had in mind. So, Maya where do we go from here?"

How am I supposed to know? This is terrible. I feel so absolutely helpless.

"Maya you and I can continue, or we can give him a few minutes and see if returns. What do you think?"

I think that I don't know what to do. I think I have an alcoholic boyfriend who is probably not coming back. I think that I don't need for you to ask me anymore questions. Why is Jamie putting me in this position? All I know isI want to get out of here. Why is Jamie putting me in this position? The only thing I really know is I don't know a damned thing. I lie.

"Give me a few minutes, I think I can get him back."

"Take whatever time you need. I'll work on my notes."

I get up from my chair and instead of feeling relief, I ask myself why did I tell this lady I was going to bring Jamie back? I already know that will not be happening. I walk out the door and look around for Jamie. I don't see him inside anywhere. I look toward the exit and see a group of people outside smoking cigarettes. I walk to the door. Outside there are two groups of people, mostly men. He stands on the fringe of one group. I approach him and gently place my hand on his shoulder.

"I ain't going back Maya."

"I know it was rough, baby but..."

"No buts, no nothing. I ain't going back. I been doing fine for the last few weeks and I don't need this crap."

"But she may be able to help you."

"How? How she gonna help me? Asking all those stupid ass questions. What my parents got to do with me drinking? Huh? Do I remember stuff that never happened! What in the hell has that got to do with anything?"

From the other group a voice calls out to me. "Maya?"

A voice from the past calls out to me. "Maya?

"Maya? Girl is that you?"

Jamie looks at me with an expression that says who in the hell is this? I can't immediately make out the voice. I turn and look into the face of someone I thought I'd never see again, and a part of me wishes I didn't see him now. This face brings back a flood of memories. It has caused me nothing but pain and anguish. It is the face of Ant's father Tony. I blurt out with machine gun rapidness.

"Tony? Tony what are you doing here? When did you get out? How long you been out?"

He runs up to me with that lying, deceptive smirk. He grabs me around the waist and gives me a hug. I look at Jamie who is still unsure of what he should be saying or doing. But he does know that he doesn't particularly care for this person named Tony. I immediately stiffen to his embrace, which is way too long. He finally releases me.

"Baby how ya doing? You sure looking good."

"I'm fine Tony, and how 'bout yourself'?"

"I can't complain. It feels good to be out and about among the free folk."

I look at an apprehensive Jamie. He seems to be in a really awkward situation. It's apparent he doesn't have a clue on how he should be responding. I try to ease his discomfort.

"Tony I want you to meet my boyfriend Jamie. Jamie this is Tony. Ant's father."

He looks at Jamie in disbelief.

"This is your what?"

"My boyfriend."

"Your boyfriend?"

"Yes my boyfriend."

He kinds of tilts his head and smiles slyly. I wait on them to extend their hands and introduce them self, that doesn't happen. Instead they kind of stare, like two dogs sniffing each other. I didn't realize it could happen quite this fast, but already this has become an adversarial relationship.

"Jamie you remember me mentioning Tony, don't you?"

"Nah I don't remember that."

"Sure you do."

"NO I DON'T! What is this, check Jamie's memory day?"

In a meek tone.

"He's Ant's father."

"Yeah you just said that."

"Yeah, that's me, Ant's daddy. You see Jamie, me and Maya go way back. We had a serious relationship long before you was ever in the picture."

"Yeah well that's the past. And some things are better left in the past. So what y'all had ain't nothin' to me."

"So Tony what're you doing here?"

"I got to take this class as a part of my early release. Alcohol and Drug Awareness." He laugh cunningly.

"Its s'pose to help me understand the way Alcohol and Drugs have affected my life. By me going through counseling, I was able to get out on early parole, got over a year cut offa my sentence."

I think to myself some things will never change. He's the same old Tony. Always looking for a way to scheme on something, He now turns his conniving mind to Jamie.

"So Homeboy, what you and Maya doing at the Drug Treatment Center?"

"I don't believe that's none of your business, Bro!" He retreats.

"Whoa, whoa there boss. It's all 's cool. Ain't no biggie. I was just asking 'cause I know Maya don't get high. So I figured maybe you having a lil problem."

"You can figure whatever you want."

They look at each other with utter an obvious disgust. I wonder how much is because Jamie is a white boy? I sense that this matter can get out hand really fast, with Jamie's temper. I attempt to diffuse the situation.

"Well Tony it's been nice seeing you again, but we are gonna have to get moving."

"That's cool baby, 'cause I gotta get back inside myself. But you don't need to be saying goodbye."

He looks at Jamie to gauge his reaction.

"Since I'm a free man again, I figure on maybe spending some time with my son. How is Ant anyway?"

This is not only a surprise to Jamie but it nearly causes me to fall on my face. He has never gone out of his way to spend any time with his son. As a matter of fact he has gone out of his way to avoid spending time with him. Five years ago I would have shouted for joy at hearing these words. Now you can't hear a sound just escaping from my throat. After all I want Ant to know his father. It would be great if Tony would really spend time with Ant. But I just don't believe it. don't believe Tony would do anything without having some kind of motive. He's got to have something in it for him.

"Ant is fine, but what do you mean by spending time with him?"

"I mean I want to make up for all the things I haven't done. I want to be a father to my child. So don't be saying goodbye. 'Cause I plan on seeing you and Ant real soon."

I look to Jamie. I know he is totally against this idea, but how can I refuse Tony. I mean he does have the right to see his child. He's Ant's father.

"I...I...I guess that will be okay. I'll give you our number and you can call me before you plan on coming over."

I reach into my purse and search for a pen or pencil. This is making me extremely nervous.

"I tell you what babe, if you still up on Flint Hill I can just drop by. What's the best time to catch you and Ant at home?"

Jamie has heard enough of this idea. He intervenes.

"Nah I don't think that just dropping by gon' work out."

"Now is that right?"

"Yeah that's exactly right. What you do is this, before you get ready to visit OUR home, you pick up the phone book and call us. We're in the book."

"Your home?"

"That's what I said. Our home."

"So you two stayin' together?"

"That's right. We live together."

"On Flint Hill?"

"That's right."

"I'll be Damned! You two living together on Flint Hill. Okay boss. Ain't no biggie. So Maya what's the best time to catch you? What hours do you work?" Jamie interrupts.

"You don't have to worry 'bout her hours. If you wanna visit Ant, you just call us on Saturday or Sunday. When both of us are at home. So you just plan on visiting our home on the weekend."

He looks at Jamie and smiles with his best, screw you white boy smile.

"And what if I don't wanna wait for the weekend to see my child?"

"Then you wait anyway. You good at waiting. You been waiting a minute now."

"Is that your business Opie?"

"If it concerns my woman, it's my business."

"Whether she your woman or not I don't know 'bout things such as that. I do know that boy is mine, and he's gonna be my boy 'til the day I die. So, homeboy, I'll come and see my boy whether you there or not."

Feeling anxious about this entire situation, I seek to bring it to a peaceful resolution.

"Tony we ain't rearranging our entire schedule 'cause you might come by. You can call us this weekend and we'll set it up so you can come by and see Ant."

"That's cool baby." He looks at Jamie with contempt. "I'll be in contact."

He smiles and walks back over to his group. I look at Jamie whose facial expression communicates in a low drained matter.

"Maya?"

"Yes."

"Can we go home now?"

History Lesson

The past couple of days I feel like I'm about to lose my damn mind. My nerves are so bad that my insides are trembling. I can't sleep, can't eat and can't think straight. I'm pacing, biting my nails and just irritable as hell. Tony is supposed to come by today. He's supposed to be here any minute.

I don't know if he'll show up. I mean he hasn't had any contact with Ant in years. If he's the same old Tony, he probably won't show. If he's the same Tony, all of this is just a lie. He's just mad at me because I'm with Jamie. He's just trying to mess things up. The first time in months that Jamie and I were getting along and in he waltzes into the picture. Tony doesn't give a damn about Ant, or me or anybody else. He just didn't like seeing me with Jamie.

To put it mildly, Jamie isn't taking this entire situation too well. In reality he is as mad as a still sober drunk hearing it's last call. He and I had been through it with this whole bigoted town. Finally when the hatred gets to a tolerable level, if hatred can ever be considered tolerable, in steps a new character. Someone who we know hates our relationship, but someone who we have to allow into our lives. At least, in my opinion, he has a reason to come into our life.

Jamie doesn't see it that way. He doesn't won't Tony in our home. He doesn't want him in the same town. Hell he doesn't want him on the same planet. His overall mood is that of out and out resentment. Over the past year, I thought I'd seen all of Jamie moods and feelings. Some of them very good and some not too good. But I had never seen him this jealous.

As I look out the window anxiously awaiting what I hope will not happen. Jamie enters the living room from the back bedroom. He's pretty much in the same mood he's been in the past few days. He's been pissed off ever since I got the call from Tony. After that call, I told Jamie that he'd be coming by to spend some time with his son.

"Where's the boy?"

"The boy's got a name Jamie."

"I know he's got a name. It's the same as that sorry bastard who's s'pose to be coming by our home. So where is Ant or should I call 'em Little Tony?"

"I sent him down the street to play with Kamaru and Omar."

"Shouldn't he be here waiting for his daddy? Or did you tell him yet? Did you let him how that his loving daddy was coming over?"

"Why are we still discussing this? Why?"

"Cause I'm bettin' you haven't told Ant nothin'. I got money that says You didn't trust the bastard enough to tell his child that he was coming by. 'Cause you didn't want to have to tell him afterwards why daddy didn't show. You don't have enough faith in Papa Tony to even tell the boy, that's what I'm betting."

"Jamie we done been over this twenty times. Tony has a right to come by to see his son. He's Ant's daddy."

"He might have the right to see his son, but he don't have the right to be called nobody's daddy. And even if he got the right to see 'em, it don't mean here. Let him do it somewhere else."

"I say he don't have no right to set food in this house. Not when I am helping pay the bills here. If he wanted to see 'em, Then he ought to just come by and pick 'em up. He ain;t sent a dime of support to you since I've known you. Now he wants to step up and be a daddy. He wants to come into our house and play daddy. You tell that son of a bitch to start paying child support before he can see the boy and I bet you money he takes off. Hell we'll never see him again." I move toward him away from the window.

"I'm not gonna do that. If he don't give me a dime, I'm not gonna keep 'em away from his son. The boy needs to know who his daddy is. My daddy left me when I was just a child, not much older than Ant. I don't want him to go through that. I want him to know his daddy."

"Daddy my ass! Just 'cause he got you pregnant doesn't mean he's a daddy."

"And just 'cause he's messed up in the past doesn't mean he shouldn't be given a second chance. And what's most important is it could help Ant. That's who I'm thinking about. He's been having such a hard time. He needs to know that his daddy cares about him."

"And how's he gonna feel when his daddy doesn't show up for another six months. How's he gonna feel when he figures out his daddy's con game! How the hell is he gonna feel when he learns his daddy is a low life son of a bitch!"

"You don't know that Jamie."

"Don't know it. You dreamin' Maya. Dreamin'. Didn't he say his self that he'd just got out? Didn't you tell me just this week that Ant wasn't his only kid? Didn't you tell me that all his life he's been a lying, no good dog! People like that don't change Maya, people like him don't give. They use Maya! All they know how to do is to use people. They'll use anybody they can. He used you, and now he want to use that that boy to feel good. He's just searching for a quick fix. He won't be here for the long haul, and you can bet on that."

"If that happens then I'll deal with it. But I'd rather that happen, than him not know his daddy at all."

"Why?"

Before I can respond, the sound of a knock on the door temporarily ends this lively discussion. We both turn our attention to the door. Through the open blinds you see a man standing on the porch. Through those same blinds his image is divided into multiple sections. He appears to be a man broken into many parts. His broken image is a distorted reflection on the glass of the door. It is Tony. Knock, knock, knock. "Just a minute."

I walk slowly to the door. It feels like a death march. Except a dead woman shouldn't feel their pulse pounding in their head. I tell myself I must be cool. I tell myself do not let Jamie get to you. I pull the door open. There as big as life, smile on his face, is Tony.

"Hey baby, you gonna invite me in or what?"

"Yeah, c'mon in Tony."

He steps through the door and for now back into my life. Hopefully, back into his child's life. He looks up and spies Jamie standing across the room. Instantly the smile disappears. On his face emerges a cold, hard stare. I look over to Jamie. Although they are different colors, at this time they are the same. They both wear the same icy expression. They view each other with scorn. Let the pissing contest begin.

"You remember my boyfriend Jamie?"

As disrespectful as possibly, he smirks as he addresses Jamie. I can't help but think that if Jamie was a brother Tony wouldn't care as much. Or should I say hate as much. If he was a black man, he might dislike Jamie, but that hatred would not be present. In a small way I understand, but I can't tell Jamie. As much as Tony dislikes him, I realize no black man is going to won't a white man raising his child.

"Yeah, I remember him. He's easy to remember."

Jamie continues to stare, without acknowledging Tony. It would be comical were it not so much tension in this room. It's like some kind of test of wills. They are both determined not to blink first. The good thing is that Tony has never been a fighter, also Jamie outweighs him by 25 pounds and is two inches taller. So I'm pretty sure no punches will be thrown.

"You mind if I have a seat Maya?"

"No sit on down Tony. That's a nice car you driving. What is it a Grand Am?"

"Yeah it's a Grand Am, it's Mama's. She let me borrow it since I was coming to see my son."

He walks over to the couch and has a seat. The entire time he keeps his eyes focused on Jamie. The snarl on his face has been replaced by a smirk. Jamie moves to the area vacated by Tony.

"Ant is down the street playing. I'll go get him."

"You don't have to do that Maya. I think I'll go outside and get some fresh air and a smoke. I'll walk down the street and send him back up."

"You sure?"

"Yeah...I'm sure."

He looks at Tony for a last time, turns and exits the room. He moves out unto the porch and calls out for Ant. After doing this two or three times with no answer, he decides to walk down the street and find him.

I walk over to the door and see, Jamie step off the porch and head down the street. In his hand a cigarette. I can't see the look on his face but I'm positive that it's not a look of contentment. I take comfort in knowing that I'm doing the right thing for the right reason. If you keep doing that, things will somehow work out.

"This is turning out better'n I thought it would. That was real slick how you got rid of that white boy. My girl."

He smiles real greasy like. As slick as a possum in a persimmon tree.

"I ain't your girl. You resigned that position."

"Don't even go there girl. Like something for real is up with you and Opie? Don't tell me you done gone over to that side?"

"I didn't go over to no side Tony. I happen to love Jamie." "Damn. He must be eating that pussy pretty damn good." I ignore him.

"I hear tell that's all them white boys good for. So if it ain't nothing but some good tongue, hey I'm a modern kinda guy, I can be down for a little sixty nine to take back what's mine."

"What?"

"You know what I'm saying. It's the nineties. I don't mind giving a lil' head, that is as long as I get a lil something in return."

Of all the nerve! Of all the damn nerve!

"Fool! You gonna come into a man's house and hit on his woman for some..."

"Hey, you was my woman long before Master John comes into the picture. So if anybody infringing on anybody it's the white boy. Just like back in slavery days. Crackers breaking up black families. And you can say what you want, me and you got history. We got a child together: We damn near a family."

"Family! Family my ass! What you proposing to me Tony? Is that what I'm hearing?"

"Hell no. What I'm saying is maybe you ought to think 'bout you and me hooking up again. This thing ain't gonna last. Whitey just got a lil' jungle fever going on. He's gonna go back on you. Watch what I'm sayin' sooner or later he's gonna go back on you. Watch what im sayin' sooner or later he's gonna give you your walkin' papers."

"Jamie loves me. And I love him."

"You always was a sucker for love. But you ought to think 'bout what's best for Ant. I'm his daddy nobody can deny that. From what I remember, the boy looks just like me."

"That don't mean a damn thing!"

"Well this means a damn thang, you know and I know it can't be good for him being raised by you and your Caucasian. How a cracker gonna raise a black child?"

"Hes got a black Mama and I'm black enough for the both of us, and besides that I don't wanna talk 'bout it Tony."

"Im not asking you to talk 'bout nothing but think about what I'm saying."

I'll be damned. Although it's no surprise, it is now apparent. This isn't about Ant at all. It's totally obvious to me that this is about Tony trying to get me back. To get back at Jamie would be an added bonus.

"I ain't thinkin' bout a damn thing. You had your chance to do right by me. I would've done anything for you. But that was then. The only thing I want from you now is to do right by your son. Ant needs you, not me. I don't need you and I don't want you. I got me a man who's taking care of business, and he's doing it with more dick than ya'll ever have. So, he got you beat there too, my brother."

"Oh so it's like that?"

"Yeah it's like that!"

"So you saying there ain't no way you and me can get back together?"

"That's what I'm saying."

"Not even for the boy?"

"Not even for Ant."

"Alright! Be like that then."

He rises up off the couch and steps toward the door. I ask myself what's this about.

"What you doing Tony?"

"I'm leaving I got better things to do than to sit here playing this messed up game. All these brothers in the world and you fall in love with a po' peckerwood. Cracker don't even have his own place, gotta move in with you. And here you fall for him. You sick Maya. You got that slave mentality home girl. I mean it. Yup all the times back when we was his property, Ol' Master would just come in and take our women. Now our women just go to Master on their own. Slave mentality."

He laughs scornfully as he continues toward the door.

"Our women volunteering to be screwed by Master John. You one sorry ass bitch! Sorry ass cracker loving bitch. I'm outta here."

So much venom that if a rattlesnake was to bite him, the snake would die.

"Whaddaya mean you're outta here? You can't leave. What am I s'pose to tell Ant?"

"Tell 'em whatever you want. It don't matter to me."

"But he's your son."

He laughs.

"I got three more just like him and two daughters. Can make another one just like him anytime. So it don't mean nothing to me."

This has got to be the worse. I ask myself how can anyone be so cold hearted and callous?

"You've done some low-down mess in your life Tony, but this has got to be the lowest."

"Well, I don't know if it is or not, but homegirl I guess I can say the same 'bout you. When you leave the brothers for a Caucasian, I figger this brother don't owe you nothin."

"And I ain't askin' for nothin'."

"You askin' me to play daddy, while the white boy gets all the perks. I came over here for you. If I had a deal with Junior, then I would've done that. But you know you ain't about that. It's as simple as this. If whitey gonna get all the pussy let him play daddy. 'Cause I'm out."

He moves to the door, turns and looks back at me.

"If you change your mind, call my mama's place. I'm in the book."

He heads down the steps to his mama's car. He gets in and like that speeds off. Like some kind of cruel magic act, the father of my child just disappears. As he turns the corner, as if it was perfectly timed, Jamie comes back into view. Walking behind him in the innocent manner of a child is Ant. Rage and anxiety shouldn't be mixed. Together they will cause a terrible concoction that can serve no purpose to aid in healing. I ignore them and wipe the stinging tears from my face.

As my two men reach the porch Jamie veers up knowingly at me. He doesn't have to ask where is Tony. He knows he's long gone. Why he's long gone, Why he's gone, well that doesn't really matter much. Jamie's just happy that he's gone. The look on his face says I told you so. He leans against the porch and waits. Ant leaps up on the porch with a thud. He smiles at me.

"What you want Mama?"

I can't help but smile, anytime I look at my little Ant. He always causes my face to light up. The harsh reality of this situation is he's better off without Tony. The whole world is better off without Tony. My boy deserves so much more. He deserves better than what the world has given him.

"Mama? What you want with me?"

"I was just seeing if you was ready to come home."

I pause as I look at Jamie.

"No we was just fooling you."

"Fooling me. Fooling me for what?"

"'Cause later on I'm gonna take you to McDonalds for a Happy Meal."

"Can I have a Sundae too?"

"I think that can be worked out. But you have to be real good."

The gigantic show of teeth indicates he has forgotten all about the visitor. The visitor who long ago forgot about him.

"I will Mama. So what time we going?"

"Oh 'bout an hour or so."

"Aww. Why we gotta wait that long?"

"Why you gotta ask so many questions? We gonna wait 'cause I got to change clothes. And you gotta get cleaned up"

"Mama what you wearin' is fine for McDonald's, and I don't need to wash up to go through the drive through."

"You just don't want to take a bath."

"A bath? Mama I need a Sundae and a Apple pie for taking a bath."

Both Jamie and I laugh. He's really pleased that Tony left. For whatever reason he knows what Ant is going through. I guess with his father being dead, he can relate to not having a father.

"I tell you what, you can get the Sundae and the pie, and you don't even have to take a bath."

"That's off the hook Mama. Can I go back down the street and play why you get ready?" I smile.

"I guess so. We'll come and get you when we're ready. Okay."

"Okay."

He leaps off the porch, running down the street screaming. "I'M GOING TO MCDONALD'S." Jamie steps up on the porch and gives me a big hug. \

"Well baby you handled that real good." I allow him to continue hugging me as we move back into the house. His support is both surprising and well needed. He seems to understand how this might have affected Ant.

I had been so hopeful that this would work out for Ant. But hope can be nothing but a wish, and for me wishes very seldom come true. Regardless, my burden doesn't seem so heavy when someone is there to help carry the load. I am so thankful for Jamie at this time. I show my thanks by turning to him and giving him a big, long, soulful kiss.

"Damn! I don't know what I did to deserve that, but I'm sure gonna do it again and again, and again."

I grind my pelvis against his, and reach behind him and grab his butt. Looking up to him, I seductively announce.

"What you deserve is more than a kiss. I'll race you to the bedroom." Totally surprising me, he sweeps me up into his arms and kisses me tenderly.

"Maya Baxter, I love you so much."

"I love you even more"

"That's not possible."

"Well let's just go find out."

He carries me into the bedroom, as he does he softly kisses me on the neck, and the cheek and on the shoulder, and as soon as we get those pesky clothes off, all over.

Accidents Happen

Wasn't nothing special about today, absolutely nothing at all. Just like every other day. The alarm went off. I get up from bed, leaving Jamie. I get Ant ready for school and watch him head out. I drive into work and put in eight hours. I put up with the dust, the noise, and the stares. The stares are getting better. Only the die hard bigots still find the time to be concerned about me. Most of the people at the plant don't really care a whole lot anymore.

After work I pick up Ant from the After-school program. Since we had all those problems earlier this year, it's easier to keep up with him this way. He and I head on home. By now Jamie is gone to work. It always peaceful when it just the two of us. I still love Jamie with all of my heart, but it's hard.

Since he'd quit going to counseling after only two meetings. It wasn't any surprise to me that the drinking would start back. I'd expected it would happen. His argument had been "those counseling people are crazy. All they wanted to do is talk about my family and stuff like that." He didn't see how that was going to help him stop drinking. Besides he didn't really feel like he had a problem, so there was no need for him to continue with the counseling. So pretty soon it was one or two beers to relax after work.

He'd started coming home a little later each night Friday, Saturday, and Sunday. Or maybe I should say, early each morning. He had made friends with several of the guys on the second shift. I guess being a softball star had really helped him fit in. Either that or color doesn't matter that much when you getting high. Regardless it seems like I was the only one still catching a little hell about who I was sleeping with.

When I got the call I wasn't exactly sure of what I should do. The only thing the hospital lady told me was that Jamie had been hurt at work, and he'd asked for me. She also told me that it was nothing life threatening so I shouldn't be too upset. That was easy for her to say. As soon as she told me to not get upset, I naturally got upset.

Once I got my head together, I called Tanesha and she agreed to watch Ant. As soon as I could, I packed some clothes and dropped him off at her place. She actually said something about hoping Jamie wasn't hurt too bad. That was undoubtedly the nicest thing she'd ever said about him. Working in that mill, I guess she knows how bad those machines can chew a person up.

Tylerville has no hospital. So Jamie was taken to Greenville Memorial, about twenty miles away. The drive to the hospital was terrible. Even though I knew he going to be all right, I could still feel my hands trembling. That's not a good thing when you're driving on a crowded highway. Especially when your vision is blurred by the moisture in the corners of your eyes.

I finally arrived at the hospital, after a short wait,I was allowed to go up and see him. I pushed open a heavy, creaking door. Lying in a small twin bed with his arm all wrapped up was my significant other. I told myself no tears. I needed to be strong for Jamie.

He look up at me with that crooked mischievous half smile.

"Damn baby, you look like you feeling worse than me."

I cautiously move over to his bedside and not knowing exactly what to do nervously ask,

"How you doing"

He exaggerates.

"I'm pretty damn good for a man who almost got his arm pulled off."

His words make me shudder. I catch myself to stifle back the tears.

"Now don't go gettin' all sentimental now. Everything's gonna be fine."

"But your arm, Is it gonna be okay? I mean how bad is it hurt?"

"Hell right now it feels just fine. I s'pect the medicine they pumping in me has got a lot to do with that. It's giving me a serious buzz."

He smiles. Always that perfect crooked smile. Even though he's weak, and even though he's hurting, he is still able to melt my heart with that blessed smile.

"How can you joke about it?"

"Ain't no sense in crying 'bout it. I figure in a month or two this ol' thang will be as good as new. I'll just take whatever time off I need, draw some workers comp and maybe even get some disability. So I'm not gonna let it get me down.

The doctor said they couldn't operate 'til tomorrow. They gotta let the swelling and stuff go down. When the machine grabbed a hold of me it tore a some of the muscle from the bone, and dislocated it. But once they operate and set the bone, the doctor says eventually it's gonna be as good as new."

I've known Jamie for the better part of a year now and I still can't figure him out. If it had been my arm caught up in one of those machines I'd be screaming loud enough for them to hear me in Columbia. He lies here flat on his back, as calm as calm can be, thinking about how he can get some money out of this situation.

"When did you have time to think 'bout worker comp and all that stuff?"

In an extremely drowsy, and fatigued voice.

"Hell I don't know. I'm a poor man. A poor man always got to be thinking 'bout money. Baby just between you and me, if I can come up with a way to sue those bastards at the mill, I'm gonna take them for everything I can. All I need is to get some people to go along with me. Everybody in this town knows that machinery is as old as dirt. I was thinking that if I get a few people to say the machinery was broken, or dangerous then I can possibly get a fat settlement."

"And what you gonna do with that settlement?"

"Now what anybody do with a lot of money? They spend it. They use it for all kind of things. They use it to make their life better. I was thinking we can put some money down on a house."

This statement completely catches me off guard. Even though we've talked about marriage on one or two other occasions, this is the first time Jamie ever seriously talked like we was totally committed. It's one thang when a man talking through his dick, but when a man start talking through his wallet, he's serious. And all it took was a narcotic IV drip.

Even though I love him deeply, in spite of that, I had always put a limit on thinking about a future with Jamie. My past just wouldn't let me. It's one thing to love this white boy, but to marry him is another thing entirely. It's something you just don't allow yourself to think too much about.

"Did you hear me baby?"

"Huh"

I was asking you if you know any good lawyers in the area?".

"No, no I can't thing of none."

"Well that's okay. We'll find someone. So don't worry. A lot of people might look at this in a bad way. They'd probably be cussin' and screamin' and carrying on. Not me. Nah. I see this as a chance. A chance for you and me to improve our lives."

He yawns and close his eyes.

"I feel so tired."

"You want me to leave, so you can get some rest?"

"Nah baby, stay a lil' while longer."

Just as these words come out of his mouth he again yawns and closes his eyes. I sit there patiently waiting for him to open his eyes, or start back talking. The seconds turn into minutes, and the minutes turn into an hour. The entire time I just sit there and look at my baby. He looks so content. The only thing that's missing is that gorgeous smile.

Finally, over the intercom a voice announces that visiting hour ends in fifteen minutes. I debate on whether I should let Jamie know I'm leaving. I decide not to. I rise up from the chair and quietly move over to his bed. I take a second to look at him one more time.

I can't help but love him. Through the good and the bad times, I very much love him. I bend over and kiss him gently on his forehead. He partially opens his eyes as if from a fairy tale. He smiles. This time there's no cockiness, no playfulness, not a single thing that has always categorized that smile. This time there is simply a smile that I sense says thank you.

"Did I fall asleep?"

"Yup. You sure did."

"I'm sorry baby. Why didn't you wake me up?"

"I didn't want to disturb you. Besides I don't think I've ever seen you so restful looking."

He tries to shift his weight upward but winces slightly in pain.

"Ow."

My heart skips a beat as I reach over to comfort him.

"Jamie! You can't be moving around like that. You gonna hurt yourself."

"I was just trying to sit up so I can talk to you. I mean you drive all the way up here and spend your whole evening sitting with me 'cause you're worried. And what do I do? Well I go right off to sleep."

"But that's alright. There's no other place I'd rather be than right here with you. Now you lay down and get some rest and I'm gonna head on back home."

He looks at me in surprised manner.

"You fixin' to leave?"

"Didn't you here the announcement that visiting hours was just about over?"

"I didn't hear nothing but some ZZZZs. You gotta go now?"

"I'll be back tomorrow. As soon as I get home from work and shower, I'll be heading right back down the highway. Ain't nothing on God's green earth gonna keep me from seeing you. Okay?"

"I guess. Well my surgery is scheduled for first thing in the morning. So tomorrow evening sounds real good. So I can expect to hear from you around five or so?"

"If I don't make it no sooner. Now is there anything you need me to bring with me tomorrow?"

He smiles with that mischievous crooked grin.

"Well if you can bring your beautiful, sweet self, a long dress, with no panties underneath, it'll sure help me feel better."

I smile.

"If it'll make you feel better, I'll do it for medical reasons and that's all."

"Hot damn!"

As he yells out he winces slightly.

"Baby I love you so much."

I lean over to kiss him goodbye.

"And I love you twice as much. Well I guess I better be gettin' down the road."

"I'm gonna call you 'bout four. I want to remind you of what toput on."

"I love you, and you don't have to remind me."

"Back at you and I just like reminding you any ol' way."

I walk out the door and continue down the hallway. I feel so good. I didn't imagine when I first got here that I would be positively floating leaving out. I move past the faces of the people dressed in white and think how wonderful it is to be loved. It occurs to me that for once color doesn't matter. I am in love and he loves me. The hell with the rest of them and what they might think.

What followed was one of the longest nights I'd ever known. It was followed by an even longer day. I couldn't get Jamie out of my mind. I don't know why, but I feel like I love him even more now that he needs me. Every time I'd picture him laid up in that bed, my heart just goes out to him.

The next few weeks or even months, he's going to rely on me more than ever before. He will need me and I want let him down. I'm going to show him how much he means to me. I'm going to take care of him like he's never been taken care of before.

It's kind of funny, but some people were even kind of decent to me today. Janetta even came over and told me how sorry she was that Jamie had gotten hurt. Nothing like a loved one nearly getting his arm torn off to bring about a little sympathy.

Finally, the day comes to an end. As soon as I arrive home, I take the fastest shower in human history. Then I get dressed in about five seconds. Just as I start out the door, the phone rings. I debate whether or not I should just let it ring. I decide to pick it up.

"Hello."

I smile immediately as I recognize Jamie's voice on the other end.

"Hey baby. How you doing today?"

I'm feeling great. You doing okay?"

"I'm doing fine since I hear your voice. I was just on my way up to the hospital. I should be there in 'bout 20 minutes or so."

A short pause.

"That's part of the reason I was calling. I just got through talking with the doctor. He says the surgery went like a charm. Things went so good, they say I can possibly go home tomorrow. I was figuring since you gotta come back up here tomorrow or the next day to pick me up, it'd be okay to just skip coming up today."

"I don't mind coining both days or even three days."

"I know you don't mind, but I just felt like you need to take care of Ant."

I interrupt.

"That's not a problem. Ant is over Tanesha's and she'll be glad to keep him another day."

"I know but I was just thinking that I'd get some rest. It's kinda hard going to sleep with somebody in the room."

"You didn't have no problems last night?"

"Yeah but I'm feeling kinda of groggy from all the medicine and I was thinking I'd just crash on out early. So you just stay home tonight and I'll see you tomorrow."

I pause not really understanding his decision.

"Well okay, if that's what you want me to do. But I wanted you to see the dress I'm wearing for you."

"Damn! I'd forgot 'bout that. But if you give me a rain check I promise I'll make it up to you."

"I don't know. I left off the panties, just like you wanted me too!"

"Aww baby don't tease me like that. You know I want you here with me, but I'm just not feeling up to it tonight."

I decide to just accept his decision. Maybe it would be best if he got some rest tonight.

"Well okay then. I guess I'll see you tomorrow."

"I 'preciate you understanding baby, and I promise I will make it up to you"

I smile

"There ain't nothing for you to make up. Anything we can't do tonight we'll do it and do it again, and again tomorrow. I just hope that arm won't keep you from having some hot fun."

"Baby, that's only one part. There's not a thing wrong with the rest of me. 'Specially the most important part."

I hear him laugh over the phone. I can picture that smile.

"I love You, Maya and don't you ever doubt it."

"I love you too. More than anything in the whole world."

"Bye bye."

"Bye."

And the phone goes silent. I reluctantly hang the thing up. I pause to look around. All day long I'd been excited about visiting Jamie at the hospital. Now there would be no visit. It's kind of funny in a way, but the visit was more important to me than it was to him. He is lying flat on his back after surgery and I need him more than he needs me. I think to myself, that's not funny, that's pretty pathetic.

I walk over to the couch and sit. I try to think what can I do? Absolutely nothing comes to mind. My entire focus the past two days has been to take care of him. I hadn't worried about my child, not about myself, just taking care of him. And now he doesn't need my help.

I wearily arise from the couch and walk back into the bedroom. I look at myself in the mirror. I ask the question who the hell are you? The answer is I don't really know. I ease out of the dress. This makes me feel stupid. No panties, and for what? This certainly wasn't my idea. I do it for him and he says "not today."

I put the dress on a hanger and prepare to put it in the closet. I look at my clothes on one side and his on the other. I guess that's how it's supposed to be. I take a second look at his clothes and think to myself, if he comes home tomorrow he doesn't even have clothes to wear. The thought occurs a second time. He doesn't have any clothes to wear home.

A smile crosses my face. I suppose he couldn't have thought about that. If he had thought about that I know he would be wanting me to bring him some clothes. Well I just want bring him a damn thing. He wants me to wait until tomorrow. I'll just wait until tomorrow. Yet I delay from hanging up the dress. The no panties dress. I ask myself should I take him some clothes? I know he said not to come but he had to have forgotten that he doesn't have any clothes to wear home.

I sit down on the bed naked, with the no panties dress in my hand. I think maybe I'll get to show this dress off after all. Once I explain things to him, and I know exactly how I'll do it. I think I'll pull up the dress to my boobs and put all this sweet pussy in his face. His arm may not work but I bet his imagination still does. I rationalize it's all in how you explain things.

Should I go, or should I not go? I feel so lonely, but decide this shouldn't be about me. I feel so empty but this should be about Jamie. But he has no clothes to wear home tomorrow, and I don't even know what time to pick him up. He forgot to tell me what time to pick him up.

It's obvious to me that Jamie is too distracted to remember all these things. It's up to me to take care of him. If it were left up to him, he'd be coming 'home naked and no telling what hour of the day. The decision is made. I'm putting my dress back on, to hell with panties.

I march back over to the closet and pick out a pair of blue jeans and a shirt for Jamie. I get dressed for the third time today and with the clothes in my arms I head back into the living room. I locate my car keys and head out the door. I'm going to the hospital.

The entire twenty plus minutes of the drive I debate whether or not I should be doing this against his will. At least a dozen times I think I should just turn the car around, but this old car seems to have a mind of it's own. I tell this foolish car it shouldn't be doing this. The car refuses to listen. So we drive on.

I arrive at the hospital and gather up Jamie's clothes and my purse. I walk through the door and to a desk. I look up at the sign directly in front of me. It reads Information Desk. That's what I'm searching for, information. As of this moment I don't seem to have any answers. Maybe more information will give me some type of solution.

At the desk sits this old lady who looks like she should have retired five years ago. Along with her is this pale Stringbean with glasses. This lady has no breast no figure no anything. On her face is so much make up, that it had to be put on with paintbrushes. Why is it that the most unattractive women in the world think that if they put on extra rouge and lipstick, that they will somehow become pretty?

"Hello young lady can I help you?"

"Yes'm. I'm here to see my boyfriend Jamie Cook. He had surgery today on his arm and I'm not sure which room they moved him to."

"Well I'll just find out for you."

The older lady types something on the computer. While she does this the Stringbean looks up at me while looking down at me. I look away. She's probably jealous because she doesn't have a man. A man would have to be damn desperate or blind to want her. The old lady obtains the desired information.

"Young lady he's in room 468-D."

"Thank you ma'm."

"But you can't go see him yet."

"Ma'm?"

"You can't go in just yet"

"Why not? Is he hurtin'?"

"I don't think so, but he already has 3 visitors and that's the limit."

"3 visitors?"

"Yes ma'm."

"Who?"

The Stringbean enters the conversation.

"Were not allowed to give out that kinda information. The only thing we can tell you is that he already has 3 passes out, and that's all we can issue."

"But there is nobody, I mean he doesn't, he's never mentioned anybody else."

"Well that's not our concern ma'm. But you are welcome to wait."

"How long do I have to wait?"

The Stringbean looks at me as if I was from another planet. She proceeds to speak to me like I was a five-year-old child.

"You have to wait until his other visitors return their passes. As soon as they do that, then you can go on up."

I'm dumbfounded. "Do I sit over there?"

"Yes'm. You sit over there."

I walk over to those ugly, hard plastic chairs. That's my world, some people are leather recliners. My life is an ugly, hard, plastic chair.

Two seats down from me is a man who has a pair of bi-focal glasses on that are so thick he can probably see through walls. Two rolls back are a Hispanic looking woman with a small child. They appear to be watching some show about a judge. I try to ignore them as I try to think who could be visiting Jamie.

I sit and wait anxiously for another one of my endless hours. My whole life seems to be full of hours like this one. Time never passes normally for me. It either drags like a snail when things are going bad. Or speeds by like a racehorse when things are going good. The only problem is I haven't rode that horse enough times in my life.

I look at the clock. It continues to taunt me, to pick at me. Twenty minutes to five. The hands look like a sad face. I feel like the face on that clock and I don't even know why.

Why didn't Jamie want me here? And who is up there with him now? Who is in that room, taking my place? I again look up at the sign and the word Information. All I seem to have are questions rolling around in my head. Where is my damned information! Over and over, I ask myself the same questions. Each time I ask these questions, I get the same answer. The answer I get is no answer at all.

What will I say to him? What will I ask him? Hell he doesn't even know I'm here. He doesn't even want me here. The man I love asked me to stay away. Why? So he could see someone else? Who does he think he is? I gave up everything for him. I gave up my life, my people all for him. And now he tells me to stay home. I'll show his ass. Son of a bitch!

I look up for a brief second and notice these people exiting the elevator. It's an attractive lady with what might be her child and her mama. She's a pretty pecan tan color. The boy and the older lady are a lighter complexion, redbones. I look at them for a moment. I think the child's mother looks upset by something. Someone close to her is probably hurt really bad. The little boy is especially cute. He's got this angelic face with soft curly looking hair. He is probably a few years younger than Ant.

I think to myself I hadn't even checked on my baby today. I need to call Sis to check on Ant. I look around for a payphone. There is one just on the other side of the exit door. I stand and begin to move toward it as soon as I do another person beats me there. I think how typical. I move back to my seat, as I do, I take a second glance at the lady and her family as the three of them head out the door back into their own life. At least someone around here has a life.

My life, the thing that I call a life, is really an existence. The reason is because it's hard to really be alive when you are less than whole. Every time I think anything different some man shows me otherwise. I exist to be used and abused and told to stay away. Don't come today baby, I need the rest. Rest my ass!

I look up again at the taunting clock. It is now almost five o'clock.

"Ma'm"

I look back to the desk. Is she talking to me? The little old lady repeats herself.

"Ma'm"

She's looking at me. She must be talking to me. I look around. The Hispanic lady is gone. Ol' Coke bottles could be mistaken for a lot of things including a human being, but not for a woman. I answer.

"Are you talkin' to me?"

"Yes'm. I was letting you know that you can go up now."

I stand and walk to the desk. I don't know what else to do. I look around. I had planned on paying attention to see who brought those passes back. I need to know these mystery people. But I hadn't noticed anybody but those two ladies and that little boy. She can't be the one. I mean she's black. Just then the irony strikes me, well fool so are you.

She can't be the one. Jamie can't be fooling around on me? I mean he's with me almost every night. Every night, that is every night after he's out drinking with the boys. No that can't be it. He can't be doing anything on the side. One I been doing is taking care of his pecker. I have been giving that boy so much loving since our little breakup, that he can't be screwing around. I mean how? He's with me seven days a week.

But even as the thoughts seep into my mind, the doubts begin to grow. Hasn't every man I ever dealt with cheated on me? Hell almost every man I ever met either cheats or tries to cheat. So what makes Jamie different? Maybe since he got himself some dark chocolate, he wants a lighter shade?

"Ma'm, are you going up?"

I look at the Stringbean. She's talking but I don't really hear her. I look at her and I look at her and I look at the door. The door where Miss Pecan Tan and her mama and her curly hair brat just went out ten minutes ago.

Should I ask her? Should I ask her about my man? That's stupid. What am I going to say to her? Hey mystery lady, you screwing my man? You giving him some of that light chocolate stuff? Does your mama and your baby know you got yourself a white boy?

"Miss are you going up?"

"Did that lady who just left, did she return the past? Is she the one who was up visiting with Jamie? Is she the one?"

The two ladies look at each other wondering what they should say. The Stringbean is the first to respond.

"Miss it is against company policy and HIPPA regulations to give out that type of information."

"Policy my ass. All I wanna know is did she just turn in this pass? Was she up there with Jamie?"

"Miss I done told you once already. We are not allowed to give out that information. We could lose our jobs if we were to tell you what you're asking."

I look at The Stringbean in my best go to hell look. I can see she enjoys this particular aspect of company policy. She reaches this slip of paper to me. I stare at the paper. The sheet could have just provided another woman access to my supposed man. How can one small piece of paper be so significant to my well being? I take one final look at the paper and at the bitch holding it. I turn and haul ass out the door.

Even though I'm in a bit of a daze, I know what I need to do. I hurry across the parking lot searching for those people and their car. Maybe they haven't left yet. Maybe they hadn't made their escape. I search for their car, of course this is made more difficult by the fact that I don't know what their car looks like. I don't even know where I left my own car. I continue walking. My steps are fast, but going where?

Since I cannot find them, I decide to just get away. I need to find an escape. At the same time I try to come up with a different possible interpretations of what all of this means. But I keep returning to the only logical possibility. Jamie got him some stuff on the side. He's cheating on me. And what about that little boy? If you mix white and pecan tan you get a curly, haired, redbone brat. Oh my Goodness! He's got a baby!

I stop again to find my keys. I ramble through my purse. Inside I find the keys along with some birth control pills. This seems a bit ironic. I start back walking and looking. I'm finally able to locate the car. As I approach it, I'm not paying attention to the traffic. I see nothing. Luckily, I hear the slight squeal of braking tires on pavement. My heart, already pounding, tries to explode right out of my chest. This is too much. Briefly I'm frozen right in my tracks. Finally, I take an instinctive step back. The car driver seems unaffected. I look into her eyes as she shakes her head in bewilderment. She must be wondering, what is going on with me?

After the Calm

Even though it's late May, it feels like Summer. I look all around and see the Pansies all but dead, their annual death ritual just about complete. I wonder if they feel any pain? I guess I'll never know if they suffer with the coming of Summer's heat.

Today I feel very much like I imagine they feel. Even if we feel the pain, what can we possibly do about it? It's not like we have the option of pulling up our roots and relocating. It's not like they can change, maybe decide to be a Marigold. I think to myself, I'm definitely a Pansy and Pansies do not look forward to any Summer. Especially not the Summer of a year that has been trying and troubling. This time Winter's discontent has wounded Spring's hope and all that leaves is Summer's agony.

I'm late. I'm late and don't know what to do about it. I'm two weeks late and that has never happened to me before. Well one time before, when I was pregnant with Ant. This morning I woke up nauseated. That's actually better than yesterday. Yesterday I was down on my knees, vomiting and praying at the same time. Vomiting because I'm probably pregnant, and praying to hell that I'm not.

I hadn't told Jamie any of this and he hasn't picked up on the fact that I've been noticeably sick. These days he's in his own little world. I didn't have to tell Ant. He asked me what was wrong? I told him I must be coming down with a virus. I wish with all my heart that it was only the flu.

Right now, I don't know what to do. I tell myself I cannot have another baby. More and more the logical decision seems to point toward having an abortion. But I ask myself, will I be able to stand the incredible guilt. It's agonizing just thinking about that alternative. It eats away at my fragile psyche. But then I look at our situation and I think how can I bring a baby into this mess? I'm simply not sure if Jamie can be a father to a child, to his child. One child without a father can be a tremendous responsibility. Two children, is totally impossible.

I find that there is still a part of me that, in spite of everything, still loves him. I tell myself if only Jamie would straighten out. He continues to talk about getting married and I believe he is sincere. However, being sincere doesn't necessarily mean it's the right thing to do. I find that sincerity from an addict somehow loses its quality. If I could only count on him getting a job and staying sober, then I would be the happiest person in the entire world. This baby would be a joy and a blessing. My decision would be so easy.

I'm afraid to tell him what I suspect and know. I'm afraid he'll do me like Tony. I'm also afraid he'll stay. I'm afraid he'll be angry. I'm afraid he won't care at all. I'm just afraid. I know he has a right to know, but I'm afraid to tell him. I don't know what decision he might push me to do. We honestly don't need to add anything else to this disaster of a relationship.

In a strange kind of way, it is again pretty amazing to see your whole life fall apart before your eyes and not be able to do a damn thing about it. I wonder how many times can a person put their life back together? Right now, it feels a lot like being in the middle of a hurricane or earthquake, except God didn't create this mess. As Jamie slips further and further into the midst of pain pills and liquor, I see no realistic solutions.

He's angry all the time. It doesn't matter what it happens to be about, he's just pissed at the world. I walk around on tippy toes , afraid to move. I'm never exactly sure what I should do or say. It doesn't really matter because he's going to curse and scream, and the other day he hit me again. It wasn't as bad as in the past, but he still hit me.

On the days when he's not angry, he moves around like some kind of zombie. The worse thing in the world that could have happened has happened to him. Being out of work he has so much time on his hand, too much time. I don't know how he finds doctors who'll write prescriptions for those pain pills. Damned scandal and a shame. What is wrong with these doctors?

Some days my man looks like death warmed over, and yet, until recently they still wrote the prescriptions. He has prescriptions from at least three doctors in three different counties. When those pills are gone, he's gets them off the street. He's pawned just about everything in the house. Last week it was the bracelet he'd given me. He pawned that beautiful, beautiful bracelet. His first real gift to me. Back then it showed me how he felt about me. Last week it showed me how he feels about the pain pills.

He claims his arm is still bothering him but it seems fine when he wants to do anything but go find a job. I think he's given up trying. Since the Mill won't hire him back, finding a job around here is really hard. He wasn't eligible for Worker's Comp or other benefits either because they found marijuana and Zanax in his blood test. It seems he'd been lying about just a few beers.

On the days he's not angry, nor a zombie, he's sick. I had seen Mama sick on liquor before, but it doesn't compare to these pills. When he can't get any for a day or two he starts shaking, then he gets the sweats. After that he gets the chills. Then comes the sweats again, followed by the chills. One minute the blanket's on, the next minute it comes off. After that here comes the muscle aches and the throwing up. When it gets really bad he gets nausea and diarrhea at the same time. I don't know how in the hell he works that one out.

So I go from being a punching bag, to a mortician, to a nurse all in the course of a day or two. One thing I am not is his lover. There isn't much time for love when the pills come first. There isn't much time for love when you aren't getting high you're coming down. When you're not coming down, you're sick. Such is the life of a woman in love with a junkie. I should know better, I've been down this road before Jamie with Schoolboy. But here is where I find myself. Back making the same mistakes? I pray to God each night, but I guess God presently isn't in the mood for listening to me. Maybe I done called on him too many times and I didn't hold up my end.

Life with Ant isn't a whole lot better. He's moody all the time. You can see by the way he acts that he's not happy. His daddy actually came by once after the first disaster, and gave him hope. It's so easy for children to have Hope. Then he lied and lied and lied and snatched it all away. I guess there's a part of me that's childlike. Late at night when I'm deep in thought, sometimes hope will slip back into my life.

When it does, the child in me can still hope he'll do better in school. His grades have never been super but they've fallen lower in the past few months. On the positive side they can't get too much lower. Regardless, I make sure he's there every day. Since that meeting with that Assistant Principal, I can't risk his missing anymore school. Still, I can't make him learn. He just seems lost. Sometimes I'll go over his homework with him, and the next day he'll fail a test.

I'd punish him about it, but he already seems so down. He's going through a lot. What Jamie's going through has got to be affecting him. The fighting and screaming, the sickness, all of this has got to be on his mind. Imagine a child watching all of this. There are so many questions, and the only answer seems to be getting rid of Jamie. But this isn't really an option. In spite of it all, I think I still love to him.

Almost daily, I see my son becoming more and more withdrawn. I try to get him to talk. Some days he's his usual bubbly self. Too many days he's only a shadow. I try to give him attention but I'm so tired most days. Working in that mill eight hours and then taking care of Jamie, it just takes all of the energy out of me. When I do have some extra time for my baby, I'm just not at my best. The sad part is he knows. I promise myself that as soon as this latest mess is straightened out, that I'm going to make it all up to him. That is what I promise.

Tanesha is talking about leaving Tylerville. People in town are beginning to talk about her and Marguerit might be dykes. Two weeks ago, Marguerite left her husband and children and moved in with Sis. Nobody's sure, nobody but me, if they're lovers. After all if you had a husband like Isaac the question wouldn't be why did you leave? The question would be why did you stay so long? The way he carried on, and treated her. But they need a little dirt on Flint Hill, and gossipers being gossipers, they don't really give a damn who they throw dirt on.

Sis seems to be keeping her spirits up. She actually seems relieved. However, at some point in time you have to ask yourself is anything worth all of this? What makes Tylerville so special that she needs to go through the gossip and name calling? All our life we've lived in Tylerville. All our life we have been the victims of scorn and ridicule. I reckon Sis is nearing the point where she says, enough is enough, perhaps she'll move to Greenville or even Atlanta. In Atlanta or any really big city she could simply get lost in the crowd. She could simply be what God made her.

I think the only thing that's keeping her here is Marguerite. Tanesha told me that Isaac is being an ass. He knows he doesn't want the children, but right now he's keeping Marguerite from seeing them.

Apparently, he can't stand the talk or the thought that what's being said around town is actually true. That Tanesha's tongue was better than his dick. Sis says Marguerite is taking it very badly. She's missed time from work and from church and just doesn't seem to be her usual snotty self. If I had the time, I would almost feel sorry for her.

Tanesha is really doing her best to help her out. You can see that she really does love her. The problem is, she's finding out what I already should know, love can't conquer all. Anyway, she feels like it won't be long before Isaac lets Marguerite have the kids. If and when that happens, my only sister will probably be gone.

I know it sounds selfish, but I hope Tanesha decides to stay. I realize the gossip is painful. I also realize it's brutally hard to love someone and not be able to be with them all the time. Absolutely no one in this town knows as well as I do, what happens when you break down barriers, but Tanesha has always been the tough one. If anybody can take it she can. It takes something like this to make you realize just how much you love and need someone. She is a part of me, and I don't know if I can function without her. I know if she leaves I'll see her again, but it's not the same. I have always known that she was right there if I needed her. Greenville, I could probably adjust to without major trauma. If she moved to Atlanta, I'd probably die.

Anyway, the day had started off piss poor, and kept on getting worse. Jamie was waiting on a call from some doctor. It turns out that it was his last doctor. Apparently, his suppliers had finally wised up. He was hoping the doctor would call in a prescription for him. I was also hoping he'd be able to get something worked out. When he gets this way there is no talking to him. Detox or treatment was out of the question for a man who doesn't have a problem. He was already irritably and getting sick. So he needed something now.

Ant was back in his bedroom staying out of sight. He'd been around Jamie long enough to know when to get the hell out of the way. I wish I had that luxury. The entire atmosphere was tense.

"Ringggg, ringggg, ringgg,"

Sick or no sick he flew over to the phone. I stand back. I do not wish for him to think that I'm listening to him. Although I'm listening to him.

"Hello! Yes this is Mr. Cook."

As I look at him beads of perspiration appear on his forehead. His eyes are sunken and his hands are unsteady. You can see the anxiety. You can feel the desperation.

"Yes ma'm I know he just filled the prescription two weeks ago, but like told you earlier, I accidentally dropped them into the toilet. And it didn't seem like such a good idea to take 'em after that happened."

He listens to the person on the other end.

"Ma'm, who would want to make up something like that?"

He pauses to listen.

"Ma'm, I can't help it if I been going through a bit of bad luck. I mean how was I s'pose to know that my friend would steal my pills the last time. I didn't know he was like that."

By now he's pacing with the phone in his hand. "Yes, it is quite a coincidence."

He listens.

"No I don't consider it a big coincidence. I don't believe in big or small coincidences, just coincidences."

He listens.

"Lady if ya'll just listen to me. What I'm telling you is the gospel truth. I know it may sound a little funny, but I promise to you on my Mama's grave, I accidentally dropped the pills in..."

He's cut off before he can finish this obvious lie. His mood is quickly turning from desperation into a crazed fury. He recognizes that things are not going well for him. He can't manipulate this nurse.

"Ma'm if you'd just hear what I'm saying. We don't have a whole lotta time 'fore the pharmacy closes."

A short pause.

"Fine then! That's fine! I tell you what, just lemme talk to Dr. Mynacus myself."

He's nearly screaming now.

"I said I wanna talk to Dr. Mynacus. You think everything I say is a lie. I don't wanna hear nothin' else you gotta say."

Another pause.

"What you mean? Listen hear lady, you got no right to keep me from my doctor. This is a medical emergency! I demand to speak with him right now! I need my goddamn medicine! I tell you what, if I get sick and have to go to the hospital, I am gonna be owning that damn clinic. I am going to sue you bastards for everything y'all got. You tell Doctor Manascus that! You people get me hooked on the stuff and then when I need it you cut me off."

I look at him. His face is distorted. He looks like an animal that is preparing to devour some prey. I'm extremely glad that the person on the end of that telephone line is on the end of that telephone. I assume from his response that the nurse has terminated this call.

"Hello, hello. Hello. Damn! That sorry bitch! That sorry bitch hung up on me. She hung up on me! Bitch!"

He slams the phone down.

I sit there taking all of this in. Jamie is so enraged that he'stotally unconcerned about my presence. He is wholly focused on his needs. Right now he needs a fix that I can't give him. He looks at me, or rather through me.

"I gotta get outta here. I gotta go. Lemme borrow your car for a hour or so."

I've heard this lie before. Getting high time is different than regular time, One hour can be anywhere from four hours to all day. I'm not about to give him my car. I have to think fast.

"Go where Jamie?"

"Don't worry 'bout that Maya. Just let me borrow the car."

"I've got some things I need to do today. I can't let you have the car right now."

"Can't they wait? If I don't find a way to get some medicine real soon, I'm gonna get real sick."

"I got bills to pay and shopping to do."

"I'm tellin' ya that my arm's hurting like hell and no medicine. So you telling me that shopping come before me getting sick? Is that what you saying Maya?"

I know not to respond to this question. There will be no rational way to deal with him now. He is just one wrong word from losing it.

"Jamie I gotta do some shopping for Ant. The boy is growing right outta of everything."

"Well why don't you get your sister to run y'all shopping?"

I pause. He has caught me off guard. I need a moment to respond to this statement.

"Tanesha might have something else to do. You know she's helping Marguerite out."

In a snide manner, he responds.

"Yeah I heard how she helping Marguerite out" Wisely, I ignore him. "Well you call her and see if she's busy."

I reluctantly walk over to the phone. I can't think of any way to get around this request. As I dial the telephone number he stands right over me. Inside my head I'm hoping, no make that praying that she's not home. The phone rings only once.

"Hello."

I don't recognize the voice.

"Hello, this is Maya."

"Oh Maya, this is Marguerite. You must want Tanesha. She's in the bedroom. I'll go get her."

A pause as Marguerite locates my sister.

"Hey Sis, what's up?"

She sounds remarkably upbeat. I guess having Marguerite around is helping her mood.

"Ah, I was just wondering if you was busy today."

"Nah, I ain't busy. What ya need?"

"Well. Jamie wants to borrow the car to run some errands, and I was just wondering if you could maybe run me off to do some shopping for Ant?"

"Are you kidding? I'll do anything to see my favorite sister and nephew. Y'all come on over we'll shop 'til we drop."

"You sure it's no hassle?"

Jamie jumps in.

"She said it was alright?"

"Is that him? I ain't doing this for his sorry for ass! I can't stand the lazy, white son of a bitch."

Needless to say I don't tell him Tanesha's thoughts. She continues.

"I'm doing it 'cause I want to see my people."

"Well if it's no problem, we'll be on over there in 'bout thirty minutes."

"Sounds like a plan Sis. We'll be waiting on y'all."

"We"

"Me and Marguerite."

I had forgotten about her. I can't stand that flat-faced dyke.

"Okay Sis. I'll see ya'in a lil bit."

"Bye."

"Bye."

I hang up the phone. He immediately pounces on me. "She said yes, didn't she?"

"Yeah she said she'd do it."

"Good, good. So how long 'fore you're ready?"

"Lemme get Ant ready, and we can head on over."

"Alright, just don't take too long."

I escape to Ant's bedroom. I stand in the doorway and gaze down at him. He's stretched out over the bed, watching the television. Batman is doing battle with the Joker or the Riddler, or some dastardly villain.

"C'mon Maya let's go."

Ant turns and looks toward the sound. His face twist into a disapproving sneer. It's obvious that he doesn't like Jamie's tone. He looks at me as if it to ask again, Why does he have to put up with this bastard? He puts up with it because Mama is engaged to a person who has some problems. He puts up with it because He doesn't have a say in the matter. I should be speaking for him, but the only thing I can say doesn't matter. I should be speaking for him, but the only thing I can say is it'll get better. I keep hoping for the best, but the best never comes this way. As a matter of fact, since his marriage proposal nothing but trouble has come this way.

"What's he so mad about?" I lie

"He's not mad sweetie."

"Yeah he is. He's always mad."

"He's just a li'l upset over his medicine."

"Why he gotta be mad all the time?"

"He's not mad all the time."

"It sure seems like he is. Every time he looks at me he's mad. Every time he talks to me he's mad. Every time he opens his mouth nothing but bad stuff come out."

I let his words sink in. I know that there is some truth to them. However, I can't afford to reflect on them too long. Jamie is not in the mood.

"Ant get your shoes on. We're going over to Auntie's for a while."

He rises up from the bed and looks underneath it for his shoes. He locates one of them. The other one apparently is not underneath the bed. He looks behind the television. It's not there. I walk over and help him in the search process. I don't want any more incidents before we flee. I open the closet door. I don't see a shoe. It's impossible to see anything. Inside Ant has thrown his clothes everywhere.

"I don't see it Mama."

"Well keep lookin'."

I kneel down and sort through the clothes. I decide not to discuss his untidy closet with Ant at this time. This is ground we've covered before. Luckily, I come across the culprit. I study it for a moment. It is worn. As a matter of fact they are raggedly. He could use a new pair. I start shifting around in my mind these weeks' bills. What can wait? Or better still, what will wait? I decide I'll use part of the grocery money and get my baby a new pair of shoes. It looks like baloney and grits for dinner a few days, and peanut butter sandwiches for lunch.

"Here it is Ant."

I hold it out to him. He wearily walks over to get it.

"I think we're gonna go to the mall and find you a new pair of tennis shoes."

A rarely seen smile appears upon his face.

"Yeah Mama. Can I get a pair of Nike Air?"

"I don't think so."

"But Mama you promised."

"Boy I promised you no such thing."

"Yeah you did Mama. You said that if I cleaned up my room every day you'd give me a special surprise."

"And how in the world does that mean, I'm gonna buy you a new pair of one hundred dollar sneakers?"

"I'll take care of 'em Mama. I promise. That way they'll last a long, long, time."

"I said no. I'll get you some nice sneakers, but they want be none of them Air Jordan's."

"But Mama, everybody be wearin' Nike. They improve your hops."

"Well you'd better improve your hops with something less than fifty dollars' I just can't afford anything higher than that."

"If Jamie was working then we could get me some Jordan's."

"What?"

Aw hell, without looking in the direction of the sound. Without turning that way. I recognize the tone of a voice that was not pleased.

"What you say boy?"

I look to Ant who appears to be frozen by fear. He eases over to me for protection. I try to downplay the incident.

"Don't be gettin' mad at him Jamie. He don't understand 'bout your accident."

Jamie takes a menacing step forward.

"I bet if I start wailing on his ass with a stout belt he'll understand."

"I don't really think that's necessary"

"Damnit Maya don't tell me what's necessary! I don't needno snotty nose child talking 'bout me."

"He doesn't understand that's all"

"And you just taking up for him. What you gonna do when we get married? You gonna take up for him when he's wrong. 'Cause if that's the way it's gonna be then you got another thought. The surest way for a kid to go bad is to take up for him when he's doing wrong."

"It's not like that Jamie."

"The hell it ain't! And I'm not gonna put up with it."

Making a quick decision I change the conversation. I remind him of his present goal.

"Why don't we discuss it later after you go and get your medicine?"

He redirects his attention. He decides that his highest priority should target his pills.

"Yeah, yeah. Okay, we'll do that. We'll get it straightened out later."

He scornfully takes a final glance at Ant. Who now stands meekly beside me.

"I'm going on to the car.I'll wait for y'all there. Try and hurry up 'cause I feel my arm starting to hurt and them cramps comin' on."

He walks out of the room and to the car. I look down at Ant as he stares at me, It looks as if he is ready to cry.

"I hate 'em Mama. I hate 'em."

"Don't say that Ant. It's not the real him. He's sick right now."

"I don't care. I hate his white ass. I wish he would die."

I kneel down and hug him tightly. He buries his head into my shoulder.

"It's gonna be alright honey. As soon as his arm gets better. Ya'll see."

"No it won't. It won't never get better. If you marry him things gonna get worse. Mama don't marry him. Please don't. I don't want you to."

Even as I listen to the words pouring out and I see him saying them, I still can't believe what I'm hearing. However, another part of me realizes why my baby is saying these words. I don't know how to respond. So, I say the words that I hope will make my son feel better.

"Don't worry 'bout that Ant. Mama's not marrying nobody, no time soon."

I hold out my bare hand. "Look I don't even have an engagement ring."

He seems to be somewhat relieved by this demonstration.

"So let's you and me head on out to your Auntie's and maybe I'll get you them Nike tennis shoes"

"Jordan's"

"We'll see how much they cost. Maybe we'll catch a pair on sale."

I rise up from my knees and delicately kiss him on the cheek. He seems to be feeling much better now. As we exit the room I secure my pocketbook and proceed to the car. Sitting underneath the steering wheel is an anxious and irate Jamie."

"I was 'bout to give up on y'all. I tell you I'm getttin' sick and you slow around like I ain't got nothing better to do. Your time ain't my time!"

I smile and slide into the passenger side of the car. I hand him the keys from my pocketbook. He turns the switch once, twice and then a third time. It fails to start. I notice that his nose is starting to run. He kind of wipes it with the back of his shirt. I think how nasty. He turns the ignition switch once more, then repeats the procedure. The engine finally kicks in.

"Thank you Lord. When I get better we gonna trade this piece of junk in baby. As soon as I get better you and me gonna turn things around."

He leans over and gives me a peck on the lips. I force myself to not pull away. I think that's a strange response. Why would you pull away from the man you suppose to love? The answer is that at this point in time he isn't the man I love. He is just a shell of the man I fell in love with.

"Where's the damn gas in this car?"

Roads

The drive over to Tanesha's place seems more distant. I have a theory that when you aren't happy the roads get longer. I can't prove this, but ask any woman who's well traveled. She'll tell you that anytime you're in an unhappy relationship, the journey gets bumpier and the destination farther away.

Unfortunately, it gives me too much time to replay Ant's words. I play them over and over in my mind. One minute I'm thinking about marrying Jamie. The next minute I'm thinking about leaving him. I tell myself he can change. Then I ask myself why hasn't he.

I think about how things were when we first got together. How special he made me feel. I think about how he changed the last time after I left him. He was doing so well until the accident. If it weren't for the accident he wouldn't be on these pills. If he weren't on these pills, he and I would still be happy. We could be happily awaiting the arrival of our child.

I tell myself, he's gotten off the liquor and drugs before. There is no reason to not believe he want do it again. He just needs some help. What kind of woman would I be to leave him now that he needs me? After all he loves me enough to ask me to be his wife. That's more that I can say about any of the other men who have darkened my door. He loves me and I love him and my baby hates his guts.

We pull up into the parking lot beside Tanesha's car. I also recognize Marguerite's car. Ant is so anxious to get away that he doesn't even wait for the car to come to a complete to stop. He unbuckles the seat belt and bolts from the car. He reaches the door and begins knocking.

As I open the door in preparation of joining him, Jamie stops me.

"Ah Maya, I ah, need to borrow fifty dollars for my medicine"

"I don't have no fifty dollars Jamie."

"I'll pay you back. I'm gonna be finding a job real soon."

"It's not 'bout paying me back. I got just enough money to buy Ant some new shoes, and that's with me stretchin' the bill money."

"Well how much you got?"

"I don't know seventy or righty dollars, something like that."

"Well just gimme forty then. Lemme hold half of it."

"I can't do that. Kids shoes aren't cheap."

"I know they ain't cheap, but I'm telling you I'm getting sick and I need to get something real quick."

"And I'm tellin' you that Ant needs some shoes. His are just about to fall apart."

"I know they ain't cheap, but I'm telling you I'm getting sick and I need to get something for it. Besides you can get some good shoes at Pic n' Pay for ten or fifteen dollars. Look just like them expensive ones."

"I'm not getting none of them cheap shoes for my baby. His feet too flat. All I can give you is twenty dollars and ya'll just have to make due."

"Twenty dollars want last through the day."

"It's the best I can do Jamie." In a nasty, sarcastic tone.

"It's the best I can do. Damnit! I'm getting sick!"

I find myself alarmed by his tone. I open the car door, look away from him and notice Tanesha standing on the stoop. She

looks concerned. She must've heard Jamie's shouting. She steps toward the car. At this time I really appreciate her being there.

"What does that nosy dyke bitch want?"

"She's my sister Jamie."

"That don't make her any less of a dyke."

She comes within ten feet of us, as she stares at us I get up from the car seat, exit and move toward her. She's the first to speak.

"Hey Sis, everything okay?"

Jamie in his presence state takes offense to her comment. Right now it wouldn't have mattered what came from her mouth, my mouth or anybody's mouth. Jamie would be offended. He answers Tanesha for me.

"Everything just fine Sis."

"I ain't your damn Sis!"

"That's right. I here tell you gettin' more pussy than me. Maybe I should call you brother?"

"Your white ass mammy gettin' more pussy than a faggot like you. So I guess you better call her daddy."

He screams.

"You better watch your mouth bitch!"

I try to intervene. I start pulling Tanesha away from the car. She reluctantly comes along with me. I look up and see Marguerite. This is the only time in my entire life that I've been glad to see her. Somehow, she realizes what's going on and comes to help me.

"C'mon Nesha. You don't need to be out here arguing with this fool."

"I ain't scared of this no dick bastard. He thinks he can talk to me any kind of way at my house. He thinks he can scare my nephew for no reason. A junkie bitch!"

"Bitch! You keep it up now. Just keep it up."

Both Marguerite and I continue pulling on Tanesha and manage to get her close to and into the house. Seeing his foe gone Jamie angrily pulls off. Once inside the house Tanesha jerks away from us and throws herself down on the couch. She looks at me.

"I done told you Maya. He's not gonna be doing Ant any kind of way. He, ain't gonna be threatening that boy. So if you won't take up for him I sure as hell will."

I think to myself, so that's it. I look over to Ant who is observing this entire spectacle. Ant done came in here and got everything fired up. He must've told Tanesha what happened at the house. I wonder how much more he's been telling her. I innocently reply.

"What?"

"What my ass! I know what's been going on here lately. You think I don't know. The bastard ain't woking and all he's doing is getting high everyday. Then he's got the nerve to threaten a child. My flesh and blood. What kinda man is that? What kinda man you in love with?"

I remain quiet. I can't answer that questions. And even if I dare answer it truthfully, I'm not sure if I would like that answer. I sit down across from Tanesha. I decide not to get too close to her. Marguerite moves over to her and places a calming arm around her shoulder.

"Nesha, girl you gettin' too excited. Calm down."

"I can't calm down. Not as long as Maya tied up with that sorry son of a bitch."

I find myself unable to put up with another word. I'm tired of the criticism and the put-downs. All my life I've had to put up with the world's crap, and for what? I'm tired of putting up with Jamie, and I'm tired putting up with Tanesha, and I'm tired paying a price for something I didn't ask for and damn sure don't deserve. Hell I'm just tired, sick and tired.

"Stop it. Stop it right now. Jamie and I are trying to work this thang out. He's got his faults but I am going to try and stay with him. No man's gonna be perfect. I'm not perfect, you're not perfect and nobody else is. Right now he's going through a hard time and I'm not gonna leave him when he's s down. We're gonna find a way to make it work."

She looks at me and just shakes her head. I know she's thinking this has got to be one sick bitch, but I don't care. At this time, at this point in my life I shouldn't care what she's thinking or even what she's about to say. Still, I wait for a response. I continue to wait, but no response is forthcoming. She simply turns to Ant.

"C'mon in the kitchen baby, I know you hungry. Auntie's got some country ham in the oven that's just finished baking. I'm gonna fix you a big ol' ham sandwich, and a Pepsi. How that sound to you?"

"That sound's good Auntie."

She rises up from the couch and exits into the kitchen with Ant.

"That sounds real good Auntie. When I finish that can I have some desert?"

They leave Marguerite and myself in the living room. This is really an uncomfortable situation. In all my life, all the time I've known Marguerite, we'd never had any real serious conversation. Since I'd discovered her and Tanesha's little secret, I surely didn't expect us to become bosom buddies. I look over at her and she back at me. Hell I don't know what to say, and neither does she.

"You know she loves you."

"Huh?" She clears her throat.

"I said you gotta know how much she loves you. And it's not just you but Ant too. I mean she loves y'all more than she loves herself. She talks 'bout y'all every single day. She's always worried and upset wondering what she can do to help y'all out."

"I know she loves us, but that don't give her the right to constantly butt In and put my man down. Just 'cause y'all don't…"

I catch myself before I say the words, but it's too late. She knows exactly what I was about to say.

"Say it Maya, you might as well say it. Just because Tanesha and me don't need no man."

"I didn't say that."

"You might as well. Everybody in this town is." She pauses to compose herself.

"Most of my life Maya I done felt out of place. Most of my life I done had to hide who I am, and what I am. Just 'cause other people wouldn't understand. They wouldn't understand that it's okay for two people to love one another without one of us having a dick and the other one having a pussy. I love your sister Maya, and more and more each day I discover that I don't care who knows it. I love her not 'cause I'm some kinda of sex fiend. It ain't even 'bout sex. I love your sister 'cause she makes me stronger. She makes me a better person. Can you understand that?"

I nod my head, not knowing what else to do.

"She makes me a stronger person 'cause I know, whatever I'm going through, I don't have to go through it alone. Your sister is the type person who will shoulder a burden for someone else. She'll shoulder a burden even though it might be dragging her down. It's not 'bout what she can get outta the deal. It's 'bout doing what's right by the people you love. I love her 'cause she helps me to love myself. When you stop loving yourself, it's kinda like ice melting on a cool day. It's real slow. It's so slow that you don't know when it starts to melt. Pretty soon ain't nothing left of what used to be you. That's how it is when you don't love yourself Maya."

She pauses to ponder her words.

"A long time ago I had stopped loving myself. I used to always think that I was ugly, and not worth anybody truly loving me. Now I know different. I know that I must be pretty special if someone like your sister can love me. She stopped me from melting away."

If I didn't know what to say earlier, I really don't know what to say now. I just sit back and continue to listen.

"Sometimes when we make love, we'll just hold each other so close. She senses that I need that security. Without me sayin' a word, she'll sense exactly what I need. It's those moments, those times when I'll just bust out and start crying for no real reason. 'Cept maybe for the first time in my life, I'm just so happy. Even two dykes deserve to be happy Maya." She pauses.

"I remember one time when I was telling her 'bout all the stuff Isaac used to do. Wasn't long before the tears just starting spilling down my face. Next thing I know is the tears start forming in her eyes. Well it turns out she's got scars too. She tries very hard to keep 'em locked inside, those deep dark secrets. But that time they got away from her. That time she couldn't keep 'ern in that dismal isolated place where she'd buried them"

"What you talking 'bout Marguerite? I don't know 'bout no secrets."

"Of course, you don't. For as long as I can remember Tanesha, the baby girl, been trying to take care of you. She had to be strong. After she told y'alls Mama and that did absolutely no good, she decided that she had to be strong. So she made it a point to never tell you. She made it a point to keep it a secret for your sake, but that night she couldn't help herself."

"Couldn't help herself from what?"

"She didn't want me to tell nobody, especially you."

"I don't care 'bout that. If there is some big important secret, then I ought to know. I'm her sister. Now tell me."

"Well it's like this. When she was thirteen years old Miss Ju Ann took her somewhere. She took her to meet this man."

"What man?"

"She took her to meet her daddy. Her real daddy."

"What you mean her real daddy? My daddy is her real daddy."

"C' mon now Maya. You gotta know the truth when it comes up to you and smacks you in the face. Your daddy's not Tanesha daddy. Her daddy is as bright skinned as she is."

Even though I'd suspected and known that Tanesha and I probably had different daddies, I never really accepted it. It didn't matter. Mama was our Mama and in these necks of the woods, that made us sisters. I look at Marguerite and think to myself, at least he's not white.

"She met him down in Spartanburg. He was real sick. That's the only reason she took her. Miss Ju Ann felt like she should know him before he died"

"So she went to see 'em. What happened that was so terrible?"

"She told me she didn't know what to expect. They got to this place where he was staying, Tanesha says it was like a nursing home for poor people. Well she goes up to see him. She introduces herself and explains that she was there to see him 'cause she'd heard he was sick and she just wanted to know a lil' 'bit 'bout him.

Even on his dying bed that sorry yellow bastard wouldn't acknowledge her. He called her a mistake, and says he'd never claim her. Said he was drunk when he used to screw your Mama. He knows he was drunk 'cause that was the only way he'd put his thang in any trashy whore. So here she was trying to find out 'bout who she was, and all he could do was to spit out poison.

When she left that room on that day she was forever changed. She told me that after that day, with all she'd been through with men, she didn't have no use for 'em. See Maya, it was a man who made her not really fit in. It was a cold hearted horny son of a bitch, who she only met, once in her entire life, who along with other men help shaped who she was. He'd had more power over her life than she did. All those years, putting up with those idiots on Flint Hill Thinking she was part white. I don't think to this day that she has ever forgiven your Mama for two things, laying down with that man, and for all the abuse that went on all those years." This catches me by surprise.

"What you mean abuse? What abuse?"

She glances at the door to make sure Tanesha isn't around.

"I told her I wouldn't tell nobody. I promised."

I demand in a whisper of a voice.

"Tell me Marguerite! You gotta tell me."

She sighs heavily.

"Did you think you was the only one? All them low down dogs your Mama used to lie down with. Did you think they only wanted one of y'all? Did you ever wonder what they did when you got old enough to get away from' them? Didn't you wonder what went on when you was not around?

Well, I'll tell you what happened. As soon as she grew some boobs and got a li'l round ass, those bastards went crazy over that cute yellow bone girl of Miss Lil' Gal's. The reason they took your loss so well was they decided Tanesha was their new favorite. It went on several times for almost a year starting when she was 12 years old. And the only thing your Mama did was to look the other way. How do I know that? Well one day she finally told Miss Lil' Gal about it and you know what she was told. She was told to be more careful around them men. To be more careful around them men. Ain't that a bitch!

So in order for it to be stopped, she had to stop it herself. In order to stop it she took matters into her own hands. She told me that she started carrying a butcher knife, even when she went to bed at night. Had to pull it on two of them bastards, including Mr. Rob, before they got the message. No teddy bears for her at night. A damned butcher knife became her stuffed toy.

And she could never tell anybody else about it. She could never talk to you about it. She knew firsthand how bad it had affected you. She told me all about the nightmares and the pain. So she didn't wanna burden you with it. Kept that burden all to herself.

And you know what the worse part of it is. The worse part is every now and again she'll see one of those men. Yeah every now and again she'll run into one of them. And you know them bastards will actually smile and try to speak to her. They will actually try to carry on a conversation 'bout the good old days. About Ol' Lil' Gal. When that would happen, well for the next week she wouldn't be able to sleep. For the next week she'll be as nervous as a fat turkey the day before

Thanksgiving. So Maya, now do you understand? Do you understand why Tanesha cried? Do you know why she's the person she is?"

I look toward the kitchen doors and try to fully comprehend for the first time the person who is my sister. For a decade she has carried this weight with her. I'd been so busy focusing on everybody else that I could never really appreciate the person who was always there for me. The only thing I can think of is God bless her, God bless my sister.

Bam! Bam! Bam! I'm startled by the pounding on the door. I look in that direction and spot Jamie. He pounds on the door for a second time. I think to myself what does he want? Then I remember that I never gave him that twenty dollars.

I reach for my pocketbook, knowing full well what he wants and realizing this is the easiest way to get him out of here before Tanesha comes back. He continues banging on the door even though he obviously sees Marguerite coming to open it. I stand and walk over toward him. He immediately pushes past Marguerite without saying so much as a word. In his eyes is lust, not for me but for something more vital to his current needs. These eyes are sunken and tired. He is pale and sickly looking. He has beads of sweat popping up on his forehead and appears to be suffering.

"You forgot to give me the money Maya. Now I'm cramping all over and getting sick as a dog."

"I forgot."

"Damn that. C'mon give me some money."

Just as those words fall from his lips, Tanesha reenters the room. She stands with her arms folded and icily views the scene before us. As she does, I hand Jamie a twenty-dollar bill.

He hungrily snatches it from my hand.

"I need fifty."

"I don't have fifty. I gotta buy Ant some shoes." In a cold, uncaring fashion.

"Buy 'em next week."

He looks at Marguerite and Tanesha, and inquires to them in a very negative manner.

"You ladies mine if I talk Maya alone?"

"This is my house, if you wanna talk alone then go to your house. But I forgot you ain't really got no home."

He looks at her in the most loathsome fashion possible.

"C'mon Maya let's go out on the porch and talk."

I, hesitate. The expression on his face suggests I not go outside. I hesitate.

"Maya you don't have to go nowhere."

"Was I talking to you? You need to mind your own damn business."

"And you need to take your beggin', junkie ass on outta my house!"

He steps toward her. I feel the need to intervene before things get totally out of control. Unlike myself Tanesha wants back down, especially from a white boy. I step between them. Marguerite must be sensing the same thing. She takes Ant by the arm and attempts to leave the room.

"Go on with Aunt Marguerite sweetie."

He initially resists but decides to go on after Tanesha instructs him to do so. I now find myself alone between the two combatants. Verbal hatred spewing from both of their mouths. Tanesha walks forward, this is her house and she's not about to be intimidated.

"Bitch you better quit messing with me. This is between me and Maya!"

"Get outta my house you worthless son of a bitch. Get out!"

Before I can react, before Tanesha can react, Jamie totally loses it. He reaches back and with all of his might, hit's her in the face with the back of his hand. She screams out in pain. The blow knocks her to her knees. It draws blood from the corner of her mouth. I instantly react by bending down to assist her. He takes a step away so as to survey the damage. He looks as if he's unsure of what he has just done.

Tanesha is temporarily dazed. I scream my anger at Jamie. Without thinking, I rise up and confront him.

"What are you doing? What are you doing? You can't be beating on my sister."

He shoves me back.

"And she can't be talking to me like I'm some kinda of dog. I ain't gonna put up with that from nobody. 'Specially no woman."

"Just go Jamie. Leave."

"Give me the money and I'm gone."

I recognize that I no longer have my pocketbook in my hand. He realizes the same thing. We both go for the pocketbook. I grab hold of it a split second before he does. This causes him to try and snatch it from my hand. The strap breaks.

"Gimme the money Maya, I ain't playin' with you."

"No! This is for my baby."

As soon as the words leave my lips I regret them. I regret them not because I don't mean them, but because of the response. He takes the back of his hands and smacks me. I refuse to let go. He balls up his fist and hits me on the left side of my head. The pain explodes through my temple. I howl out in pain, but manage to hold unto the purse.

I scream to Tanesha who's not there. She has left me. Out of the blue Marguerite runs in shouting.

"You better get your ass outta here Jamie, I done called the police and they'll be here any minute."

In a last ditch effort to get the money he tries to kick me in the stomach. His foot mostly misses its target. Seeing this Marguerite runs over and leaps unto his back, knocking him off balance. They stumble and fall to the floor. Marguerite catches the brunt of the fall and is temporarily stunned.

While all of this madness is going on Ant has come from the kitchen to try and help. He runs over and grabs Jamie by the leg and plunges his choppers, as deep into Jamie's thigh as is humanly possible. This time it's Jamie feeling the pain. This time it's him who screams.

However, this bellow is in anger. He turns on Ant kicking him off his leg on to the floor. He begins to pound on him. Ant futilely accepts the beating, he has no choice. If that wasn't bad enough, he raises his leg and kick Ant in the head.

A loyalty that I've never felt before leads me to attack. I run and throw my entire fury into the assault. I use all of my might to try and assist my child. I grab him around the neck and pull with all of my God given strength. In doing this I choke him.

My aggression causes Jamie to turn away from Ant. He knocks me to the floor and prepares to redirect his assault. I am terrorized.

Suddenly, to my amazement he turns away from me. He stops. He's focused on something else. He backs up a step. Then I hear the words.

"You son of a bitch! You po' white, dirty son of a bitch! You come in my house and beat on me! You kick my baby in his head like he's dirt. I'll teach you to hit us."

Bam!

Almost immediately there's a piercing sound, no doubt in my mind, it has to be the most horrifying scream my ears have ever heard. I look up to see his hand on his shoulder. There is something red coming from underneath his hand. He looks at his hand, with eyes the size of a Kennedy fifty cents piece, as the blood covers it. He stares at it a second time as if this can't be real. He simply can't believe that he's been shot. Just to make sure he's not mistaken, Tanesha takes aim and fires the 38 a second time. This time the bullet finds it's mark in his side. Again, he screams out in pain. He staggers back. Tanesha stands with the gun raised, preparing for another strike. Her eyes are fixed and emotionless, I guess they are kind of like a shark before it strikes.

"Son of a bitch! Son of a bitch! Maya! She done shot me. Maya, that bitch done shot me."

He staggers and falls down to the floor. At least I thought it was the floor.

"AHHHHH! Get him offa me! Get this dead bastard offa me!"

It seems that Jamie had fell right on top of Marguerite. It would seem that that Marguerite, current sexual preference or not, didn't approve of his being in this particular position.

I look up at Tanesha who's standing perfectly still, except she now drops the Pistol down to her side. The look in her eyes is one of closure. This collision has been almost a certainty for some time now. Today, a full-fledged wreck occurs. This was more than Jamie she'd shot. This was for all the pain men had caused her all of her life. It's as if she's decided I killed all of those bastards. She took care of all the demons with those two shots.

I move over to him and lift his head. His breathing is heavy and the front of his shirt is changing colors. I don't believe I've ever seen this much blood before, except maybe once when it was hog slaughtering time. I try to comfort him. I take the blouse off of my back to try and stop the bleeding.

"Oh baby my poor, poor baby. Please God don't take my baby."

Between heavy difficult breaths and agonizing suffering, he manages to speak. He seems genuinely afraid.

"Don't let me die Maya. Please don't let me die."

I search the room for some sense in all of this. Tanesha has now made her way to the couch and sits down. She is unsure if she has just killed a man. Still, she appears to be unremorseful. As a matter of fact, she looks on in a manner that is totally distant, totally disassociated.

Marguerite is trying to regain her composure. She has just gotten off the phone from calling the paramedics. She can't believe all of this has occurred. That makes four of us, especially Jamie.

Marguerite runs over to me, in her hand is the metal fireplace poker from the fake fireplace. I ask myself what in the hell is she doing? Is she going to finish Jamie off? She pulls me up from Jamie. She's thought of an idea. She grabs me by the shoulder. Her hand feels like a vice. Almost shouting, she announces.

"We've got to protect Tanesha!"

"What?"

"I said we've got to protect your sister. Put this in his hand."

I look at her totally confused. Why does she want me to put this in Jamie's hand?

"Put it in his hand before the police get here."

I continue to hesitate not knowing what to do, or why I'm doing it. Marguerite senses this. She bends over and puts the poker in Jamie's right hand. He weakly rolls his head over toward her, and then closes his eyes. This frightens me. Marguerite stands and grabs me by my shoulders.

"We've got to protect Tanesha!"

"What?"

She shouts!

"Listen to me! I said we've got to protect your sister. When the police get her, we've got to say he was coming at her with this. You got it?"

I look at her totally confused. Why does she want me to say that? And why did she put the poker in his hand? She shouts at Ant and myself.

"We got to say, he was beating on us trying to take your money, with all these bruises on us that will be easy to believe. Then he picked up the poker to scare us. He was coming after us and that's why Tanesha shot him. Ya got it?"

Ant nods his head. He's got it. The child has got it.

I continue to hesitate not knowing what to do, or why I'm doing it. Marguerite senses this. She stands up and grabs me by the shoulders. This frightens me. She shouts!

"Listen Maya, we don't have time for you to act scared! We've got to protect Tanesha. You know the only reason she shot 'em was 'cause he was beating on us. He was beating on all of us."

I nod.

"Then we've got to protect her. When the police get here we gotta tell 'em he had beat on all of us, tryin' to take money. We've got to tell them that he is a junkie with a drug problem, beating us for money. He picked up the poker and was a waving it 'round and threatin' to kill everybody. That's when Tanesha went got the gun. He was just about to hit Tanesha when she warned him to put the poker down. He drew back like he was going to hit her and that's when she shot 'ern. You got it?"

I nod, but I'm unsure of what I expects of myself.

"Do you understand Maya? We've got to be straight on this. You've gotta backs us up. It's your time to take care of your sister."

I again nod. She walks over to Tanesha and Ant again repeating what she has just said to me. Tanesha shakes her head. It appears that the alibi has been established.

I kneel down and resume holding Jamie in my arms, praying a second time for God to spare his life. As I do this, Ant walks up to me with tears in his eyes.

"Mama I'm scared."

"So am I."

It seemed like the police were never going to get there. Then it seemed like they came quickly. They arrived a few minutes before the paramedics, and helped comfort Jamie. Then they begin to ask the questions.

Marguerite and I gave them the answers. Marguerite was really good at it. She explained everything and even pointed out the bruises. They took a lot of pictures of our injuries. I didn't say too much, but when I did I felt terrible. To me it seemed like they knew I was lying. Lord my heart was going a mile a minute. If they hook me up to one of them lie detectors, I'm going to break the machine. But Ant and I stuck with the story.

Worse of all, I felt like I was betraying Jamie. In spite of everything, I still care for him. In spite of everything I don't know if it was right for Tanesha to shoot him, let alone shoot him twice. I don't know if I could've kept telling that lie if the paramedics hadn't gotten him out of that house. I don't know if I can keep telling that lie. I don't know what I'm going to say when I have to look at Jamie. God I feel like I'm being torn apart. And then things got really confusing.

Mama

This is an absolute mess. Whether they believed us or not, the police took Tanesha in for questioning. We thought that with all three of us saying the same thing they wouldn't. But they did it anyway. Even though they said it sounded like an obvious case of self-defense, they couldn't be responsible for making that decision. So they told us she'd be held until Magistrate Tillman could see her tonight or tomorrow.

Tylerville is too small to have a full-time magistrate. So if you do anything to get arrested on the weekend, and you don't belong to the same church as Magistrate Tillman, then you sit in jail possibly until Monday morning. If you belong to Flint Hill Baptist Church, well the Lord may be with you but not the Tylerville's Magistrates Office.

All Marguerite and I could do, was watch as two redneck bastards forcing a person we deeply love into their control. One thing I can tell you is they thoroughly enjoyed the entire experience. I can't remember the last time someone was arrested in Tylerville for shooting another person. They probably felt like they had captured a big, timed gangster or someone. The way they handcuffed her made her wince in pain. When they got her to the car they practically shoved her into the back seat. Marguerite and Ant started to cry like babies. I had begun before them. I think that made them even rougher with her. Then they tell us we can't post bond until the Magistrate set the amount..

After they saw the bruises on Ant's face, a second county police car came and contacted social services. It wasn't too long after that when a social worker from the Department of Social Services came and talked to Ant for about twenty minutes. They decided it would be best if he stayed in their custody, for the time being. They claimed that there was enough evidence to support an ongoing child abuse petition against Jamie, but he needed to be observed for twenty four to forty eight hours. Another good thing for Tanesha, but terrible for me.

When they put my baby in that car I thought I was going to go slap crazy. I tried to be strong for him, but I couldn't. When he started screaming for me, I completely lost it. I mean I cried to the snots came out of my nose. They wouldn't tell me where he was going, only that it was routine procedure considering the circumstances. They wouldn't even tell me where my baby is being held or whom he's with. You don't know anguish until you see your child being taken away from you.

Jamie was rushed to the Emergency Room and then up for surgery. After a short time to clear my head, I followed them to the hospital. They wouldn't allow me in to see him. I was told that everything was okay and I should just go home and get some rest. Yeah go home and get some rest. The shot in his shoulder turned out to be a flesh wound. The shot in his side nicked his kidney but didn't do any serious damage. The major problem is to make sure there is no infection.

The funny part of this whole thing is they have him on a Dilaudid drip. After all of this to get his medicine, Jamie ended up getting his medicine.

When I drove home that night I felt like the loneliest person in the world. perhaps the only person who might be lonelier was Marguerite. She had given up her man and her children for love. Now the person she loves, we love, might be going to jail for God only knows how long.

Sitting in that house all alone, under these circumstances, you have to be very careful. You have to be careful that your mind doesn't start playing tricks on you.

When it started happening to me I wasn't really sure if I was dreaming, or having a nightmare, but I was sure that something wasn't exactly right. It hadn't happened in a while, except when Jamie got his arm messed up. I'd attributed that to being back in the hospital where Mama had died. Lately, I'd pretty much forgotten about her. I guess with all that stress I should have expected a return visit. Somewhere during a sleepless night, with my nerves completely shot, an old acquaintance comes to visit me.

"Well you sure screwed this one up."

"Huh?"

"I said, like always, you sure as hell screwed this one up." "Mama?"

"Well who else you think it is?"

"I don't know. I just hadn't thought 'bout you for a long time."

"You think you can get rid of me that easy? You think I ain't watching over y, all? If you ain't a piece of work."

"I just forgot Mama."

"How can you forget 'bout your own Mama? I think maybe you wanna forget? Is that it Maya? You wanna forget all 'bout me?"

"No Mama, that's not it."

"It sure seems that way. it seems to me that I ain't heard from you in a long, long, time. So, if you ain't trying to forget me, then where have you been the last few months?"

I pause to answer the voices that plague me. I find that there is no answer, except for a lie. I tell myself it is no use in lying to a spirit. Even if the spirit is a phantom from your past. I don't know how but phantoms can somehow tell when you are lying. At least this one can.

"So what you gonna do?"

"Do? Do 'bout what Mama?"

"Do about your dyke sister being in jail, do 'bout your bastard son being in a home, and do 'bout your no good ass cracker boyfriend being in the hospital."

"I don't know Mama. I don't know what I can do."

"I be damned! Is that your answer for everything? I don't know. Your life is a damned mess. A total disaster and all you can say is I don't know."

"But I don't know Mama. I don't know if I can do anything 'bout it."

"You know what you can do. You can take responsibility for what you caused. It's your turn. You've ain't got me to blame for this one!"

"I never blamed you Mama. I didn't,"

"Liar! You always blamed me. You blamed me for your daddy leaving. you blamed me 'cause we were poor. You blamed me 'cause I did what I had to do to survive. So don't lie to me! You blamed me and I took responsibility. So you take responsibility."

"Take responsibility for what Mama?"

"For what? You the reason Tanesha's in jail. Not me. You the reason Ant is gone. If you had listened to what was right, you would not have been with that sorry white boy. You should have learned from the past."

"But I love 'em Mama."

"Love 'em. What is there to love? He beats you. He's an addict. When I went with a man at least I could get something outta it. What are you getting besides his dick? Let a man get in your drawers and damn if you don't give 'em your heart and soul." I say nothing.

"For a dick, not only do you ruin your life, but you take your sister and your child with you. And right now you ain't doing a whole helluva lot of good for your white boy. Some things never change and one of 'em is whatever you touch falls apart."

I hold my head down in shame. I got used to doing that when Mama was still alive. Right now it's as if she was still here with me. The realization hits me, as long as I live she would be with me. As long as I take a breath, she'll still be with me.

"That's right as long as you breathe, I'll be with you. When you look in the mirror, I'm with you. When you get up in the mornings, I'm with you. When you go to bed at night, I'm with you. I'm here to tell you there's no getting around the fact that you are my child. I'm here to tell you it's time to stand up and accept what you've done. So it's time you take responsibility. Everybody would be better off can't you see that? It's time to take responsibility."

"No Mama."

The words continue to echo in my brain.

"Take responsibility. Take responsibility. I can't do what you're asking Mama. I can't."

Then, they gently fade away. "I want do it Mama. I want do it."

"Take responsibility Maya."

I look up and see the sun shining brightly. It's a new day that holds no promise for me or anybody I love. I tell myself it was only a dream, and it meant absolutely nothing. But even as I say those words to myself, I don't believe them. You can't lie to a phantom, or to myself.

I find it extremely difficult to make up my mind. Where I should go first? What should I do first? Should I contact Social Services? Or should I go to the jail? Should I visit Tanesha? Or would it be best to visit Jamie first? I can't decide? One minute I lean in this direction. The next minute I lean in another. I'm being pulled in multiple directions.

When I called Social Services, all I got was an answering service. I was told to leave a phone number and a short message explaining the nature of the call. I left the number, but no message could fully explain the nature of this call. I couldn't imagine any words that would define a soul that was soulless, a soul that had been drained of it's spirit. How could they possibly account for the torment that I was going through? So I left a message that said,

"This is Maya Baxter. I'm calling about my son."

I spoke some other words and pretty much begged the mysterious person who might receive this message to please call back.

After two nerve filled hours the weekend on call person responded. She told me that she was not allowed to give me the information that I needed. She told me that Ant was fine. That pending completion of the investigation he'd remains where he was. And that someone would be in contact with me later today. Then she hung up.

What disturbed me the most was the cold, matter of fact manner in which she dispatched me. It was so routine, so unfeeling. How could people like this care for my baby? She might as well have been telling me about how she took care of her houseplant. I bet if she has any, they all dead. This lady didn't seem like she had the time, nor the heart to care for any living thing.

I thought about Jamie and Tanesha. I was dreading a visit to see either one of them. Since I had more time to visit Jamie in the evening, I decided I'd check in on Tanesha. Poor Sis, she must be feeling terrible. To wake up one day and have your freedom suddenly taken away from you. In spite of everything that had happened to her Tanesha always seemed to be a person who was certain about life. Now she sits it a filthy jail cell, her future an absolute uncertainty. The reason...she chose to stand up for me. How can I possibly forgive myself if she has to go to prison?

I get into the car and head downtown to the Tylerville Court House. I park in the back and walk up a few stairs. Inside the building, the corridor is slightly darkened. I guess it's appropriate that the lighting is poor. Many people who enter have futures about as bright as this hallway.

The building is way over eighty years old. The roaches are slightly over ten. The jail itself is made of four small rundown cells, a reception area, and two offices. One office holds a computer and some files. The other holds two desks and a coffeepot. One of the desks makes up the Chief's office. The other is shared by two shifts of alternating deputies.

The Tylerville City Police force is mostly a name. The Country Police provide most of the real police force. The Chief and his men mostly watch prisoners, mostly drunks, and wife beaters. Those are two major activities on the weekend in Tylerville. Today Chief Ross must be feeling mighty proud. He's got himself an attempted murderer.

The deputy is sitting at the desk when I walk in. He stands and walks over to me. He's about forty-five or so, slightly balding, bespectacled and paunchy. He looks like he'd be good at killing small animals and calling it a sport, drinking Pabst Blue Ribbon beer and rebuilding the motor on his pickup truck.

"Can I hep you ma'm?"

I clear my throat. I can't remember the last time I've felt comfortable about anything. So naturally if my heart was a car, I'd be stopped for speeding.

"Yes sir. I'd like, if possible to see my sister."

"And who is your sister, mam?"

I want to ask how many women you got in the place, instead I simply point out that my sister's name is Tanesha Baxter.

He thumbs through a small notebook as if he works for some big city police department. As he does this he calls out her name.

"Tanesha Baxter, Tanesha Baxter. Here it is. Tanesha Baxter. And you say you're her sister."

He peers down over those ugly, plastic frame looking glasses at me.

"That girl in the jail is your sister?"

"Yes sir, she's my sister."

"Well y'all sure don't look alike. Hell she could almost go for white. Of course ain't no doubt 'bout you being a Black."

"I guess not."

"Well visiting ain't for another forty minutes. You can't see her until then. We don't allow visitor's 'til three."

I look at him in disbelief. Maybe three people in the whole place and I can't see her. I don't know what to say to Bubba.

"Yup that's the rules ma'm. No visitors 'til three o'clock. So you can wait in here or outside, or come back later on. Your choice."

My head starts to pound. I can't concentrate. Go or stay. Right now the simplest decision has become more difficult than ending the war in the Middle East.

"I reckon I'll stay sir. That's if you don't mind."

"Suit yourself."

He turns and walks to the coffeepot. He pours himself a cup and puts in four spoons of sugar, and some cream. He sits down at the desk, props his feet up and begins reading the paper while sipping on his diabetes juice.

I move over to a kitchen chair and sit down. For over half-hour I look around. I look around at the same clock, the same desks, the same counter, the same dirt, the same disgusting walls, until I know every nook and cranny. At five minutes to three the deputy slides up to the counter and announces the first good news I've heard all day.

"Ma'm, I tell you what. I'm gonna do you a lil' favor. I'll let you go on back early so you can spend some extra time with you sister."

I look up at this disgusting face. That's all it is to me now. A thoroughly disgusting face. I smile appreciatively as if he'd done me some enormous favor.

"Thank you sir."

I rise up from my throne. My behind has left an imprint in the chair and the chair has definitely left an impression on me. I follow Bubba around the corner and down a short hallway. Through another door are the jail cells. In one cell is a white man I don't know. He looks worse than I feel. I guess considering where we are that is to be expected. Homeboy done caught pure D hell.

In the second cell is a face I know but presently I'm not familiar with. My sister doesn't look like herself. She looks troubled and very vulnerable. She smiles weakly. I can't help but think how this is all my fault. In a voice that is totally void of any emotions, he in a matter of fact tone declares.

"Y'all got fifteen minutes."

He opens the cell door and leaves. I run into Tanesha's arms. The overwhelming significance of the moment hits us both. The next thing I know we're embracing as if we've been separated for an eternity. The hug lasts until she leads me to her bed. We sit. The mattress is about as thick as a pan of cornbeard. She immediately takes the role she has filled her entire life. She pats me on the back and begins comforting me. I sob onto her shoulder as she wipes her own tears away.

"Don't worry none Sis. It's gonna be alright."

I have trouble speaking. My voice comes in short choppy bits and pieces.

"I, I, I feel so bbbad 'bout everything. It, it it's all my fffault."

"Now stop it Maya. Stop all the crying and stop blaming yourself. Won't do no good to start blaming nobody. The fact is this, what's done is done. One of the guards told me that Jamie gonna be okay. So we don't have to be worried 'bout him. We don't need to be lookin' back! We just need to stick together. Everything will work out find if we all stick together. If we keep on sayin' the same thing, over and over, in a couple days things are gonna be fine."

I pause to consider her words even as I nod in agreement with them. If we all stick together everything is going to be just fine. I guess Jamie must be nobody. If I stick to my story, he'll be mad as hell, but I doubt if he'll be fine. After all we've been through, I know that this will truly be the end of us. If I stick with this lie, he and I are finished. The father of my expected child will be gone. But what else can I do? It's too late to change. I've gotten in over my head. We all have.

If I change my story now, not only will I be in hot water but so will Marguerite and Tanesha. There is no easy way out of this mess.

"To make this thing work, I had to sign a warrant against Jamie."

"What?"

"I had to take out a warrant against Jamie. Sayin' after he beat on us, he was threatening us with that fireplace poker."

"But why?"

'Cause my defense is self-defense and the only way that works if I was acting to keep him from killing one of us. Besides it's not like all of it is a lie. He did hit me and you, Ant and Marguerite. He beat up on all of us."

"But he wasn't swingin' no fireplace poker at us."

"I know he wasn't, but you can't just shoot a white boy just 'cause he slaps you around. You gotta say he was trying to kill us. The fireplace poker makes the shooting justifiable."

I cover my eyes and shake my head. This is all too much.

"It's the only way Maya. I know you still care about him but..."

"I don't just care about him Sis. It's more than that. I know you don't approve, but I can't help it. This whole thing would be so much easier if I didn't care so much. But I guess things aren't s'pose to be easy for me. How in the hell would I know how to cope if things were to suddenly get easier?"

I look into the face of an all encompassing stare. I see a mixed vision of anxiety, anger, disappointment and fatigue. It's obvious that she can't believe I'm second guessing this lie. Her point of view is so simple. It shouldn't be such a difficult matter to frame the man I love?

"It ain't easy Sis, 'cause you make everything so damn hard! Don't you make this thing hard Maya! You my flesh and blood...right now I need you more than I ever needed anybody else before. I gotta know that you gonna be there for me?"

I pause.

"Maya don't you let me down. Don't you leave me hanging?"

"But he could get serious time for this."

"Well deserved time, Maya."

Obviously, we didn't hear the sound of those flat feet as they approached us. These feet are the type that never brings good news. Here was old Bubba to once again let us know that behind these walls, he was the boss.

"Alright ladies. Your time is just 'bout up." Bubba announces as he reenters the area outside of Tanesha's cell.

"Can we have another five minutes? I need to tell my Sister one more thing to do for me."

"No ma'm. Can't do it. The Chief says ten minutes and I've been kind enuff to give y'all fifteen. So that's all I can give y'all."

"I'm not asking for much. All I want is a few minutes."

"Ma'm, I don't mean to sound disrespectful or nothing' but you ain't done nothing' special to be locked up here. Now you and your sister gonna have to talk. with one another on Monday. So Missy you just tell your sister goodbye and I'll get on back to my work."

I stand. I look at Bubba and then back at Tanesha. I hate to leave her all alone. She is so anxious and afraid. She's so fearful that I want be able to hold up my end. I know she's afraid because she's unsure if I'll be there for her. She's afraid that I will crack under the pressure. She knows she'll be able to count on Marguerite. She's afraid of Maya. I give her a brief hug. She whispers to me.

"Go by the house and talk with Marguerite. She'll help you feel better. She understands what you're going through. Sis, I'm depending on you."

I nod affirmatively to her as I move away. Even though I feel no one understand exactly what I'm going through. I don't even know what I'm going through. I look back at her until the bars fade into one. I then walk behind the deputy out of the holding area. As I prepare to exit the building, Bubba announces.

"I tell you what Missy. Y'all sure don't look like no sisters. At least not none I've ever known."

I look at him not knowing how I should respond to his brilliant observation. I decide that no response is the best response. I walk out the door. I depart from Tanesha's prison and into my own. I think about Bubba's statement. He's right we don't look nor act like sisters. It's hard to be family when one of you is always locked away in some kind of prison.

I stand on the steps of the jailhouse and look up to the heavens for some kind of divine intervention. It fails to come . Maybe it's because of all clouds moving in, clouds of turbulence. I reason that God won't look down upon his lost children through these kinds of clouds. I feel so very tired. Yet I have one more stop to make.

Mama's Too

I don't know how I thought this day would turn out, but I didn't think it would be quite like this. As I rub my tired eyes with the palm of my hands, I recall and shiver at the events of the last twenty-four hours. First the son of a bitches at Social Services want even let me see my child. See him, they want even let me talk to him. Then my own sister, my only sister is near breaking down. Right now she doesn't trust me to take care of her. The one time in our life when I can help her, and she can't be sure that I will. Why? Because if I do, I must destroy the man that I might still love. The man who has fathered my unborn child. Damned if my life doesn't sound like a soap opera.

So here I am, back at the Greenville Hospital. In a way it's ironic. If it were not for Jamie being treated here with the pain medicine, then perhaps he would have never become addicted. If it weren't for the addiction then our worse problem would have been only the waning hatred of ignorance bigots. I guess we didn't realize when we had a good thing.

The good news, and it was the only good thing to happen today, was that Jamie had been upgraded from stable to fair condition. He'd been moved out of the Intensive Care unit to a regular room. This meant that he would be all right. He would be just fine. It also means he can now have visitors.

When I got to his room I found myself paralyzed. All of a sudden my feet refuse to move. Not a single step further. My arms couldn't find the strength to open that door. The only part of my body that was currently working, is an overactive brain.

I asked myself what would I say to him? Hello darling I still love your junkie ass and I'm happy that my sister didn't kill you. If we ever did get married it would be some wedding. The Maid of Honor had tried to blow the Groom's ass off. I'd heard of shotgun weddings before, but never a pistol send off. I breathe in heavily and proceed to knock on the door. I don't know why I knocked it isn't like Jamie's going to get up and let me in. Initially there's no response. I knock again and this time there is an answer. It's a woman's voice that comes from the darkened room. I assume it's a nurse. It's not, She opens the door, being careful to block my entry.

I manage a quick glance at someone who's lying on the bed. I see tubes leading to his arm. I think this is Jamie. The lady steps toward me, easing me back into the hallway. She's joined by a younger woman. Although she's a shade darker than the older lady she's definitely resembles her.

"Can I help you?"

I look closely at them. It would probably be more accurate to say I examine them. The two women look closely at me. The older lady is perhaps fifty years old and light complexion. The other looks to be in her late twenties. I can't help but feel that there is something strangely familiar about them. This- is weird because they're not from Tylervilleand that's pretty much the extent of my world. The older woman speaks a second time.

"Young lady, can I help you?"

"No ma'm. I was just looking for Jamie, I mean James Cook's room,"

In a stern quizzical tone, the younger one speaks.

"What you looking for James Cook for?"

I pause. Something tells me that I shouldn't say too much. As secretive as Jamie is about his past I don't want to say the wrong thing to the wrong people. Especially these people. I know them from somewhere but I'm not exactly sure where.

"He's a good friend of mine. Why you askin'?"

"I got my reasons."

"Can I come in and we discuss them?"

"I don't know if that's any of your business. So lets hold of a minute on you coming in."

"I've been living with him for the past year."

The older lady jumps into the conversation.

"Then you must be Maya? He's been askin' 'bout you."

This announcement surprises me. She knows my name, but who in the hell is she?

"Yes, that's me, so Jamie told you about me?"

He told me about you awhile back. He wrote and told me all about you. He told me how you look and how much he loves you. He wasn't able to say much to us today, but he asked for you right away. Says you can help straighten out the mess. So to make a long story short, I know 'bout you cause I'm Jimmie's Mama."

"And that would make him my brother." I shake my head no.

"Oh. Well this can't be the same James Cook. The one I'm talkin 'bout is white."

"It's the same one and my brother ain't white!"

I'm confused by this exchange. I thought I was agreeing with her. If her brother isn't white and my fiance is, then it can't be the same person.

"You mean there are two people with the same name in the hospital at the same time."

The expression on mom's face, along with shaking of her head says that no such coincidence exists. This only serves to add to my state of confusion. It's obvious that although these people are light skinned, they are black, Yet they claim to be Jamie's family. At this point I don't know how to respond to them. So we stand the three of us, in a hallway outside of Jamie's room. The lady claiming to be his mother is the first to speak. Her words while soothing are quite disconcerting.

"Sweetheart there's not two people with the same name. We're talking 'bout the same person. He's my son and her brother, and I'm gonna guest that from all you're saying, Jimmie hasn't told you a whole lot 'bout either of us."

I nod my head in agreement.

"Jimmie told me y'all was dead. So no he hasn't told me nothing' bout nothing'."

Jamie's sister interrupts my brief conversation with the mother. She gently pulls mom a few steps away. I strain my ears to listen in on the conversation.

"Mama I don't know how much we ought to be saying to her? We don't even know this lady. You need to be careful."

"She's Jimmie's girlfriend."

"She's Jimmie's girlfriend who he choose not to tell nothing Jimmie's girlfriend who knows something 'bout what happened and hadn't step up with the police to help Jimmie out."

"He's told me how much he loves her over and over in his letters."

"In his letters. That ain't nothing' Mama! He ain't even told her 'bout us. She don't even know nothing' bout us. She didn't even know he wasn't white. And we don't know what she knows 'bout that fight. So what makes you think Jimmie wants us talking to her?"

"It want hurt nothing' to talk to her."

"Well you just need to be careful with what you say to her."

This pisses me off. Who in the hell does this bitch think she is? Hell it sounds like she's screwing Jamie. Talk about being over protective. But I hold my tongue, realizing how much she cares for her brother.

"Lord child give me credit for some sense. I'm just gonna talk to the girl. Shoot she might be able to tell us something 'bout what happen to my boy."

As I hear those words I feel a bit panicky. I also realizes how much she obviously loves Jamie or Jimmie or whatever his name happens to be. You can see the love and concern etched in her face. They coil and curve through a face that has known worry and frustration before. She is a beautiful, but troubled lady. She walks back over to me. Her daughter hesitates.

"Baby I'm Pearline Watson, and this here is my baby Emma Blakeney. We are pleased to finally meet you."

I'm not sure what I should say. I simply try to be pleasant. Until this very moment I didn't know these people existed.

"Thank you Miss Watson."

"Shoot now, you don' t have to go all formal on me. Just call me Pearline or Miss Pearl. That's what everybody back home calls me."

"Okay Miss Pearline. I'm Maya Baxter. I don't really know how much Jamie has said 'bout me, but I just want you to know that I do love him very, very much."

I look over at Emma. She's still playing the role of ice queen. She reluctantly acknowledges my right to exist.

"Miss Pearline do you think it'll be alright for me, I mean us to goin and see Jamie?"

"I think maybe we ought to give him some time. He just went back to sleep and he needs his rest."

"I know he needs some rest, but Miss Pearline I'm so worried 'bout him. I need to know how he's doing? I need to know that he's okay? I'm just about to go totally crazy. If I could only see him for a few minutes."

"Ya'll be able to see 'em in a lil' bit Maya. Just be patient. Let's all of us have a seat over here and talk for awhile."

She points to a waiting section down the hallway. Even as I answer her, I'm thinking what does she want to talk to me about? What does she want me to say?

"Yes'm, that'll be fine."

The three of us move to the waiting area. I again ask her the question. "How is he doing?" The sister answers.

"He's doing just great considering some bitch tried to blow his ass all to hell!"

I think, now that girl sounds like Tanesha. Maybe that's why she seems so familiar.

"Now Emma you don't have to be saying it like that."

"Well that's what happened Mama. My brother is laying in there hooked up to machine, damned near too weak to talk, hogtied to a bed 'cause some low life bitch tookin' shot him. I just wish I could get my hands on her."

I look down at the tile on the floor, avoiding eye contact. I must have spent half of my life looking down at floors trying not to look into the eyes of someone or something. I'd just like to spend one day, one damn day looking right into the face of whatever might come my way.

"Don't let it get to you Mama." I look at the older lady and can't help but feel her pain.

"When your baby is hurtin', well then you hurt too. Here my baby's laying in that bed with his legs shackled…"

"What you mean shackled? Shackled how? Shackled to what? I don't understand."

Miss Pearline looks up at me. Her eyes are deeply saddened.

"We didn't get the whole story, but before Jimmie fell back to sleep he told us that them bastard done charged him with Assault and Battery with Intent to Kill and Simple Assault. They say he took'n beat up on this lady and threatened her with a fireplace poker."

"Yeah that's what the Police say! Before he fell back to sleep, Jimmie says he didn't do it. And he's never lied to me. Ain't got no reason to lie to me. Anytime he'd be in trouble in the past, he'd always tell me what really happened. He always tell me the truth."

This is all occurring way too fast. Since I don't have a clue as to what I ought to say. I keep my mouth closed. A part of me feels certain they're expecting something from me. But I can't even think about helping them. Even as Miss Pearline looks at me with those eyes that reveal unmentionable anguish, I know I cannot ease her pain. I have made up my mind. I simply can't.

"Maya? If you can, if you know anything about what happened, please help my baby?"

I look at her as best I can. That's not exactly true, more accurately I try to look through her. I'm afraid if I look at her my eyes will give me away, I briefly turn away, only to find the burning, penetrating glare of that evil bitch Emma. I think to myself that they know, they know what we did. I immediately turn back to the slightly more preferable face of Miss Pearline.

"No ma'm. I don't know anything that'll help Jamie." She sighs, and Emma curses.

"Well bless you anyway baby. I'm just glad you're here for my Jimmie. I know he's gonna be thrilled to see you. I know right now he's gotta be awfully scared."

I nod in agreement and in relief. I tell myself he hasn't told them. They don't know the whole truth. If they did then Emma would be cursing me out and calling me a damned liar.

"Maya I'm gonna tell you something don't nobody know but me and Emma."

"Mama! What you doing?"

"I'm gonna tell her something."

"Mama don't do it! It ain't your place to be tellin' her `nothing' bout Jimmie!"

"Chile I just want her to understand."

"I don't give a damn if she understands! It ain't her place to understand. If Jimmie had wanted her to know, he woulda told her hisself! You don't have no business talking 'bout family business to a stranger."

"For goodness sake Emma. The girl is supposed to be marrying Jimmie. She has a right to know."

"Then damnit Mama let Jimmie tell her. If she can't help 'em, she ain't got a right to know nothing more than what she already knows."

"It don't matter who tells her."

"Then let Jimmie tell her! Let him make that decision."

I now know how a ping-pong ball feels. This back and forth has my head, throbbing. What is it the old lady wants to tell me, that the Ice queen doesn't want me to know? It can't be any more astonishing than finding out my fiance is actually black, or at least half black, or half white or half something. It can't be any more surprising to find out that Jamie is Jimmie or Jimmie is Jamie. What other secrets are hidden in this closet? It can't be that many more secrets because there is not enough room in that one space.

"Fine then. Let's go back in and see if Jimmie is woke. He can tell her everything."

"Okay then let's do that."

The two of them are the first to rise. Feeling like an outsider I look to Mama for permission to be included.

"C'mon Maya. We're going back inside."

Like an obedient child, I join them. We make the short journey back up the hallway and into Jamie-Jimmie's room. As we enter, initially the eyes have to 'adjust. Only one small reading light is on. In a way it's like going from daylight to darkness. I struggle to make out the form on the bed. It's funny how this image imitates true life. At this time I really can't make out the figure, because I don't really know whom it is. I've never really known.

Miss Pearline walks over to the side of the bed. She gently places a hand onto what I assume is Jimmie-Jamie's shoulder. As my eyes begin to focus, I notice a chair in the corner of this small room. I choose this spot. I hope to be away from the center of attention. I gingerly ease into the chair, as I do, Emma moves over to the other side of the bed, across from Miss Pearline. She looks down upon her son, watching over him as any loving mother would watch over their child. He, perhaps sensing her presence, responds to her touch. He weakly calls out.

"Mama."

"Yes baby?"

You still here"

"We both here Jimmie. Me and Mama." He recognizes the voice and smiles.

"That's my girls."

I notice the smile on her face as my eyes have now made the adjustment to the low lighting. I am seeing more clearly. I also notice the IV in his arms. Damned if this boy hasn't spent the last few month of his life with an IV in his arm or a pill in his hand.

"You think we're gonna leave you?"

"I just figured y'all would be gone by now."

"Well you can't get rid of us that easy. Ain't that right Mama?"

"That's right. And this time we got somebody else with us."

"Who's that Mama?" I shudder as she responds.

"It's Maya baby. It's your sweetheart Maya."

He tries to rise up, but as he does the pain suggest that he doesn't. He's reminded of the exact reason he's in this bed. He calls out. His voice is weaker than usual, but there is a noticeable edge to it. He searches out for me.

"Maya? Is that you? What you doing here?"

I stand at attention, and take a single step towards him.

"I'm here because I wanted to see you. I had to see that you are alright."

He attempts to sit up again. This time although in obvious pain, he manages to slide up on the pillow. Miss Pearline sensing his discomfort assists him in his effort. You immediately know that this isn't the first time she has come to his aid, she is used to doing for him.

"Be careful baby. You don't wanna loosen them stitches."

He turns his head ever so slightly. He manages to look directly into my eyes. At this moment, I appreciate the fact that the lights are not too bright. If they were brighter he'd be able to see a lying, dishonest soul.

"I'm glad you're here baby. I need you."

Instinctively I move over closer to him. I still remain a step away from the bed. I don't feel comfortable getting between a Mother and her child.

"I'm sorry Maya. I'm sorry for all the pain I cost you."

What the hell? Of all the things I had imagined Jamie-Jimmie saying to me, I'm sorry was not one of them. I don't really know how to respond to this comment. My sister shoots Jamie and he says he's sorry. I move forward and tenderly hold his hand. When I do, I notice the metal bracelets on his ankles. It's really kind of a strange situation. He's tied to the bed by shackles and a narcotic drip.

"I know I've said it before but I'm sorry baby and I'm gonna make it up to you."

"You don't have to apologize. I know you didn't mean for things to work out like they did. Nobody wanted to see you in the hospital."

"It's not just this. It's for everything. I know you must be thinking bad about me. I mean here I lied to you 'bout my Mama and Emma. 'Bout me being white. But it was a reason for that Maya. I was gonna tell you before we got married, but it looks like I don't have to do that now."

He looks over at his Mama and then to his sister. Miss Pearline simply smiles and nods to him. Emma cautions him.

"You don't have to do this Jimmie. You can always wait to do this." I turn and glance at her.

"Nah Sis. This is something that I shoulda already done. I can trust Maya. I love her and I hope she still loves me. I know she won't do nothing' to hurt me."

I nod in agreement with him, even as I feel the guilt of my part in a lie.

"Maya the reason I didn't tell you 'bout my past, 'bout my family, 'bout who I am 'cause of the problems I've had."

Once again Emma seeks to protect him from me.

"Jimmie I'm not sure if you should be doing this. She's not family."

Not yet she ain't, but if she'll still have me, she will be."

"I just wish you would think about it some more before you tell her everything."

"I have thought about it, and I know what I'm doing."He pauses to think. I pause to breathe.

"You see Maya the reason I kept everything as a secret was 'cause of some trouble I'd gotten into back in Georgia. The truth is I'm on parole. I had to do a some time for Assault on a Female and domestic violence. My wife, ex-wife, had me do time on them charges when I shouldn't have. The last time I went to court, it was her fault. It shouldn't have happened. They took a year out of my life for some lies she told on me. That bitch told so many lies in court that it made me sick. That whole year I spent locked up, just made me madder and madder. She didn't even let my kid write to me. When I finally got released, the only thing I could think about was gettin' me some payback."

Even though I listen intently to his words, I still can't believe what I'm hearing. Ex-wife, assault, child, parole I'm literally afraid of what he's going to say next.

"I know I shouldn't have did it."

Emma again seeks to minimize any negative aspect of her brother's behavior.

"Don't blame yourself Jimmie. Anybody who'd spent a year of their life in jail because of a lie has a right to be mad."

"I know Sis, but I still shouldn't did it."

He again looks at me.

"Went I got out I had been drinking. I went and found her. I went straight to her house. I didn't really plan on beating her that bad, but I guess a year worth of hatred had built up in me and the liquor didn't help. Once I got started it was like I couldn't control myself. Well, the long and the short of it is I beat her up bad, real bad."

He pauses for a brief moment. I guess this is to recompose himself.

"Then it hit me. I knew if I stayed there, I was going right back to prison. I was gonna be going back for more than a year. So I panicked. That's when I took off. I couldn't go back Maya, I couldn't. I woulda had to do the time for parole violation and for another Assault. Maya, I can't go back to prison.

Realizing what would happen if I got caught, I basically moved around from place to place, scared to stay anywhere too long.

Except when I landed here in Tylerville, when I met you. If it wasn't for me falling in love with you, then I guess I'd still be on the road." He pauses to examine my response.

"I reckon love will make you take a risk. Anyway, when I fell in love with you I decided I needed to stay awhile. That's when I just kept on playing up that white boy angle. Wasn't nobody lookin' for no white boy. Emma here, well Sis takes after Mama. Me, I take after my daddy."

"I s'pose you can call him that. You see my daddy is white."

He pauses to look at his Mama.

"We don't talk about it a whole lot, outta respect to Mama. Mama and Daddy they never married. You see daddy was this big, timed businessman in Northeast Georgia. He traveled a lot. I guess he found it lonely on the road."

He again glances up to his mother. She seems to be okay by this conversation.

"Basically, for a number of years, he took care of that loneliness by having himself two family. We was his back up family. Had his self a ready-made family back in Savannah. A ready-made white family. He always said he loved us and loved Mama. But this was Georgia right after the Civil Rights movement.

Mama used to tell us that daddy couldn't leave his wife and family for a black lady. It woulda destroyed his business. So he made his decision. Eventually he eased completely outta the picture. We was his little dark secret. Wasn't worth his time, only a check every month. That's what my daddy was Maya, a check."

"I'm sorry baby, I'm so sorry. Y'all deserved better than that. I take the blame for all of it."

"Don't blame yourself Mama. He had a mind of his own. He made his own decisions. He didn't wanna be a part of our life and that's on him. Anyway, I'm tired of talking 'bout him. As far as I'm concerned, he can go to hell.

So, it comes to me that everybody in Georgia is looking for Jimmie Watson a light skinned black man. I decided it was time for Mr. Cook to help me out. So, I came up with this idea. I decided to take on the bastard's name and start over in South Carolina.

And that's how and why I passed. I became Jamie Cook, a white man. Believe me, I never wanted to fool you or nobody else about who I am. I consider myself Black and I am proud of that fact. But being white has kept me out of prison. Being white was necessary."

If it's possible, which it's not, my face has to be as white as Jamie's. This is truly amazing. This is beyond amazing. This is incredible. Even so, I ask myself, why is he now telling all of this to me, and where is all of this going?

"Maya I know it was wrong, but I had no choice. If you think I enjoyed this skin game then you're mistaken. For me to be raised black, to have put up with all that I had to put up with, believe me the last thing in the world I ever wanted to do was to go for white. I spent most of my life hating my daddy and hating myself. I didn't belong Maya. I didn't belong anywhere. Especially in the white world."

This time the tears belong to him. But for some reason they don't appear to be totally genuine.

"What am I Maya? What am I? Mama's black and daddy's white, so what does that make me?"

I don't answer. This is one of those questions you don't answer.

243

"It makes me one mixed up bastard."

"Jimmie! Don't you dare talk about yourself like that. You know better."

"I'm sorry Mama. I don't mean to hurt you."

"Don't concern yourself with me baby. It's you I'm worried 'bout."

"I know it Mama. You and Emma have always put me first and I truly love y'all for that."

He returns his focus to me. As he does he again struggles to sit up higher in the bed.

Both Miss Pearline and Emma move on both sides of him. They manage to get him sitting in a semi-upright position. While all of this is going on, I slide to my right, away from his face. He smiles as he speaks to me.

"See Maya. See how much they love me."

I think maybe too much.

"I know Jamie."

"They'd do anything for me. But they can't help me now. The reason I been telling you all of this is 'cause of how much I love you and how tired I am of lying to you. Maya I hope you love me as much as I love you. I need you so much. I need you more than ever. The truth is this. Maya you're the only person in the world who can help me."

He pauses seemingly to assess my response.

"You see these Maya?"

He pulls back the cover to give me a full view of those shackles. I find myself looking at them but not seeing them.

"The police came by earlier today Maya. They came over and charge me for trying to kill Tanesha. They say I tried to kill her Maya. They say I tried to kill her with a fireplace poker. Maya you know that ain't true. You know I hit her but didn't have no fireplace poker when she shot me. You know damn well I didn't try to kill your sister with no fireplace poker."

I don't know what the shortest time period is that can be measured. don't know if it was a millisecond, or something really shorter. I do know that as fast as is humanly possible Emma begins to curse and scream. I think to myself that the temper thing must run in the family.

"What! Did I hear Jimmie say that your sister is the bitch who's got him in all this trouble? I know damned well you ain't stood here talking to me and my Mama 'bout Jimmie, and all the time it was your sister who shot my brother! Uh, uh. Bitch you gonna tell me something!"

By now we are nose to nose, or more appropriately, she is nose to nose with me. Miss Pearline steps in and plays referee. She grabs Emma by arm and pulls her back. I'm certain this isn't the first time she's had to play this role. I try to defend myself.

"I didn't know what to say to y'all."

"How 'bout saying the truth bitch! How 'bout that. You think you and your damned lying ass sister gonna send my brother back to prison? You think y all gonna send him back to prison for nothing'!"

Through this explosion I hear the voices of Jamie and Miss Pearline trying to restore the calm. They are unsuccessful. Emma breaks away from Miss Pearline and tries to swing at me. I step back. Just as I do the door opens. Miss Pearline grabs hold of Emma a second time. Through the open door walks in a nurse. She can't believe what's going on, and neither can I.

"What's going on here? What are you people doing?"

She walks over to us. It's Miss Pearline who responds to the question.

"We're sorry ma'm. We're just having a lit' disagreement."

"Disagreement. I can hear y'all clear down the hall. Half this wing can hear y'all's little disagreement."

"I really am sorry ma'm. We'll keep it quiet."

She looks at Emma and me.

"You'd better or else I'm gonna have to get security up here and have all of you removed. Do I make myself clear!"

Again, Miss Pearline is the one who answers.

"Yes ma'm, we understand you perfectly clear."

She takes one last look at this now peaceful scene, turns and walks out the door.

Jamie-Jimmie is the first to speak. It could best be described as a statement where the pot is calling the kettle black.

"See there Sis. There you go again with that damn temper. This is between me and Maya."

"Between you and Maya! Was Maya the one who visited you at Kirkland Prison almost every Sunday for a year? Was Maya the one who sent you money for cigarettes and snacks? Tell me that!"

"I know you love me Sis, but please lemme take care of this."

A troubled silence ensues.

"Maya you gotta help me. The police are gonna come back over tomorrow and fingerprint me. Once they run those fingerprints, they might find out all about my past. If that happens then they gonna know everything. Maya I'm gonna have to do time for that Georgia parole violation and for this mess with Tanesha. Baby I can't go back to jail. I can't go back!"

I stand there listening to the frantic plea of a desperate man. The look on his face says it all. I honestly believe that if I were to say something he doesn't like he'd somehow get up out of that bed and knock the hell out of me. Therefore, I say nothing.

"Maya, I know it's your sister, but it's not right what she's doing. I mean if she'll drop them charges and stop all the lying, I promise I want even testify against her. You and me and Ant can take off. We can get married and just get the hell outta Tylerville. Maya you know the truth. All I'm askin' you to do Is to tell the truth! You need to tell the truth before it's too late. Maya I need you to go to the police station and tell them exactly what happened. I need you to convince Tanesha. I need you to do it today!"

I look at the faces in this room. In Jamie I see the face of hopelessness. He realizes the door is shutting tightly upon him. He's could be back in prison really soon. And that is all too clear.

In the eyes of Miss Perline there's fear. In her face I see the love and the pain only a mother can know. Her only wish is that her son be okay. She's terribly afraid that she'll lose her son.

Finally, I look into the eyes of Emma. I see resentment. She feels contempt for me. She totally hates that I, and not she, am Jamie's only hope.

The room now sounds a bit like a distorted echo chamber. Bouncing from wall to wall are the sounds of hopelessness, fear, and resentment. Each of them speaking different words but all expressing similar necessity. The sounds merge into one frantic message.

"Maya? Maya? Tell me you're gonna do it? Maya you gotta say you're gonna do it?"

I don't know what to say or how to say it. I feel a sick, nauseated feeling in the pit of my stomach. There is also an intense, tight feeling all around my heart. My head, it feels as if it's in a three-prong vise, and everyone turning it tighter and tighter. Until something finally breaks.

As I walk briskly out the door, I can hear the screams. As Emma's shouts of "come back here bitch" grow weaker and weaker until they are no longer a sound but a voice inside my consciousness. It reminds me that I must somehow take responsibility.

Takin' Responsibility

I didn't shoot nobody. Didn't beat the hell out of nobody. So it doesn't seem fair that I'm under so much pressure? I can't even seem to get my breath. The simple task of taking a breathe has become difficult. My mind goes from throbbing to racing. To say my thoughts are racing is an understatement. Hell, they got back to Tylerville way before my old car.

As I enter the town limits, I pass the old mill. It's closed today as the hours have been getting cut back lately. Indirectly, in a way it too can be considered responsible for this damnable mess. This is where I met Jamie-Jimmie. In truth I can blame the mill for a lot of things but it somehow doesn't seem fair to blame it on this. But I blame it anyway. I think about how it allowed all of those people to jeer and insult Jimmie-Jamie and me. It is where Jamie-Jimmie hurt his arm. If it were not for the mill things would have certainly been easier. Maybe Jimmie-Jamie wouldn't have felt the need to get started on drugs. Maybe he would've been a totally different person.

I drive on past Red's Grill. Standing outside are several good old boys. I look at them and they stare back at me. I know they're talking about me. That's what they're doing. They're talking about how them two Baxter girls and their dyke girlfriend shot that boy and now they're lying about it. I can tell by the look on their faces. I know I didn't see anybody's face for more than a fraction of a second, but I can tell.

I bet the whole town is talking. I bet all of them, black and white are trying to figure out a way to take care of us once and for all. They think they can hurt us. They're all in it together, they are conspiring against us. They took my baby, put my sister in jail, and somehow, they must have given me something when I was in that hospital. That's why I feel so sick. I don't know how they did it, but they gave me something to make me sick. I can see it clearly now, they are out to get us. But when did they have the time to give it to me.

I come to the bypass and think about heading home. But I'm not sure if Flint Hill is still home. Very few of them want me. They've all wanted something bad to happen to me since I took up with that white boy. The white boy who happens to be a black boy or mixed boy. It's a fact, for the last year, everybody on Flint Hill wanted things to go bad between me and Jamie-Jimmie. The only person, outside of my family, who I could count on, was Caressa.

That's it! I want go home. That's what they want me to do. But I will fool them. I will fool them all. I'll go see Caressa. She'll understand. She has always understood. She knows about how bad love can be. She is the only person who ever accepted the fact that I fell in love with a white boy, who happens to be a black boy or a mixed boy who looks like a white boy. She understands why I turned away from the so-called brothers on Flint Hill. Those so-called players.

I turn on the corner of Green Street and State Avenue. Caressa lives about ablock from here. I notice the people hanging in front of the liquor store. This is one of the spots where everybody hangs. Here they gossip and talk about the latest news. Today they are again talking about Lil' Gal's daughters. I know they're talking about me. I can feel it. They think they can get me, but I'll show them all.

I turn onto Caressa's street. The houses look drab and worn down. That's because they are drab and worn down. They use to be mill houses. A long time ago white folk stayed here. But not anymore for as long as I can remember, Flint Hill has been all black. I pull up to Caressa's house.

In the yard is a car that I don't recognize. Actually it's more like a piece of junk. It's a Nineteen eighty something Chrysler Lebaron. It fits with this neighborhood. As I get out of the car I notice Che Che playing on the porch. She is Caressa's oldest, about 10 years old. She recognizes me and jumps off the porch, running out to greet me. She looks lonely.

"Hey Aunt Maya." "Hey Che Che."

I notice her hair is kind of nappy and needing a good hot comb. Her jeans also need to be ironed.

"Mama's in the house but she's got company."

"She does."

"Yes'm. It's her boyfriend."

I wonder who the latest flavor of the month might be. Then it occurs to me, maybe they sent him. Maybe her company is part of their plan to take care of Tanesha and myself. If they get to Caressa they know I will have nobody. It's all apart of their plan.

"His name is JoJo."

I pause for a second, who the hell is JoJo ? Caressa never mentioned anything about a JoJo. My thoughts are going at the speed of light. I tell myself that I have to slow down. I breath in slowly and exhale. This doesn't make any sense. I think this can't be happening.

"Yes'm. I think he's from Seneca. He stays with us on Saturday and Sunday."

"Oh. So where is your brother and sister?"

"They daddy came and picked them up on Friday. They staying at his house this weekend."

"Okay. So what your Mama doing in there?"

"She and Jojo been drinking a lil' bit. So she sent me outdoors." "Well maybe I should come back a bit later."

"You can go on in. She was just talking 'bout how she hope you was doing alright. She was sayin' how she was going to stop by and see you on account of your sister trying to kill your boyfriend and that had to make you mad."

Mad, I don't believe that quite expresses what I'm going through.

"Well I'm gonna go on in and see her and just let her know I'm okay."

Before I can move to the door, Che Che looks up at me with her big brown eyes. I feel a bit of sadness. She reminds me of someone I know very well. Because of that I know those eyes are going to experience so much pain. It goes with the territory of growing up black, female, and poor.

"Aunt Maya you got a dollar?"

I smile. I actually smile. If this isn't the first time today, it's got to be the second. I reach into my pocketbook and pull out a wrinkle dollar bill. I hand it to Che Che who thanks me and quickly dashes off. I holler at her.

"Where you going girl?" She yells back.

"I'm going to the store and get some Cracker Jacks."

"Well don't you need to let your Mama know?"

"No ma'm. She let's me go all the time."

She resumes running up the street. I watch her as she bounds out of sight. I smile, until I think of Ant. Then the throbbing in my temple starts back up.

I knock on the door. No one answers. I knock a second time and still there is no response. I decide to try one more time. Before I can, the door squeaks open. In the doorway in a flowery colored nightgown stands the only person in this world who loves me, who's not locked away. Of course she happens to be as drunk as a marine on leave, and just as loud. She standing there with a housecoat on even though it's evening time. She looks old. I happen to know that we're the same age. For whatever reason I focus in on how old she looks. I reckon more than the Baxter family is catching some kinds of hell.

"Homegirl!" She seems genuinely thrilled to see me.

"Yep it's me."

"Homegirl! I be damn! Jojo, it's my homegirl. Gal, we was just talking 'bout you. Wasn't we Jojo?"

She turns and looks behind her. On the couch is a skinny, gray haired black man. He looks to be twice her age and as if he's dead. A drunk corpse lying on the living room couch. He tries to respond to Caressa but this requires too much energy. So he simply grunts and groans.

"Ummm."

"Aw shet the hell up Jojo, with your drunk ass. C'mon in Maya. Have a seat on the couch."

She tugs on her housecoat, pulling it closed and leads me into the house. I look at Jojo lying all spread out on the couch and decide to search for a seat somewhere else. Caressa doesn't have another chair in the living room so I suggest that I get another chair.

"I don't wanna wake up your friend. Why don't I just grab a chair outta the kitchen?"

"Girl you know I ain't gonna have that."

She walks over and taps Jojo on the head. When this doesn't awaken him she begins shaking him.

"Jojo! Jojo! Wake your drunk ass up!"

"Ummm."

"Ummm my ass, you wake your drunk behind up!"

He sits straight up on the couch and she flops down beside him.

"I ain't drunk and I ain't sleep. So, you take your fat ass and leave me alone."

"Well move your po' drunk ass over then."

"He don't have to do that Caressa. I can just stand right here. I won't be staying long. I was just stopping by to talk for a minute."

Jojo finally becomes aware of my presence.

"Who's you?"

"Fool this my friend Maya."

"Maya who?"

"The Maya who I been telling you 'bout." "The one who shot her boyfriend?"

"She didn't shoot him fool. Her sister shot 'em."

"I don't give a damn who shot 'em, don't you be gettin' no ideas in your head."

This is a bit too much. I decide that it was not a good idea to stop by Caressa's place.

"Caressa I'm gonna head on home. You got company and I got some important stuff I need to take care of."

"Don't hurry Maya. You ain't got to leave 'cause of drunk ass Jojo."

"I done told you, I ain't drunk."He looks over at me."

"You a pretty lit' thang too. Since your boyfriend all shot up if you wanna get together sometime just let me know.'

As he utters his last dumb drunken comment, Caressa reaches over and pops him on his head.

"Oww. Bitch I done told you 'bout that shit."

"You think you gonna sit here in front of me and hit on my best friend? I'll whip your drunk ass!"

"I wasn't hitting nobody. I was just kiddin' 'round a lil' bit. Trying to make the girl feel good."

"I bet you were. Can't get your mind offa pussy even when you can't do a damn thang with it."

"I told you I wasn't doin' nothing' but playin' 'round with the girl. You think I'm gonna say something to another woman with you sitting 'side me?"

I've had enough of this. Two drunks arguing over nothing. I done had enough of addicts for the rest of my life. This is something I can get away from. I make up a quick excuse to aid in my escape.

"It's no biggie Caressa, besides I've really gotta go. I'm s'pose to meet up with Marguerite to get something worked out for Tanesha's bail."

"You ain't gotta go Maya. If Jojo says another word I'll reach over there and knock his dentures slap down his throat."

I begin to move toward the door. As I do Caressa struggles up from the suddenly pleased couch. I take another step and find myself next to the door.

"I wasn't paying him no attention. He really ain't bothering me. I just gotta get up with Marguerite."

I open the door.

"You sure?"

"Yup I'm sure."

"Well I tell you what, as soon as Jojo goes to sleep I'll call you. It want be but a lil' bit. Then we can sit down and talk awhile."

"You don't have to do that."

"Girl please! This me you talking too. You and me go back as far as I can remember. You know I'm gonna be there for my Boo."

I smile. Caressa always could make me smile. No matter that it's the shortest time from smile back to frown in the history of mankind.

"I know it."

She reaches out and gives me a big tight bear hug. As she does I smell the liquor. It seems to be soaking right through her pores. I remember Mama being like that before she died. Caressa really drinks too much. She let's go of the embrace. I exit out the door and let go of my last attempt for understanding. I get into the car and back out of the driveway. As I head up the street I see Che Che cracker jacks in hand playing with some other kids. I smile to her. She smiles back. In spite of the JoJo's in her life, all she needs is a soda or a piece of candy to make her smile. Children are like that. Che Che is a lot like I was as a child, and Caressa reminds me of Mama. Too much of my childhood was spent around Jojo's. Yet as a child, I never felt so terrible as I do now.

"Blame me all you want. You gotta take responsibility for this mess."

"Huh?"

"I said go 'head and blame me if you want. I ain't taking no blame."

Before I realize it, I'm again talking to the only blood kin that is able to talk to me. Presently she is the only one that is allowed to speak to me. The voice is very recognizable. I look around. All I know is I don't want to hear from her. I tell myself that they aren't real. I'm simply going to block them out.

"You can try to ignore me if you want. But you can't ignore yourself. This is on you Miss Maya. This is on you." I try to ignore the voice.

"Do you actually think you can get rid of me that easy? Do you think I'll just go away? I'll never go away! Never! There's only one way you can get rid of me." The aching in my temple resumes.

"If you wanna help your sister, if you want the pain to stop, you gotta take responsibility. If you want me to leave, then you gotta take responsibility."

I scream at her.

"Take responsibility for what Mama? Take responsibility for what?"

"There's only one way Maya!"

I feel a tightness in my chest, along with a numbing sensation in my arms. My hands tremble on the steering wheel. I have to pull the car over. I'm hyperventilating. I tell myself she isn't real. She isn't real and she can't control me anymore. I struggle to catch my breath. I look around half expecting to see her. Either she's gone or she's hiding from me.

I make the decision to not go home. As much as I dread it, I turn the car around and head toward Tanesha's place. Tanesha told me to go see Marguerite, besides I don't want to be alone. My only choice is Marguerite. I drive the few miles unsure if I should. I determine that it's for the best. In case the police need to question us again. We can compare stories to see if there are any holes in our plan.

As I arrive in the parking lot I do not see Marguerite's car. I think to myself, shouldn't there be some of that yellow Police tape? Small town police, don't know how to do nothing right. I think that maybe Marguerite isn't here. For a moment I don't know what to do.

Still, I exit the car and head to do door. I knock, there's no answer. I knock again and again, still no answer. I then realize that I have a key.. I locate the key and turn it in the door.

I enter the darkened, isolated apartment. I feel a chill. I turn on the light and it takes a moment for my eyes to adjust. I realize that suddenly night is fast approaching. I look around. I can't help but look around. On the floor is a blood stain. It is Jimmie-Jamie's blood. It mocks me. Why didn't Marguerite clean it up? The police took all their pictures, they took Tanesha's gun, they took the fireplace poker, and they took anything they even thought was related to this case. Except they didn't take Jamie-Jimmie's blood from the carpet. That and the truth.

I now begin to feel that maybe this wasn't such a good idea to come back here. I sense the walls closing in on me. I know the walls aren't moving, but I feel the walls moving. A raging debate begins in my head. Should I go or should I stay? I tell myself that Marguerite will be here soon. As soon as she gets here I won't seem so all alone.

Then I realize that I have not spoken to anyone about Ant. The on call Social Worker said someone would be calling me. In all of the craziness of today, I think what if I had missed the call. I find myself screaming at the top of my lungs. What am I doing to my baby? How could I have forgotten about the call?

I panic, again, I seek guidance for myself. I just need something to calm my nerves. That's all. I just need something to help with these nerves. Tanesha always has something in the medicine cabinet. I'll just. go and get something to help settle my nerves.

I walk through the living. room. Careful not to step in the blood stain. But it seems to be everywhere, could it be spreading? Is it getting bigger? It doesn't matter that it is dried up, I don't want to walk on it. I don't want to get Jimmie-Jamie's blood on me.

I open the bathroom door, catching my reflection in the mirror. I look into the medicine cabinet. Inside as usual are several kind of pills. I take out a king-sized bottle of aspirin. I shut the cabinet. As I do I scream out in terror. There in the mirror, I see her. It's her! I 'drop the bottle and scream a second time. I fall to my knees.

"Oh God no! No! No! No! Mama why are you doing this to me?" The voice answers.

"This is the only way baby. It'll be best for your sister. It's best for your son. You're falling apart. You won't be able to help them. You're gonna mess everything up."

I realize that there is truth in what she's saying. The scalding tears begin to flow.

"This way your sister gets out. You don't have to face the police. You don't have to feel guilty no more. You don't have to worry about Tanesha or Jamie or even Ant. You know it's the only way out Maya. It's the only way."

"But I don't wanna die Mama. I don't wanna die."

"Don't think about it as dying. Think about it as ending your agony. The pain stops as soon as you take responsibility. This is your doing Maya. Everybody told you not to fool with that white boy. Your own baby didn't want you fooling with him. Now because of you, Ant is somewhere with Social Services. Tanesha told you not to fool with him. Now look at her. Because of you she's in jail. Maya, I'm your Mama. It's time you take responsibility."

I look at the pills. The label says two hundred. It looks like a million.

"After you take 'em it'll all be over. The pain will be gone."

"No Mama, No!I can't. I just can't!"

I close my eyes and try to stop my rampaging thoughts. I just wish the pain would stop.

"And it will stop. No more tough decisions no more lying. All you gotta do is take responsibility for what you've done."

I turn on the faucet. I look at the pills. I take a cup from the dispenser. I look at the pills. The water quickly fills the cup to the top. I look at the pills. Turning off the faucet, I place the cup squarely in my hand. I put it down. I look at the pills. This is crazy. I can't do this.

"Yes you can. It's the only way out."

I try to open the bottle. It's one of those childproof tops. I laugh nervously. What does a lesbian need with a childproof top? I get the top open. I look at the pills. I stare at them. For the first time in days I feel relief. I feel a calm sink over me. I pour twenty or thirty or maybe even forty pills in my hand. I pray silently to myself.

"Father God, you know what I'm going through. You said you'd never put more on me than I could handle. Lord forgive me."

I swallow about half of the pills, chasing them down with a long sip of water. I'm surprised at how easy they go down. There is a small amount of difficulty but otherwise, they go down. Again, I am overcome by a huge sense of relief, I feel as if all my burdens have been lifted. I repeat the procedure. If possible, I feel contentment. I look into the mirror, the same mirror that a few minutes ago caused me so much anguish. Now all I feel is calm. I feel totally at ease.

I think to myself, it's amazing how that many aspirin and a little water fill you up. I feel like I've just eaten a full meal. I guess contentment makes you feel full. I feel too full. It's like I'm going to burst. It's like,

"BBBllluuuhhh"

The vomit forces some of the pills back up.

"BBBllluuuhhh"

I vomit a second time. I look down on the sink. I can make out at least fifteen or twenty pills. While breathing insanely heavy, I fill the cup a second time. I pour more pills into my hand. My throat is closing up. It's more difficult to swallow, but I manage to get them down. I feel bloated and very sick, but the pills manage to stay down. I look into the medicine cabinet mirror. There she is a smile on her face. It is done.

The rest of it becomes something of a blur. I remember getting very sick and throwing up at least one more time. My entire body begins to shake and be torn apart by violent spasm, jerks and convulsions. I remember nothing else after that. Except waking up here.

I hadn't made up my mind whether I was lucky or unlucky that Marguerite came in and found my body. She must have called 911 and they were able to resuscitate me. Bless their hearts, or curse them. So now I find myself in the same hospital, the same intensive care unit Jamie was in just twenty-four hours ago. Now I taste that nasty ass charcoal. If I ever get sick enough to think about killing myself again, I know it won't be by overdosing.

Damn if love isn't twisted. I'm in the hospital. Ant's in a home. Tanesha's in jail. Jamie's heading for prison. And it's all in the name of love.

Love always has taken me on strange and painful journeys. This time a bit stranger and a little more painful. As I lie here in this bed all I can do is wonder. I question everything including love. It was love that led me here. It was love that tore my life apart. Maybe, just maybe, I love too much. Perhaps it's time to do something differently.